# POETRY, SYMBOL, AND ALLEGORY

# POETRY, SYMBOL, AND ALLEGORY

*Interpreting Metaphorical Language
from Plato to the Present*

## SIMON BRITTAN

*University of Virginia Press*

CHARLOTTESVILLE AND LONDON

University of Virginia Press
© 2003 by the Rector and Visitors of the University of Virginia
All rights reserved
Printed in the United States of America on acid-free paper
*First published 2003*

1 3 5 7 9 8 6 4 2

Library of Congress Cataloging-in-Publication Data

Brittan, Simon, 1959–
    Poetry, symbol, and allegory : interpreting metaphorical language
from Plato to the present / Simon Brittan.
    p.      cm.
    Includes bibliographical references (p.  ) and index.
    ISBN 0-8139-2156-2 (cloth : alk. paper) — ISBN 0-8139-2157-0
(pbk. : alk. paper)
    1. English poetry—History and criticism—Theory, etc.  2. Metaphor.
3. American poetry—20th century—History and criticism—Theory. etc.
4. Dante Alighieri, 1265–1321—Aesthetics.  5. Meaning (Philosophy)
in literature.  6. Symbolism in literature.  7. Allegory.  I. Title.
    PR508.M43 B75 2003
    809.1—dc21
                                                                    2002155372

*For David Lawton*

"Do you mean to say that the story has a moral?"
"Certainly," said the Linnet.
"Well, really," said the Water-rat, in a very angry manner,
"I think you should have told me that before you began."

—Oscar Wilde, *The Devoted Friend*

# CONTENTS

CONTENTS

# PREFACE

This book is intended primarily for undergraduate students of English or comparative literature (but also of history and philosophy) and for the teachers who write their courses, though beginning graduate students who have not had much real exposure to the history of interpretation will also find it useful. In my experience of teaching at universities, this last group is likely to equate to a sizeable majority. The large corpus of Renaissance criticism and theory, for example, is in the lecture hall often reduced to a few rather worn extracts from Sidney's *Apology for Poetry* concerning the first book of Aristotle's *Poetics*. Aristotle himself, one of the most influential thinkers in human history, tends to be represented by one or two sentences on "universals" and "particulars." For one thing, presenting his ideas in this garbled form can easily leave students with the impression that Aristotle was using the word *universals* to convey a modern, quasi-spiritual, or "transcendental" meaning, whereas the word actually means, roughly, "possibilities." And it may well be the case, anyway, that students learn about Aristotle only through Sidney's use of his ideas—or, rather, through Sidney's version of one or more Latin versions of one or more Greek versions of an original *Poetics* 1. It seems rather unfair on Aristotle.

If I seem to labor this point it is because what Aristotle said about poetry—that it can in certain given circumstances teach us to be virtuous—has had such enormous impact on the way later critics have thought about interpretation. This book therefore begins by looking in some detail at the respective positions of Aristotle and Plato on the value of poetry in society and then goes on to discuss what the *Poetics* has to say about the idea of representation. This discussion forms the basis upon which the subsequent chapters build.

Poetry seems to present problems to undergraduate students. This may be because of the ways the idea of poetry has been dealt with in English secondary schools and U.S. high schools. At any rate, while students are usually able to respond with active enthusiasm to prose and drama, poetry has a disturbing tendency to silence them. It is as though they feel uneasy about expressing an opinion that might be wrong. If this is so, it is certainly remarkable that a concern expressed in exegesis throughout the Middle Ages from Augustine to Aquinas should still hold such sway over a generation brought up in an environment of freedom of expression and "reader-response" theories. Something seems to be wrong. No one can deny that poetry speaks ultimately of the same things as prose and drama, yet students frequently voice the complaint that they "can't relate to it"—alarming indeed since it implies a perception of poetry as valid only insofar as it makes obvious reference to an event (an idea or situation) that lies within the personal experience of the reader. In other words, poetry is increasingly regarded as esoteric, elitist, removed from the "real" world.

It is difficult, without appearing offensive, to explain to someone that if at first reading a text seems to bear no direct relation to his or her own life, that text is not necessarily valueless; in the same way, it must be difficult (I dimly perceive) to explain physics to someone who does not know what gravity is. But it is quite illogical to expect students to understand the concept of, say, deconstruction, if they are unaware of the structures from which texts might be freed. I cannot believe that there are any serious teachers of literature anywhere who would welcome a return to the kind of critical approach that attempted to assign immutable meanings to literary texts: to do so would be to deny the intellectual achievements of the past few decades (by no means, of course, confined to literary criticism), and in so doing to deny our own place in history.

This book bases its arguments on the premise that metaphor has always been, and still is, the main device of poetry, and on the further premise that it is metaphor's capability of indefinite semiosis (not at all the same thing as unlimited semiosis) that makes undergraduate students view poetry with something approaching despair rather than with pleasure. This is no great profundity, but it does need addressing. There are, of course, histories of interpretation in circulation, but they are not specific to poetry, and recent productions tend to place such emphasis on the critical work of the nineteenth and twentieth centuries that students may be forgiven for assuming that nothing of any consequence happened in the two and a half thousand years since Aristotle wrote down the first systematic analysis of representation in the Western tradition.

Two crucial interpretive systems in particular are silently passed over. Firstly there is Origen's third-century view—the view, that is, of a father of the church—that Scripture must be read as essentially symbolic. Surely, he says, no one in their sober senses would claim the Bible to be anything other than a collection of wonderful fables—allegorical tales written down in order to teach us how to be virtuous human beings. Secondly there is the radically opposed view of Augustine, who holds the Bible to be a historical narrative that must be read first of all *literally* and only then (and only in certain cases) allegorically. I have no religious agenda, and consequently no denominational drum to beat, but to ignore an interpretive tradition that continued for very nearly eight hundred years seems frankly irresponsible; nor is doing so likely to help students understand the subsequent reactions against it. The second chapter of this book is therefore devoted to a discussion of what Origen, Augustine, and Aquinas have to say about metaphor, allegory and symbols, signs, and "figurative language." It was, after all, one and a half millennia before Ferdinand de Saussure and C. S. Peirce that Augustine pointed out the distinction between words (which he also calls "signs") and the things to which they refer.

While Aquinas was trying to ensure that spiritual allegory was contained within biblical texts, interest in the Corpus Hermeticum began to revive—a "new age" response to the interpretive and associative limitations imposed by Christian theologians. And at the same time there appeared Dante's now famous letter to Can Grande della Scala with its reading of Psalm 114 and its implication that spiritual allegory may be found also in secular poetry. Dante was not a hermetist—on the contrary, he was in other respects a follower of Aquinas—but the desire to widen theoretical limits to include the serious analysis of secular poetry in the vernacular, to which his letter testifies, can be seen as giving as much impetus to the idea of a renaissance as can the revival of interest in classical literary texts. Nor was Dante the first or the only theorist to express the possibility of turning critical attention to bear on secular poetry in order to discover spiritual allegories, but he was the most famous poet to do so, and the third chapter of this book therefore focuses on him and his contemporaries, as well as on hermetic texts and thought.

From the fourth chapter onwards, the book concentrates largely on poetry in English and on English responses to inherited (or revived) theories of allegory and symbolism: from Renaissance criticism in England to the mid-eighteenth century; then there is an excursion to Germany for Goethe's distinction between symbol and allegory; back to England for romantic theories of poetry; via France and symbolism to Eliot, Hulme, Pound, and the imagists; to a final chapter that, though this is not a book on "theory," necessarily discusses modern approaches to interpretation as far they concern symbol and allegory. This final chapter also restates, and explains, the claim I have made above that metaphor, which I use here in an extended sense to include the symbol and allegory of this book's title, is indeed still the central device of poetry in English.

The book therefore offers students an overview of what philosophers, theorists of poetry, and poets themselves have had to say about metaphor and its interpretation up to the present, very young, twenty-first century. It is not instructional in the sense that it does not tell students how to interpret (I am no Augustine). It is not in itself a theory of interpretation. Nor is it a dictionary of symbols along the lines of *rose* = (1) *blood of Christ,* (2) *love,* and so on. I have included brief readings of my own—of poems by Robert Graves, T. E. Hulme, and Ezra Pound. Their presence in what claims to be an overview of others' allegorical interpretation of poetry can, I hope, be excused on the grounds that they exemplify interpretive traditions discussed elsewhere in the book. My aim is to give students a point of departure, not arrival.

A note on "lacunae": some readers will find it odd that certain established members of the English literary canon are mentioned only in passing or even not at all. Shakespeare, for example, is here with one complete sonnet and passing references to two plays and one other poem; Dryden's criticism is discussed in some detail, but not his poetry; Pope makes no appearance. The reason for this can be deduced from the title *Poetry, Symbol, and Allegory:* this is not an anthology of poetry, nor a history of interpretation, but essentially a study of how, or whether, certain ideas about the interpretation of allegorical texts, which since classical times have been the focus of major philosophical and theological debate, are reflected in poetry. For this reason, the book is not concerned to be representative except where those ideas are concerned, so that I have been able to avoid doing any author the discourtesy of including him or her merely for the sake of inclusion. The only reason any text has been included is because I believe it to be a good illustration of an idea—again, with the sole aim of making it easier for undergraduate students to respond to poetry.

Several friends and colleagues have helped in the composition of this book, either by reading parts of the manuscript or by discussing with me some of the ideas it deals with. In particular my thanks are due to Ian McCormick and Patrick Quinn, University College, Northampton; David Lawton, Washington University, Saint Louis; Stéphane Spoiden, University of Michigan–Dearborn; Jon Cook, University of East Anglia; John Glendening, University of Montana–Missoula. I also owe a special debt of gratitude to Cathie Brettschneider at the University of Virginia Press.

Finally, I am grateful for permission to quote from the following works: *Piers Plowman: The C-text,* by William Langland, edited by Derek Pearsall, published by University of Exeter Press; Aristotle, *Poetics* 1, with the *Tractatus Coislinianus, a Hypothetical Reconstruction of "Poetics" II and the Fragments of the "On Poets,"* translated with notes by Richard Janko, reprinted by permission of Hackett Publishing Company, all rights reserved; Roy Flannagan, *The Riverside Milton,* © 1998 by Houghton Mifflin Company; and *Literary Criticism of John Dryden,* edited by Arthur C. Kirsch, published 1966 by the University of Nebraska Press.

# THE WESTERN TRADITION

*OVERVIEW*

For the poet William Blake, the Old and New Testaments were "the great Code of Art." His choice of words is interesting because it implies a particular understanding of poetry: if something is encoded, it must first be *de*coded before it can be properly understood. Also, it raises the question: why would anyone want to encode it in the first place? What is so important or secret about poetry's "message" that it needs to be hidden? From whom is it meant to be hidden? And who are the initiated who are able to unlock the code? Blake might have meant the word *code* in the sense of its dictionary definition, to indicate "a body of laws so arranged as to avoid inconsistency," but even if he did, and thought of his own art as governed by the same body of laws, our interpretations of his poems are certainly not all consistent.

Blake was not the first to think about codes in this way. Umberto Eco has discussed (*Limits* 8–20) how, in the fifth century, Augustine of Hippo — Saint Augustine — had formulated a set of rules for ascertaining when events reported by the Holy Scriptures had to be read figuratively, as symbolic of something else.[1] Augustine still believed most firmly in the literal sense of the Scriptures, but he also perceived that in some cases they were saying more than one thing at the same time, that they were speaking of something *as well as* the "historical" events they reported. Essentially he said that it is safe to assume this when the Scriptures speak of things that have a comprehensible literal sense but seem to contradict Christian doctrine. For example, Jesus really did overturn the money changers' tables in the temple at Jerusalem, but this surely cannot mean that he encouraged violent behavior. The story must stand for something else. Eventually the church fathers therefore proposed three possible ways of reading the Scriptures, three possible senses—literal, moral, and mystic—which later became four: literal, moral, allegorical, and spiritual (or anagogical).

The problem they faced was how to *limit* scriptural interpretation— how, for example, to make it impossible for Jesus' destructive actions in the temple at Jerusalem to be interpreted as condoning violence. Clearly, the interpretation of scriptural allegory had to be governed by a code, and the code itself was defined by Christian theology: we can, so Augustine tells us, have as many interpretations as we like, but ultimately they all have to point to the same infinite and unalterable truth of God's word. In other words, interpretation meant always finding new ways of saying the same thing.

When the church fathers had formulated a basic system, later, medieval commentators on the Scriptures were able to elaborate the rules for "correct" interpretation. Their problem was that, since the Bible was God's work, and since God comprises everything, the Bible must, surely, *speak* of everything, so that everything seemed to be a potential symbol. Medieval commentators responded to this dilemma by producing huge numbers of lists and encyclopedias—copies of Pliny's *Natural History;* herbaria, bestiaries, lapidaries—all volumes in which they could assign symbolic values to everything that existed in the physical world. This meant that though a flower, for example, or an animal could, depending on the context in which it was used as a symbol, stand for many different things, in the context of the Bible it *had to* stand for the "right" thing and could be interpreted only in this way. Even so, many things listed in these medieval encyclopedias had various and sometimes contradictory symbolic meanings: the rooster, for example, could stand sometimes for the risen Christ, sometimes for the Devil. But it would always be clear from the context which was the right interpretation (*Limits* 9 ff.).

Aquinas, who was both theologian and poet, added his own conditions to those Augustine had set down in *De doctrina christiana* about seven hundred years earlier. He stressed that *only* the Scriptures should be interpreted as having any spiritual sense—worldly poetry should not be treated in the same way and should be read only literally, because whatever allegorical second sense it seemed to have was merely a variation of the literal one. This variant sense he called "parabolic." According to Aquinas, even the Scriptures should, first and foremost, be read literally; only then should we ask whether they necessarily carry a further, allegorical meaning. All the same, he did go so far as to admit that, because the Bible is the work of God, because it speaks of divine mysteries, it is sometimes beyond the reach of human understanding and for this reason sometimes speaks allegorically: so we see God the Father teaching his children by telling them stories. After all, Christ spoke to the disciples in the same way, teaching through parables. In the sixteenth century we find Sir Thomas Browne making precisely the same point in *Religio Medici*.

The end of the Bible's monopoly on spiritual allegory came with Dante Alighieri. As we have seen, so far our interpreters have concentrated on the Scriptures—though they have not ignored worldly literature, their rules for interpretation have been formulated specifically to apply to scriptural texts: they have all said that their rules do not apply to anything else. Thus they have discussed secular classical and medieval poetry only insofar as it provided them with negative examples, places where their rules ceased to function because they were not meant to.

Whether by accident or by design, Dante, born in 1265 nine years before Aquinas's death, was instrumental in changing this. In a letter to Cangrande della Scala, to whom he presented the last book, *Paradiso,* of his allegorical *Divina Commedia,* he offered an analysis of Psalm 114 according to the rules laid down concerning the four senses mentioned above. There was nothing revolutionary about his reading of the psalm, but the fact that he gave it in the context of the *Commedia* was understood by many to imply a belief on his part that the same rules could be applied to his own, secular poem; in other words, that the *Commedia* could be read as an allegory conveying a *spiritual* meaning (*Limits* 16). Once this was accepted, there was nothing to stop interpreters from applying the same rules, so carefully reserved by Augustine and Aquinas for scriptural texts, to all secular literature, and so the game of find-the-hidden-meaning could begin—or, rather, it could continue, but now everyone could play.

From Augustine to Aquinas the interpretive code had been limited by and referred to Scripture, and the permitted functions of symbols were therefore limited in the same way: they could refer to anything in the physical world, but only if these things were referred to in a biblical context could they convey a spiritual meaning as well as a literal one. We can see that if it was now allowed to attribute spiritual meaning to things symbolized in a nonbiblical context, then not only had the idea of the symbol itself changed dramatically but there was now a whole new universe of symbols and "objects"—things that symbols are interpreted as standing for—whose significance was not clearly defined. It is important to remember this because it was to prove a development that, in a Christian culture, allowed the term *spiritual* to acquire meaning outside a biblical context. For the time being, though, the "new" universe of symbols was really the same one that Augustine and the medieval commentators had mapped out, only now a previously unknown (or ignored) part of it had been discovered.

All the same, if the *Commedia* or any other secular poem had a spiritual meaning, then its author must, with or without realizing it, have been divinely inspired. However, almost every poet has at some time or other claimed to be inspired by love. We could say that because God is the originator of everything then he also contains love—it exists in him. But we would be forced to admit in the same breath that in this case he also contains hatred, and indeed everything else. This line of thought, if it were unregulated, could lead us to the idea that everything is "connected"—that a relationship, a kind of kinship or similarity, exists between every object in our universe. And if we believe this we can see everything as in some way standing for everything else. What would connect everything together would be its divine origin or "essence." Outside the church, this way of thinking, the so-called hermetic tradition, gained currency during the period of Renaissance humanism in Italy, and it is highly important for our study because, though it has undergone various modifications, we can still recognize its effects on poetry and on theories of interpretation as late as Romanticism.

Whatever form it took in the real world, whether animal, bird, plant, or precious stone, the medieval symbol had stood ultimately for God's work and God's word. The world was "univocal," speaking always and only of its creator. In this sense God was knowable. But in the hermetic tradition, where all things seem connected to each other, God is self-contradictory since he contains everything, a universe of ideas and, it must follow, their opposite ideas: love and hatred, joy and misery, peace and war, good and evil, and so on. A God who is in this way self-contradictory cannot be knowable in the medieval sense because we would never be able to finish describing him: whatever terms we used would only ever partially define him. In this tradition, symbols cannot speak of one thing without speaking, not of something else, but of *everything* else.

A similar approach is reflected in the definition of symbolism formulated much later by the German poet Goethe: "Symbolism transforms the experience into an idea and an idea into an image, so that the idea expressed through the image remains always active and unattainable and, even though expressed in all languages, remains inexpressible." For as much as Goethe professed to dislike romanticism, we find William Wordsworth sounding rather like him when he claimed, in his preface to *Lyrical Ballads* (1802), that poetry must be composed "in a state of vivid sensation" (*Ballads* 241). And in the twentieth century we find the poet Robert Graves saying something very similar: poetry is the "unaccountable product of a trance" (*On Poetry* 286).

If we know what we want our symbols to refer to—that is, if their objects are knowable—we hardly need to be "in a state of vivid sensation" (not to speak of "a trance") when we order them into a poem. It seems then that at least one twentieth-century poet refers back more than a thousand years to the view of poetry as a way of talking about something that is inexpressible because it is unknowable. As we shall see, there are many more; and as we shall also see, they are to be found even among those who at first seem vehemently opposed to anything in poetry that might be labeled "mysticism."

The French symbolists of the nineteenth century differed from the Romantics in claiming quite categorically that poetry (their poetry, at least) spoke of something attainable. Symbolism failed to differ from Romanticism in that it was unable to offer an explanation of what this attainable thing might be, except to call it an ideal world. For the symbolists, as for Plato, the real physical world was inhabited only by shadows of the ideal one, which was a world of essential Ideas, or Forms. Utterly unlike Plato, they held that poets could lead us into this world through symbols.

The symbolists' "heirs" in the English language were, most notably, W. B. Yeats, Ezra Pound, T. S. Eliot, and the so-called imagist poets. Eliot, for example, made frequent symbolic use of Fire, Water, and the Rose; while Pound turned a whole personal and idealized concept of Renaissance Italy into a symbol that he used to create a contrast with what he perceived as the decadence of Western cultures. (Yeats's fascination with the occult and its relation to his highly personalized system of symbols makes him of less interest to this study: our concern here is with broad traditions only.) In England there was a reaction against Eliot's kind of poetry by what became known as "the Movement" (though they were themselves reluctant to acknowledge the existence of any such group). Donald Davie and Philip Larkin were among those who looked to certain writers of the previous generation as upholders of what they saw as an English tradition as opposed to Eliot's more "European" intellectualism. Of those they turned to, I have singled out Robert Graves because of the remarkable consistency of his work, which implies an insistence on a particular attitude toward the function and production of poetry and on a particular kind of symbolism.

### PLATO

We do not know what Plato really thought about poetry and poets. All we know is what he says about them in the *Republic, Phaedrus, Ion,* and *Philebus.* But from these writings it is abundantly clear that we are meant to hold them in such low regard that we would agree with him in having them banned altogether from his ideal state. He may himself have enjoyed reading poetry—he has Socrates admit to *privately* enjoying the works of Homer—but in the context of the education of the young and of the pursuit of philosophical truth, he has no time for it.

In book 2 of the *Republic,* which deals with individual, state, and education, poetry is first mentioned in the context of the idea of justice. The setting for the arguments given to Socrates is a conversation between Glaucon, his brother Adeimantus, and Socrates himself. Adeimantus begins to speak disparagingly of poets when he associates them with those people who are concerned with reputation rather than with justice:

> Parents and tutors are always telling their sons and their wards that they are to be just; but why? not for the sake of justice, but for the sake of character and reputation; in the hope of obtaining for him who is reputed just, some of those offices, marriages and the like which Glaucon has enumerated among the advantages accruing to the unjust from the reputation of justice. More, however, is made of appearances by this class of persons than by others; for they throw in the good opinion of the gods, and will tell you a shower of benefits which the heavens, as they say, rain upon the pious; and this accords with the noble testimony of Hesiod and Homer, the first of whom says that the gods make the oaks of the just "To bear acorns at the summit, and bees in the middle; And the sheep are bowed down with the weight of their fleeces," and many other blessings of a like kind are provided for them. And Homer has a very similar strain; for he speaks of one whose fame is "As the fame

of some blameless king who, like a god, Maintains justice; to whom the black earth brings forth Wheat and barley, whose trees are bowed with fruit, And his sheep never fail to bear, and the sea gives him fish." (*Republic* 2)

Adeimantus goes on to discuss prose writers in the same vein, but points out that the poets are the authorities to whom they appeal,

now smoothing the path of vice with the words of Hesiod: "Vice may be had in abundance without trouble; the way is smooth and her dwelling-place is near. But before virtue the gods have set toil, and a tedious uphill road." . . . And now when the young hear all this about virtue and vice . . . how are their minds likely to be affected, my dear Socrates—those of them, I mean, who are quick-witted, and, like bees on the wing, light on every flower, and from all that they hear are prone to draw conclusions as to what manner of persons they should be and in what way they should walk if they would make the best of life? Probably the youth will say to himself in the words of Pindar: "Can I by justice or by crooked ways of deceit ascend a loftier tower which may be a fortress to me all my days?" (*Republic* 2)

We must consider Adeimantus's attack in its proper context: it is in fact directed against Socrates' claim that justice is the prime social virtue and therefore a concept of great value. Not so, replies Adeimantus, since people are concerned only with the *appearance* of justice, which will of itself bring various financial and social rewards, rather than with *actual* justice. His argument against the poetry of Hesiod and Homer is that, though it seems to praise justice, it is full of high-flown metaphor and simile that divert the reader away from the essential ideas under discussion toward the things and attributes that are used as comparisons. Thus in the quote from Homer, "As the fame of some blameless king who, like a god, Maintains justice," Adeimantus's point is that we, or the young in particular, are likely to focus more on the fame and the kingship than on the justice, and that therefore we are in danger of thinking that fame and kingship are the virtues the poet is extolling. Moreover, when he talks about the line from Pindar above, Adeimantus points out that, if the poets can be believed, we might just as well forget about virtue altogether and devote our efforts to the practice of deception:

If I am really just and am not also thought just, profit there is none, but the pain and loss on the other hand are unmistakable. But if, though unjust, I acquire the reputation of justice, a heavenly life is promised to me. Since then, as philosophers prove, appearance tyrannizes over truth and is lord of happiness, to appearance I must devote myself. I will describe around me a picture and shadow of virtue to be the vestibule and exterior of my house. . . . And there are professors of rhetoric who teach the art of persuading courts and assemblies; and so, partly by persuasion and partly by force, I shall make unlawful gains and not be punished. Still I hear a voice saying that the gods cannot be deceived, neither can they be compelled. But what if there are no gods? or, suppose them to have no care of human things—why in either case should we mind about concealment? And even if there are gods, and they do care about us, yet we know of them only from tradition and the genealogies of the poets; and these are the very persons who say that they may be influenced and turned by "sacrifices and soothing entreaties and by offerings" (*Republic* 2).

Adeimantus's argument against poetry is that it is not merely frivolous, talking of things that may or may not exist (gods), nor even that it obscures the truth from us by useless and irrelevant comparison (kingship, fame). It has, he thinks, both of these negative qualities, but the main thrust of his attack is that it is actively harmful: by suggesting that evil actions may go unpunished, it encourages those actions in us. When we hear about such actions in the real world, we should react with horror. When we read about them in poetry, however, or see them portrayed by actors, we are encouraged to find them attractive. (If Adeimantus's argument sounds familiar, this is because it is still to be heard in the debate on the censorship of television and film.)

Socrates does not refute any of this but merely brings the focus of the debate back to the idea of justice itself, ignoring for the moment its representation in poetry. This does not mean he considers it unimportant. On the contrary, he agrees. But he is himself a consummate rhetorician with a wonderfully methodical mind (having Plato write your arguments for you is an advantage) and will turn to the subject of poetry when he has first proved to Adeimantus that ideas are more important than appearances. Once this has been established, he can then go on to criticize poetry for concentrating on appearances—representation by means of metaphor, simile, symbol, and allegory.

The debate continues in book 3 of the *Republic,* which deals with the arts in education. Here the argument is given to Socrates, and he begins by discussing how poetry undermines soldiers' morale, and thus the security of the state, by instilling, from childhood up, the fear of death.[2] It does this by its terrifying descriptions of the underworld. Socrates therefore holds that

> we must beg Homer and the other poets not to be angry if we strike out these and similar passages, not because they are unpoetical, or unattractive to the popular ear, but because the greater the poetical charm of them, the less are they meet for the ears of boys and men who are meant to be free, and who should fear slavery more than death. . . . Also we shall have to reject all the terrible and appalling names which describe the world below—Cocytus and Styx, ghosts under the earth, and sapless shades, and any similar words of which the very mention causes a shudder to pass through the inmost soul of him who hears them. (*Republic* 3)

For the same reason, he wants to eradicate all descriptions of "weepings and wailings" of illustrious men, reserving lamentation over worldly loss for women and "men of a baser sort," so that "those who are being educated by us to be the defenders of their country may scorn to do the like." The same applies to gods, who must not be shown bemoaning the fate of a human favorite: "For if . . . our youth seriously listen to such unworthy representations of the gods, instead of laughing at them as they ought, hardly will any of them deem that he himself, being but a man, can be dishonored by similar actions" (*Republic* 3). Indeed, laughter is generally proscribed, for "a fit of laughter which has been indulged in to excess almost always produces a violent reaction," so that "persons of worth . . . must not be represented as overcome by laughter, and still less must such a representation of the gods be allowed."

In this way, Socrates and Adeimantus between them pass from one social and civic virtue to the next—temperance and self-control as opposed to sensuality and licentiousness; endurance, piety, generosity, love of truth—all of which are shown to be eroded by poetry. So, of course, the works of Homer and the other poets are whittled away until eventually nothing remains.

Their debate on appearances leads logically into a discussion of mimesis: imitation. Poetry, they say, especially narrative and dramatic poetry, operates by imitation in that the poet necessarily adopts the voice of the character whose actions and words he wishes to portray. We have already been told how seductive poetry can be, inducing us to behave badly simply by describing bad behavior. Now we learn, in addition, that actors and poets themselves will succumb to the same corruption if they are particularly skillful at representing it, since "imitations, beginning in early youth and continuing far into life, at length grow into habits and become a second nature, affecting body, voice, and mind," and for this reason

> we will not allow those for whom we profess a care and of whom we say that they ought to be good men, to imitate a woman, whether young or old, quarrelling with her husband, or striving and vaunting against the gods in conceit of her happiness, or when she is in affliction, or sorrow, or weeping; and certainly not one who is in sickness, love, or labor. . . . Neither must they represent slaves, male or female, performing the offices of slaves. . . . And surely not bad men, whether cowards or any other, who do the reverse of what we have been prescribing, who scold or mock or revile one another in drink or out of drink, or who in any other manner sin against themselves and their neighbors in word or deed. . . . Neither should they be trained to imitate the action or speech of men or women who are mad or bad; for madness, like vice, is to be known but not to be practiced or imitated. (*Republic* 3)

The debate also makes special mention of imitating the sounds of animals, musical instruments, and natural and physical phenomena such as the sound of thunder, wind, hail, or the creaking of wheels or pulleys. But the whole of what we have seen so far from the *Republic* points to one basic distinction: on the one hand there is a "real" world (the quotation marks are important here, as we shall soon see) of physical objects and ideas, while on the other there is appearance or imitation—or, rather, an imitation that produces an appearance. On the one hand there is "truth," and on the other there are mere representations and, in a sense, lies.

The actor symbolizes the character the author wishes to have represented in the theater, and his words and gestures are symbols for words and gestures that, we are meant to believe, his character would really say and perform. The poet who writes narrative verse offers his readers words and actions, heroic or evil, that symbolize real or assumed ones.

And why is Plato so much against symbols? Because "there are plenty of beds and tables in the world"—real ones, which can be used for sleeping on and eating from. But these real beds and tables are themselves mere symbols, signs that stand for the Form—the "essence" or idea of beds and tables. It is these ideal articles of household furniture that are, for Plato, real, and therefore more important. They will not do for everyday life because if we tried to make use of them we should soon find ourselves suffering from chronic back injury and without a single unbroken plate or cup, but Plato was making the point that the physical objects that surround us could not exist without having previously existed as ideas. This works very obviously for beds and tables, which are made by human beings, but it works also for stars, hills, birds, trees, and animals (including humans), which are all God's ideas. And if humans, too, are God's idea, then their ideas must also originate in him. Everything, then, is merely a representation of its divine essence; and we can now, by the way, also begin to see how there came to be something called a hermetic tradition that imagined a relation between everything in the universe.

But Plato was not interested in hermetic traditions. He was philosophically interested in the nature of reality, and because he believed in a One, a divine origin of all things, he was able to conclude that the closer we approach this One, the closer we approach reality, or truth. For this reason, any given thing is less real than its Form. Art, which Plato sees as representation, imitation, mimesis, is no more than a copy of something: a painting of a building or a landscape, music expressing joy, a dance expressing fear, or a poem describing the wanderings of Ulysses and the intervention of the gods in his progress. A painting of a building is not a building; it is merely a painting, however photo-realistic it might be. There are several paintings by the Belgian artist René Magritte that make precisely the same point: I mean the series of "pipe paintings." In the example I have in mind, Magritte depicts, in the center of the canvas, a curved, Sherlock Holmes–style pipe. Underneath this is written, "Ceci n'est pas une pipe" ("This is not a pipe"). It's a very Neoplatonic painting. Plato's point is that art (apart from all its other detrimental effects on society) takes us one step further from the truth. It is merely a representation of a representation, a symbol of a symbol.

Some modern approaches view language in a similar way. They see words as signs that can be interpreted only by using other words, therefore other signs. In this way, meaning is continually deferred. The only way out of this situation would be to impose some set of rules for interpretation. We shall see in the next chapter, on Augustine and the Middle Ages, how an attempt was made to do just that.

Plato makes another charge against poetry when he says that in practical terms it is not really an art at all—that it is not a skill (*technē*)—since poets compose under inspiration rather than by exercising the intellect. In the *Apology,* he shows, or rather describes, Socrates defending himself against the Athenians' charges that he was a corrupter of youth and subverter of public morals. Socrates relates how he went from person to person in order to find someone wiser than himself—each one a representative of a particular group: artisans, politicians, poets, and so on—only to discover that not only could they not be called wise but they were unable even to discourse coherently on their own professions.

> When I left the politicians, I went to the poets; tragic, dithyrambic, and all sorts.[3] And there, I said to myself, you will be detected; now you will find out that you are more ignorant than they are. Accordingly, I took them some of their most elaborate passages in their own writings, and asked what was the meaning of them—thinking that they would teach me something. Will you believe me? I am almost ashamed to speak of this, but still I must say that there is hardly a person present who would not have talked better about poetry than they did themselves. They showed me in an instant that not by wisdom do poets write poetry, but by a sort of genius and inspiration; they are like diviners or soothsayers who also say many fine things but do not understand the meaning of them. And the poets appeared to be much in the same case; and I further observed that upon the strength of their poetry they believed themselves to be the wisest of men in other things in which they were not wise. So I departed, conceiving myself to be superior to them for the same reason that I was superior to the politicians.

Poetry does not derive from wisdom but from "a sort of genius and inspiration," and poets are therefore "like soothsayers." If they say valuable things, this has nothing to do with any skill on their part since they merely receive their words from somewhere else. This is an important point because it was later developed, in very different ways, both by biblical interpreters and by the poet Dante and his contemporaries.

Plato's arguments against poetry can, then, be summed up in this way:

poetry is mere mimesis and therefore at two removes from the truth;
it teaches us, by example and by rousing our emotions, to behave in the
wrong way;
it is not the product of wisdom or *technē* but of inspiration.

We can now turn to Plato's brilliant student, Aristotle, the darling of
medieval philosophers and theorists of interpretation, to see how he answers these charges.

## ARISTOTLE

The *Poetics* has had more influence on the study of poetry and its interpretation than probably any other work written; it has the distinction
of being the first work to recognize that poetry is governed by its own
rules; and it is the first work devoted solely to literary theory. It is also
recognized, both by linguists and historians of literary interpretation,
to be central to the continuing debate on the nature of language and
meaning.

The *Poetics* bases in Aristotle's rejection of Plato's theory of Forms, the
theory that produces the sequence: *Form* (Idea)—*Object* (in the physical
world)—*mimesis* (artistic representation), used by Plato to demonstrate
the distance of poetry from truth. Aristotle's rejection of Plato's theory is
not total. He retains, for example, the idea of poetry as mimesis, and he
accepts the claim that poetry arouses the emotions. His interpretation of
these facts, however, is radically different from Plato's. Where Plato uses
mimesis in the negative senses of "copy" and "impersonate," Aristotle's
claim is that poetry *represents* the deeds and objects of the physical world
in the same way that language represents ideas. This is crucial because it
allows him to make the further point that recognizing something as a representation of something else is an intellectual process. If this is so, then
we must allow that reading poetry, since it is an intellectual process, is
something that can be learned, and this, in turn, must mean that there are
rules for reading poetry; that is, rules for interpreting representations.
This would certainly explain the attraction Aristotle held for early interpreters of Scripture.

13

His comments on representation also make clear that he accepts the fact that poetry can cause pleasure (if it is any good) as something natural:

> Representation is natural to human beings from childhood. They differ from the other animals in this: man tends most towards representation and learns his first lessons through representation.
>
> Also, everyone delights in representations. An indication of this is what happens in fact: we delight in looking at the most detailed images of things which in themselves we see with pain, e.g. the shapes of the most despised wild animals even when dead. The cause of this is that learning is most pleasant, not only for philosophers but for others likewise (but they share in it to a small extent). For this reason they delight in seeing images, because it comes about that they learn as they observe, and infer what each thing is, e.g. that this person [represents] that one. For if one has not seen the thing [that is represented] before, [its image] will not produce pleasure as a representation, but because of its accomplishment, color, or some other such cause.[4] (*Poetics* 4)

A modern example of "things which in themselves we see with pain" but whose artistic representation might cause "delight" would be the spiritual desolation of Vladimir and Estragon in *Waiting for Godot* or the abuse of the character Lucky in the same play (though the bloodthirsty ghouls from *Night of the Living Dead* would do just as well). At any rate, between those two rather extreme examples there is room, so to speak, for a good deal of real-life pain and aesthetic delight.

In the same passage, Aristotle stresses that this delight is related to learning—we delight in images because we learn as we observe. But he also says that learning, in this context, means that we "infer what each thing is." There is no mention yet of learning to be a good citizen, or of learning to be just, pious, or virtuous. What he means by learning is knowing something that we previously did not know. In this sense, Aristotle seems to be equating learning with interpretation. This is important because the idea that poetry can, or must, both "teach and delight" is one that English critics of the sixteenth century took every opportunity of quoting. We shall see, however, that they were concerned with not so much with aesthetics as with moral implications.

What he writes on recognition—on learning, or inferring, what is being represented—is strikingly modern. The example he gives is of the recognition, in tragedy, of one character by another:

A recognition, as the word itself indicates, is a change from ignorance to knowledge, and so to either friendship or enmity, among people defined in relation to good fortune or misfortune. . . . There are indeed other [kinds of] recognition. For it can happen in the manner stated regarding inanimate objects and random events; and one can recognize whether someone has done something or not done it. . . . Since recognition is a recognition of people, some recognitions are by one person only of the other, when the identity of one of them is clear; but sometimes there must be a recognition of both persons. E.g. Iphigenia [in Euripides' play *Iphigenia in Tauris*] is recognized by Orestes as a result of her sending the letter, but it requires another recognition for him [to be recognized] by her. (*Poetics* 14)

The idea of the girl Iphigenia being recognized through a letter she has written, the idea of her presence, somewhere, implied by the page bearing her handwriting, is very similar to the one used by Umberto Eco in his discussion of symbol and allegory:

Originally a symbol was a token, the present half of a broken table or coin or medal, that performed its social and semiotic function [i.e., its function as a sign] by recalling the absent half to which it potentially could be reconnected. This potentiality was indeed crucial because, since the two halves could be reconnected, it was unnecessary to yearn for the reconnection. So, too, it happens today that, when we enter a theatre with our ticket stub, nobody tries to check where the other half is; everyone trusts the semiotic nature of the token, which in this case works on the basis of an established and recognized convention. (*Limits* 9)

We can see why Aristotle still attracts close critical attention almost two and a half thousand years after the production of the *Poetics*. Even what he says about knowing something one did not previously know is reflected in the modern debate on whether interpretation means knowing something *more* or knowing something *else*.

The much-quoted passage on "universals" runs, from the beginning of the relevant section, as follows:

It is also obvious from what we have said that it is the function of a poet to relate not things that have happened, but things that may happen, i.e. that are possible in accordance with probability or necessity. For the historian and the poet do not differ according to whether they write in verse or without verse—the writings of Herodotus could be put into verse, but they would be no less a sort of history in verse than they are without verses. But the former relates things that have happened, the latter things that may happen. For this reason poetry is a more philosophical and more serious thing than history; poetry tends to speak of universals, history of particulars. A universal is the sort of thing that a certain kind of person may well say or do in accordance with probability or necessity—this is what poetry aims at, although it assigns names [to the people]. A particular is [e.g.] what Alcibiades did or what he suffered. (*Poetics* 12)

Aristotle's "what we have said" concerns the nature of the plot in verse drama and in narrative poems. Some poets, Aristotle says, erroneously suppose that "because Heracles was a single person, his story too must be a single story." But "an indefinitely large number of things" happen to individuals during the course of their lives, and this leads bad poets into the error of including (in our example) every known fact, or myth, about Heracles' life in their poems about his adventures. Aristotle cites the *Odyssey* as an example of a better poem because Homer did not include everything that happened to Odysseus but left out unnecessary details that had no logical consequence that would develop the narrative a step further. Homer "constructed the *Odyssey* around a single action," by which Aristotle means the completed action, or act, of Odysseus's tortuous journey home to Ithaca. The poem's title stands for all the individual episodes that together make up this completed action. These episodes and individual incidents are what Aristotle calls universals; the superfluous details are "particulars." In Homer's poem, when characters speak or do things, their words and deeds—within the context of a narrative concerned with superhuman heroes, gods, demigods, and goddesses—are just what we might reasonably expect such characters to say and do. There is nothing mystical about Aristotle's universals.

He goes into some detail on his use of the term *metaphor*, by which he means "the application to something of a name belonging to something else." The literal meaning of the Greek word *metaphora* is "transference," and Aristotle speaks of transference (of names) between *genus* and *species*. In formal logic, a genus is a class of things that includes subordinate classes, as in the relation between the genus *human beings* and the species *men, women, children;* or between the genus *men* and the species *Italian men* or *men with blond hair,* for example. The example Aristotle gives of transference from species to genus is the line "truly has Odysseus done ten thousand deeds of worth," and he explains that the species *ten thousand* is part of the genus *many* (Homer uses the exaggeration simply to stand for "a lot").

Aristotle then exemplifies transference from species to species: "Killing a man by draining out his life with bronze" [i.e., a weapon] and "drawing water by cutting it with long-edged bronze" [i.e., a bowl]. He explains that the poet calls "cutting" *draining,* and "draining" *cutting,* both terms being species of the genus *taking away.*

He then lists transference by analogy, under which term *a* is to *b* as *c* is to *d;* for example, a man in love might say to himself "she is to me as Aphrodite is to love—she is my goddess." He would then be able to startle his beloved by telling her, "You were born of the foam of the sea."

If all this seems rather hair-splitting, we need to remember that Aristotle was the first in what has become the Western interpretive tradition to deal systematically with poetic devices; and what he is talking about—saying one thing and meaning another—is indeed the subject of this book. His ideas become much clearer from the further examples he gives of *metaphora: the shield of Dionysus* for "wine-bowl"; *the wine-bowl of Ares* (the god of war) for "shield"; "evening" is *the old age of the day*; while old age itself is *the evening of life.* There are any number of ghastly euphemisms in modern English that equate to this last example.

Finally, there remains Plato's charge that poetry—comedy, tragedy, and epic—arouses the emotions, and that this is a bad thing since we should always seek to control emotions. Aristotle certainly agreed that poetry could have a strong emotional effect on its hearers, but he also thought that this could be a good thing. In fact, a well-written tragedy can, he says, cause "catharsis"—"purification" of the emotions. The problem for scholars is that, though Aristotle gives us this description in *Poetics* 1, he offers no further explanation of it. In *Politics* 8 he mentioned it again, and promised to deal with it in the *Poetics*—presumably he did so in book 2, on comedy, which unfortunately, apart from a few fragments, is now lost to us. He also seems to have discussed it in *On Poets.* But scholars have been able to reconstruct an outline of his ideas from the comments of later writers who seem to have known the missing works directly, combining these comments with what we have in Aristotle's own words. Janko offers the following summary in the introduction to his excellent translation of the *Poetics:*

> Taking tragedy as an example, the cathartic process works as follows. By representing pitiable, terrifying and other painful events, tragedy arouses pity, terror and other painful emotions in the audience, for each according to his own emotional capacity, and so stimulates these emotions as to relieve them by giving them moderate and harmless exercise, thereby bringing the audience nearer to the mean in their emotional responses, and so nearer to virtue in their characters; and with this relief comes pleasure. Comedy works on the pleasant emotions in the same way. (*Poetics* xix–xx)

The important point is that what we are responding to is *representation*—we have already seen that Aristotle makes a very definite distinction between painful scenes in real life and their "re-creation" in dramatic or narrative verse. Of course, poetry does not really re-create events, just as Magritte's painting of a pipe does not really re-create a pipe. Even so, Aristotle would say the we are perfectly entitled to delight in looking at Magritte's painting "for no other reason than because of its shape."

Aristotle claims that we should be able to find out whether music—under which term he includes poetry—"contributes to the character and the soul" by finding out whether we become certain kinds of people because of it. That we indeed do he holds to be obvious, and he cites the songs of Olympus—that is, religious poems set to music—as an example:

> For it is agreed that these arouse the soul to ecstasy, and ecstasy is an emotion of the character connected with the soul. Again, when listening to representations, everyone comes to share in the emotion, even apart from rhythms and songs themselves.
>
> Since music happens to belong among pleasant things, and virtue is connected with feeling delight correctly and loving and hating [correctly], clearly one should learn, and become habituated to, nothing so much as judging correctly, i.e. feeling delight in decent characters and fine actions. Rhythms and songs contain especially close likenesses of the true natures of anger and mildness, bravery, temperance and all their opposites, and of the other traits of character: this is clear from the facts— we are moved in our soul when we listen to such things. (*Politics* 8)

In other words, we can learn to appreciate virtues through their representation in poetry, to share in them and emulate them, and through force of habit acquire them ourselves. Aristotle's response to Plato's charges against poetry can, then, be summed up as follows:

> Because poetry has a set of rules that can be comprehended by the intellect, the charge that it is not a real skill, or *technē,* is not valid.
>
> Poetry is certainly *mimesis,* but this cannot be called a bad thing since we can learn from representations.
>
> Connected to the second point is the one we have just discussed: poetry may well arouse the emotions, but in doing so we actually regulate them through *catharsis,* or "purification."

# RELIGION, PHILOSOPHY, AND
# INTERPRETATION IN THE MIDDLE AGES

## *AUGUSTINE*

Book 1 of Augustine's *De doctrina christiana* begins by telling us that there are two things "upon which all interpretation of Scripture depends: the mode of ascertaining the proper meaning, and the mode of making known the meaning when it is ascertained." We learn from the outset, then, that this is a work about limiting interpretation: firstly, we gather that systematic textual analysis is to be confined to Scripture; secondly, if there is a "proper" meaning of Scripture that must be ascertained, there must be other possible interpretations that will not do. The first point needs to be borne in mind because important aspects of it were to hold for many centuries. The consequences of Augustine's second point form the body of this chapter.

The first example he gives of proper interpretation does not concern a physical symbol—a rose, a shield, a burning bush—but words, a quotation from the Bible: "Whosoever hath, to him shall be given" (Mark 6:30). Augustine's interpretation is that those who have, provided they use whatever it is they have received from God "freely and cheerfully," will be given more and thus be able to continue to share their gift. He relates this interpretation not only to the miracle of the loaves with which the disciples fed five thousand, but to his own task of setting down the *doctrina christiana*:

> Just as the bread increased in the very act of breaking it, so these thoughts which the Lord has already vouchsafed to me with a view to undertaking this work will, as soon as I begin to impart them to others, be multiplied by His grace, so that, in this very work of distribution in

20

which I have engaged, so far from incurring loss and poverty, I shall be made to rejoice in a marvelous increase of wealth. (*Doct. christ.* 1.1)

It is difficult, by the way, not be reminded of the appeals to the Muses for assistance with which classical poets began their epics. Augustine would not have been pleased.

But what he establishes by relating the quotation from the Gospel of Mark to the feeding of the five thousand and to his own undertaking is that there are different ways of reading things. Augustine certainly believed in the literal sense of Mark's words, that the disciples were *in fact* able to feed five thousand hungry followers with a few loaves of bread, but he also believed that the event stood for something else, or something more. In this case the something more is the general law that "whosoever hath, to him shall be given." But so that this law cannot be read as, for example, a justification of the division between rich and poor, it needs to be interpreted in the allegorical sense Augustine gives it.

Augustine inherited a classical tradition of interpretation that distinguished between *allegoria in factis* (event or deed as allegory) and *allegoria in verbis* (word or words as allegory). For biblical interpretation it was essential to give precedence to *allegoria in factis,* since if it were accepted that the very words of the Bible, rather than the events to which they referred, were used in an allegorical sense, it would be possible to believe that the events they reported need not have really occurred at all but were simply parables invented for instructional purposes. Therefore Augustine needed to read the miracle of feeding the five thousand as *allegoria in factis:* it actually occurred, but is also symbolic of a point of Christian doctrine. All the same, he was certainly aware that he was dealing with a linguistic problem, for he gives the next chapter of *doctrina christiana* the heading "What a Thing Is, and What a Sign," and, having discussed things "which are never employed as a sign of anything else: for example, wood, stone, cattle" (and then remembering that "the wood which, we read, Moses cast into the waters to make them sweet," "the stone which Jacob used as a pillow," and "the ram which Abraham offered up instead of his son" are also signs) he points out that

there are signs of another kind, those that are never employed except as signs: for example, words. No one uses words except as signs of something else; and hence may be understood what I call signs: those things, to wit, which are used to indicate something else. Accordingly, every sign is also a thing, for what is not a thing is nothing at all. Every thing, however, is not also a sign. . . . But we must carefully remember that what we have now to consider about things is what they are in themselves, not what they are signs of. (*Doct. christ.* 1.2)

For Augustine to say that not all things are signs seems to indicate that he rejected Plato's theory of Forms, which sees all things as physical representations of their Ideas; and indeed in *doctrina christiana* he mentions Plato, or at least his admirers, only disparagingly. His first mention of the Platonists is in the context of their claim that "our Lord Jesus Christ learnt all those sayings of His, which [the followers of Plato] are compelled to admire and praise, from the books of Plato—because (they urged) it cannot be denied that Plato lived long before the coming of our Lord!" In fact this is exactly the kind of argument that Eco (*Limits* 18–19) cites as typical of the hermetic thought that gained currency during the Renaissance:

> A typical example of such an attitude is the way in which every Hermetic thinker is able to demonstrate that the *Corpus Hermeticum* is not a late product of Hellenistic civilization—as Isaac Casaubon has proved—but comes before Plato, before Pythagoras, before Egyptian civilization. The argument runs as follows: "That the *Corpus Hermeticum* contains ideas that evidently circulated at the times of Plato means that it appeared before Plato."

We might just as well argue that, because today's *New York Times* carries an article about gold smuggling during World War II, it was printed before 1939.

The important point in Augustine's distinction above is his claim that "every thing is not a sign" and his caution to consider things in terms of "what they are in themselves" rather than "what they are signs of." As we can see from the examples of wood and stone he himself gives, he is perfectly aware that every thing *can* be a sign, but in attempting to make the distinction between things and signs—that is, between things and the words that denote them—he is enabling himself to say, depending on the context: Now I mean the object *stone,* and, Now I mean the word *stone.* This is crucial to the doctrine that (1) Scripture should be read first literally and only then (if at all) allegorically, and (2) that it is only in the context of Scripture that texts can be read as allegory conveying a spiritual meaning—the point that was later stated categorically by Aquinas. This second point is in fact logical and necessary from Augustine's point of view since all spiritual meaning in the world must be contained in the ages before Christ, which anticipate him, and during his lifetime on earth: after the Resurrection the world was left to human affairs. The latest texts that could possibly be read as spiritual allegory were therefore those collected in the New Testament.

In book 2.3 of *De doctrina christiana,* Augustine distinguishes between natural and conventional signs, natural signs being those that occur without any intention of their being used as such (he gives animals' footprints, or the smoke rising from a fire, as examples). Accordingly, conventional signs are those "which living beings mutually exchange for the purpose of showing, as well as they can, the feelings of their minds, or their perceptions, or their thoughts." This class includes those signs given to humans by God, made known to us by the human-produced (but divinely inspired) Scriptures, and it is the one Augustine concentrates on. The most important group in this class is words—words have "among men obtained far and away the chief place as a means of indicating the thoughts of the mind" (*Doct. christ.* 2.4). However, some nonverbal signs denote events so mystical that they could not, anyway, be expressed in human language: Augustine gives as examples the odor of the ointment poured upon Christ's feet and the making "whole" of the woman who touched the hem of his robe. Faced with the impossibility of discussing events for which there exists no language, Augustine thinks it wise to let their signs well alone and concentrate on verbal ones. These he divides into two groups: "proper," as in the Latin word *bos,* signifying "ox;" and "figurative," as in *bos* used to signify literally "ox" but also to symbolize a preacher of the gospel, "as Scripture signifies, according to the apostle's explanation, when it says: 'Thou shalt not muzzle the ox that treadeth out the corn'" (*Doct. christ.* 2.10).

The point of his distinction between things and signs becomes absolutely clear in 2.16. Having dealt with the nature of things "as they are in themselves" and the nature of the signs that denote them in everyday language, he then moves on to discuss textual ambiguities arising from ignorance of things, by which he means ignorance of their natural qualities. For example, when Scripture tells us we should be as wise as serpents, it would be ignorance of things, "as when we do not know the nature of animals," that would deny us the understanding that the reference is to the behavior of snakes—that

> to protect its head [the serpent] will present its whole body to its assailants . . . that is to say, that for the sake of our head, which is Christ, we should willingly offer our body to the persecutors, lest the Christian faith should, as it were, be destroyed in us, if to save the body we deny our God! Or again, the statement that the serpent gets rid of its old skin by squeezing itself through a narrow hole, and thus acquires a new strength—how appropriately it fits in with the direction to imitate the wisdom of the serpent, and to put off the old man, as the apostle says that we may put on the new, and to put it off, too, by coming through a narrow place, according to the saying of our Lord, "Enter ye in at the strait gate!" As, then, the knowledge of the nature of the serpent throws light upon the many metaphors which Scripture is accustomed to draw from that animal, so ignorance of other animals, which are no less frequently mentioned by way of comparison, is a very great drawback to the reader.

The same applies to minerals and plants: awareness that the carbuncle shines in the dark "throws light upon many of the dark places in books" that make symbolic use of it; the olive branch symbolizes perpetual peace because "the smooth touch of olive oil is not easily spoiled by a fluid of another kind" and because the olive itself is an evergreen; if we know that the plant hyssop cleanses the lungs and can in spite of its insignificant appearance pierce rock with its roots, we can understand "Purge me with hyssop, and I shall be clean" (Psalm 51:7).

The same also applies to numbers. Moses, Elijah, and Jesus all fasted for forty days because the number (four times ten) indicates "the knowledge of all things": there are four seasons, the twenty-four hours of the day are divided into four (morning, afternoon, evening, night). The number ten signifies the knowledge of God and his creatures: God is a trinity; life consists of three "parts" (the "three ages of man"); and there are four elements, earth, air, fire, water, of which creatures are constituted: thus, the four elements added to the three ages of man make seven, and seven plus the three of the Trinity equals ten. The number four is time-related, and therefore worldly, while the number ten is related to spiritual matters. Therefore a withdrawal from the world for forty days signifies a mystical combination of the spiritual with a rejection of temporal pleasures. It all seems highly convoluted, but we need to remember that Augustine held these laws of things and numbers to have been discovered, not invented, by humans. It is certainly true, at any rate, that numbers and combinations of numbers play a significant role (in more senses than one) in Scripture.

Everything, then, that exists in the physical world has a potential symbolic value, but Augustine needed to ensure that the interpretation of Scriptural symbols was not left entirely to the imagination of the individual. For this reason he makes a point of composing a list (*Doct. christ.* 2.20–26) as proof of "the superstitious nature of human institutions": numerology; astrology; the worshipping of idols; "consultations and arrangements about signs and leagues with devils"; all kinds of magic and augury; amulets, charms, incantations; and the "thousands of the most frivolous practices" his contemporaries indulged in, such as making sure to step on the threshold when leaving the house; regarding clothes gnawed by mice as an omen of coming misfortune; and going back to bed if anyone should happen to sneeze as you were getting up.

Book 2 of *De doctrina christiana* deals essentially with "unknown signs"—that snake, for example, of whose characteristics we are ignorant and that we cannot, therefore, read in the context Augustine wishes us to: we cannot see why it should be a wise snake. Whatever would we do without Augustine? This question is not meant ironically: there is an answer, and it demonstrates very clearly how absolutely essential it was for Augustine to set down rules for interpretation, to formulate the code with which the mysteries of Scripture could be decoded. Without such a code, we could freely associate these "unknown signs," the things of which Scripture speaks, according to our own capabilities—our powers of imagination and our personal circumstances: the aleatory conditions[1] that influence our ability to associate one thing with another. In other words, without Augustine's code, interpretation would have been able to produce theories of deconstruction, hermetic drift,[2] and so on. Or, in a different and more alarming context, we would have produced heretical readings of Scripture and been burned at the stake by grand inquisitors.

Ignorance of snakes might have counted as an excuse (especially for people in Ireland, from which country all snakes were of course banished by Saint Patrick), but when we were faced with what Augustine calls "ambiguous signs" we would know that we had a choice between a right and at least one wrong interpretation: the odds on escaping the flames would have been against us. To resolve this problem, Augustine formulated the method of dealing with ambiguous signs that makes up the greater part of book 3. He says that ambiguity arises in two ways. Either the sign is a "direct" (nonfigurative) one that might be ambiguous because of idiosyncratic punctuation or uncertain etymology; in this case we should refer to the original language or compare translations. Those who, like the present author, lack Hebrew, will feel more comfortable with the signs Augustine says are ambiguous because they are figurative, and it is on these that he himself concentrates in book 3.

The first thing he does is to warn against interpreting literal signs figuratively, and vice versa. This means that we need to be able to recognize which signs are which, and on this point Augustine tells us that "whatever can be shown to be in its literal sense inconsistent either with purity of life or correctness of doctrine must be taken figuratively"; furthermore, on signs that have been "proved to be figurative" he says that the general principle for interpretation is that "no interpretation can be true which does not promote the love of God and the love of man."

Too strict adherence to the letter of Scripture is a form of slavery, and it was precisely this overrigorous sense of the literal that was responsible, according to Augustine, for the Jews' rejection of Jesus as Messiah:

> And although they paid attention to the signs of spiritual realities in place of the realities themselves, not knowing to what the signs referred, still they had this conviction rooted in their minds, that in subjecting themselves to such a bondage they were doing the pleasure of the one invisible God of all. And the apostle describes this bondage as being like to that of boys under the guidance of a schoolmaster. And those who clung obstinately to such signs could not endure our Lord's neglect of them when the time for their revelation had come; and hence their leaders brought it as a charge against Him that He healed on the Sabbath, and the people, clinging to these signs as if they were realities, could not believe that one who refused to observe them in the way Jews did was God, or came from God . . . he is in bondage to a sign who uses, or pays homage to, any significant object without knowing what it signifies: he, on the other hand, who either uses or honors a useful sign divinely appointed, whose force and significance he understands, does not honor the sign which is seen and temporal, but that to which all such signs refer. (*Doct. christ.* 3.6–9)

All the same, "it is better to be in bondage to unknown but useful signs than, by interpreting them wrongly, to draw the neck from under the yoke of bondage only to insert it into the coils of error" (*Doct. christ.* 3.9). There is, then, a twofold danger of misinterpretation: interpreting wrongly, and not interpreting at all. This does not affect the view that we should read Scripture first literally and then as allegory, but Augustine is well aware that there are numerous passages in the Old Testament that demand allegorical reading if they are to be understood as referring to Christ specifically, rather than to a Messiah whose arrival on earth is indefinitely deferred. He may also have felt uneasy about the obvious superfluity, in a Christian context, of long lists and genealogies such as those contained in the Book of Numbers if they were not assumed to carry mystic symbolic senses. Otherwise they would simply be lists of genealogies.

The actual rule he formulates for interpreting figurative expressions is brief, and at first reading rather obscure: "In regard to figurative expressions, a rule such as the following will be observed, to carefully turn over in our minds and meditate upon what we read till an interpretation be found that tends to establish the reign of love. Now, if when taken literally it at once gives a meaning of this kind, the expression is not to be considered figurative" (*Doct. christ.* 3.15). A text, or a reading of a text, that "tends to establish the reign of love" is one in accordance with the Christian doctrine of charity *(caritas)*, which Augustine defines as "that affection of the mind which aims at the enjoyment of God for His own sake, and the enjoyment of one's self and one's neighbor in subordination to God" (*Doct. christ.* 3.16). Symbolic language in Scripture is to be "picked out as food for the nourishment of charity" (*Doct. christ.* 3.18) since Scripture "enjoins nothing except charity" (*Doct. christ.* 3.15).

This, then, is the basis upon which the whole of Augustine's theory of interpretation is founded. Whoever reads the Bible must recognize, first, what is meant to be read allegorically and what is to be taken solely literally. But without a clearly defined and regulated code, allegory can be interpreted only in terms familiar to the interpreter—the situations, images, and associations made possible by the circumstances of the interpreter's own life. For Augustine, a learned philosopher of the church, it was natural to discuss biblical allegory in terms of other biblical allegories and to refer to the commentaries of his contemporaries and predecessors. Also, he was writing *De doctrina christiana* for the purpose of disseminating his own religion according to correct doctrine, as a kind of evangelical handbook, and his "target readership" consisted largely of monks and priests engaged in this missionary endeavor. He was perfectly aware, though, that congregations are not made up of monks and priests, and for this reason he had to allow that people make associations according to what they know and what they see every day. He implies as much in the *City of God,* in his own allegorical interpretation of Eden:

> No one can stop us from interpreting paradise symbolically as the life of the blessed; its four rivers as the four virtues, prudence, courage, temperance and justice; its trees as all the beneficial disciplines; the fruit of the trees as the character of the righteous; the tree of life as wisdom, the mother of all good things; and the tree of the knowledge of good and evil as the experience of disobedience to a commandment. . . . This is the kind of thing that can be said by way of allegorical interpretation of paradise; and there may be other more valuable lines of interpretation. There is no prohibition against such exegesis, provided that we also believe in the truth of the story as a faithful record of historical fact. (*City of God* 13.22)

Essentially, then, it makes no difference what signs we use to describe to ourselves the signs in Scripture so long as they lead to "that affection of mind which aims at the enjoyment of God for His own sake, and the enjoyment of one's self and one's neighbor in subordination to God."

This duality certainly poses problems for modern readers brought up in an environment of reader-response theories, and some students, at least, are likely to find extremely distasteful the idea that an association, personal and apparently freely made, should be disregarded or found "wrong" because it happens not to be readily adaptable to a system of religious beliefs. Of course, we could point out that any system that tries to exist without such, or similar, limitations will inevitably fall to pieces; or that each of us constantly rejects possible interpretations in the process of everyday discourses—life would be impossible if we did not. But it is also true that, because of the enormous power, both spiritual and temporal, acquired by the Roman Catholic Church until it embraced all of Europe and beyond, what Augustine said about interpretation can be said to have directly affected the lives of everyone living in Christendom. His point was that for Christianity to continue to exist, what it meant to be Christian had to be as nearly defined as possible. The obvious ambiguity of many passages in

Scripture made this definition difficult, and therefore the ambiguities had to be removed. Since the text itself was sacred and the ambiguities should not be removed physically, their interpretation must be regulated. Hence his insistence that we need to understand the nature of things—animals, birds, music: anything that Scripture uses as a sign, since this knowledge enables us finally to establish that any given sign—"dog," "ruby," "milk," and so on—could *paradigmatically,* by a process of free association, be linked to anything at all, as in the sequence: *dog—animal—human—Augustine of Hippo. Syntagmatically* however, in any logical, everyday context, we should not readily be able to infer "Augustine of Hippo" from "dog." The symbolism of the Bible must function according to a *particular* code: it must function syntagmatically, not paradigmatically:[3]

> The same word does not always signify the same thing. And when it is shown to be figurative, the words in which it is expressed will be found to be drawn either from like objects or from objects having some affinity. But as there are many ways in which things show a likeness to each other, we are not to suppose that what a thing signifies by similitude in one place it is to be taken to signify in all other places. . . . The following is an example of the same object being taken, not in opposite, but only in different significations: water denotes people, as we read in Apocalypse, and also the Holy Spirit, as for example, "Out of his belly shall flow rivers of living water"; and many other things besides water must be interpreted according to the place in which they are found. . . . And in the same way other objects are not single in their signification, but each one of them denotes not two only but sometimes even several different things, according to the connection in which it is found. (*Doct. christ.* 25)

Furthermore, "from the places where the sense in which [signs] are used is more manifest we must gather the sense in which they are to be understood in obscure passages." The implication is clear: the code that is to be used to unlock Scripture is Scripture itself. The things the Bible speaks of are to be defined according to their nature, "as they are in themselves," and ambiguities resolved by reference to these defined things. The ambiguous Bible thus becomes the ultimate closed text—speaking of itself, referring to itself, a self-defining and self-contained mirror of God.[4]

## *THOMAS AQUINAS*

In his *Summa theologiae,* Aquinas addresses Roman Catholic doctrine in a series of objections and replies. He formulates apparently logical objections to various points of dogma, and then, rather like Socrates talking to Adeimantus, sets about dismantling them. In the first part of his work particularly he deals with metaphor and interpretation. First of all he addresses the argument that "Holy Scripture should not use metaphors." The objection against metaphor (and by implication against symbol, allegory, "similitudes," and all sorts of figurative language) runs as follows:

> Metaphor is the device of "the lowest science" (i.e., poetry) and therefore is unfit for Scripture and theology, "which holds the highest place of all."
> Scripture purports to make divine truths clear and should not therefore obscure them by speaking of them symbolically, especially if those symbols are "corporeal," worldly things.
> Since the higher creatures are nearer to the divine likeness than lower ones, it should (if at all) be by means of comparison with the former that God is represented, yet Scripture frequently chooses the latter for its similes.

Aquinas responds by pointing out that

> it is befitting Holy Writ to put forward divine and spiritual truths by means of comparisons with material things. For God provides for everything according to the capacity of its nature. Now it is natural to man to attain to intellectual truths through sensible objects [i.e., objects that are perceived through the senses], because all our knowledge originates from sense. Hence in Holy Writ, spiritual truths are fittingly taught under the likeness of material things. This is what Dionysius says [in his *On the Celestial Hierarchy* i]: "We cannot be enlightened by the divine rays except they be hidden within the covering of many sacred veils." . . . It is also befitting Holy Writ, which is proposed to all without distinction of persons . . . that spiritual truths be expounded by means of figures taken from corporeal things, in order that thereby even the simple who are unable by themselves to grasp intellectual things may be able to understand it. (*Summa theol.* 1.1.i.9)

In respect of this last idea, we might point out that if Scripture were really intended to reveal divine truths to even the "simple," then ambiguities ought not to be present at all. But Aquinas's point is that divine truths are usefully, even necessarily, veiled in symbol and metaphor since this process "does not allow the minds of those to whom the revelation has been made, to rest in the metaphors, but raises them to the knowledge of truths" (*Summa theol.* 1.1.i.9). If this is so, it must mean that in the very act of symbolic representation, the act of writing, truth is revealed to the author so that writing and revelation are simultaneous and even synonymous. Furthermore, "through those to whom the revelation has been made others may also receive instruction in these matters" (*Summa theol.* 1.1.i.9). This is an important point because it equates to the proposal of the French symbolists in the nineteenth century that an ideal world could be attained through (their own) poetry. As for the "simple," "those things that are taught metaphorically in one part of Scripture, in other parts are taught more openly." Aquinas is careful to point out that worldly poetry does not work in the same way, and he does so, with unintentional irony, by echoing Aristotle's defense of worldly poetry against Plato's criticisms: whereas Scripture "makes use of metaphors as both necessary and useful," poetry employs them "to produce a representation, for it is natural to man to be pleased with representations" (*Summa theol.* 1.1.i.9).

In response to the objection that Scripture makes frequent use of "lower" creatures in its similes, Aquinas constructs an argument that gives us insight into his understanding of the nature and function of symbols themselves. First he says that this choice of symbol is good because it makes perfectly clear that the signs in question do not refer to things "as they are in themselves"—that "these things are not literal descriptions of divine truths, which might have been open to doubt had they been expressed under the figure of nobler bodies" (*Summa theol.* 1.1.i.9). But then he goes on to tell us that this method of representation is in fact a proper reflection of our worldly knowledge of God: "For what He is not is clearer to us than what He is. Therefore similitudes drawn from things farthest away from God form within us a truer estimate that God is above whatsoever we may say or think of Him" (*Summa theol.* 1.1.i.9). In contrast, then, with Augustine's idea that symbols are chosen from "like objects or from objects having some affinity" with the idea symbolized, Aquinas states quite categorically that in this context symbols function through the *difference* between them and what they speak of; in other words, they function by a process rather like that which modern interpretive theory knows as defamiliarization. The obvious dissimilarity between symbol and symbolized (or sign and signified) "shocks" the reader into paying closer attention, and by understanding "what is not," that reader will be led toward an understanding of "what is."

The next objection Aquinas addresses is related to the previous one and concerns the senses in which Scripture is to be read. Holy Writ cannot, according to this argument,

> have several senses, historical or literal, allegorical, tropological [i.e., figurative] or moral, and anagogical [i.e., spiritual]. For many different senses in one text produce confusion and deception and destroy all force of argument. Hence no argument, but only fallacies, can be deduced from a multiplicity of propositions. But Holy Writ ought to be able to state the truth without any fallacy. Therefore in it there cannot be several senses to a word. (*Summa theol.* 1.1.i.10)

This is a very useful objection to raise, and if it cannot be answered, reading the Bible will become not a process of revealing the truth, but an act of deconstruction that will peel away layer after layer of figurative untruth. Aquinas begins by reminding us that Scripture is the work of God, and God can signify meaning not only in words but also "by things themselves." We know this from the New Testament, for in the King James Version, the Gospel according to John begins:

> In the beginning was the Word, and the Word was with God, and the Word was God.
> The same was in the beginning with God.
> All things were made by him; and without him was not any thing made that was made.
> In him was life; and the life was the light of men.
> And the light shineth in the darkness; and the darkness comprehended it not. (John 1:1–5)

What does this mean? God is Word—language—and Word is God. God and Word are therefore the same thing: God is language. But Word is also *with* God, and John tells us that this Word, or aspect of Word, is Christ, since it was made flesh and sent to redeem us. In Genesis, when God creates he does so by language, by speaking: "God said, Let there be light: and there was light" (Genesis 1:3), and so on with the firmament, the appearance of dry land, plants, stars, and all the furniture of the physical universe. I know of no more succinct modern description of creating Word than that given by David Lawton:

> Well over two thousand years of linguistic study might well be condensed in one truism: given as an example, as coincidence would have it, by both the father of the Church, St Augustine, and the father of modern linguistics, Ferdinand de Saussure. When I say "ox" in English I refer to the same thing as someone who says "*bos*" in Latin or "*boeuf*" in French. I use an arbitrary or conventional sign—a random collection of sounds that the speakers of a language agree to let signify the thing "*ox*"—for that ox, a real, natural thing. The sign I use, the word "*ox,*" is not the thing to which I refer. There is no alternative; or rather, there is one alternative only, that when I form my vocal apparatus to say the word "*ox,*" the thing, a real ox, pops tumbling out of my mouth. Absurd: yet this is what God does in Genesis One, for that is precisely the nature of creating Word. (Lawton 12–13)

God does indeed, and quite literally, use things to signify what he means, since speaking and creating are for him synonymous. Or at least he did, during the first acts of creation; but also, in a different way, during the dictation of Scripture, which is Aquinas's point. But now, most importantly for this study, Aquinas goes on to define the various senses in which Scripture can be read, underlining at the same time the necessity for each. I shall cite the greater part of his reply since it constitutes an interpretive theory that was soon to be applied to secular poetry:

> So, whereas in every other science things are signified by words, this science [i.e., scriptural interpretation] has the property, that the things signified by the words have themselves a signification. Therefore that first signification whereby words signify things belongs to the first sense, the historical or literal. That signification whereby things signified by words have themselves also a signification is called the spiritual sense, which is based on the literal, and presupposes it. Now this spiritual sense has a threefold division . . . so far as the things of the Old Law [i.e., the Old Testament] signify the things of the New Law, there is the allegorical sense; so far as the things done in Christ, or so far as the things which signify Christ, are types of what we ought to do, there is the moral

sense. But so far as they signify what relates to eternal glory, there is the anagogical sense. Since the literal sense is that which the author intends, and since the author of Holy Writ is God, Who by one act comprehends all things by His intellect, it is not unfitting, as Augustine says [*Confessions* xii], if, even according to the literal sense, one word in Holy Writ should have several senses. (*Summa theol.* 1.1.i.10)

Aquinas's claim that the multiplicity of senses in which it is possible to read the Bible does not lead to equivocation rests on one fundamental premise, and it is the same premise that Augustine insisted on: the literal sense of Scripture is the origin of all other senses. He explains what he means by *literal* using the example of God's arm: "When Scripture speaks of God's arm, the literal sense is not that God has such a member, but only what is signified by this member, namely operative power." This subdivision of the literal sense is the "parabolic" sense, and it is an important distinction because it stresses again the need to attach symbolic meaning to every thing the Bible mentions; and so we can understand the urgency underlying the medieval commentators' fascination with "what is" and "what is not." But there is another claim made in the passage just quoted, and it is one that can be said to have determined the direction of literary interpretation until only very recently. It is the claim, made almost parenthetically by Aquinas, that the literal sense is to be found in the intention of the author.

So far I have used *symbol* and *allegory* as interchangeable terms. This is because the medieval interpretive tradition from Augustine to Aquinas seems to have made no difference between them. Eco explains this in the context of the attempt to limit scriptural interpretation:

The Scriptures were in the position of saying everything, and everything was too much for interpreters interested in Truth. The symbolic nature of the Holy Books had to be tamed; in order to do so the symbolic mode had to be identified with the allegorical one. . . . The Scriptures had potentially every possible meaning, but their reading had to be governed by a code, and that is why the Fathers proposed the theory of the allegorical senses. . . . The theory of the four senses provided a sort of guarantee for the correct decoding of the Books. (*Limits* 11 ff.)

To say that the symbolic mode had to be identified with the allegorical one means that symbols had to be taken to stand for ready formulated readings, or "stories": Christ's overturning of the money changers' tables in the temple at Jerusalem stands for the law against gainful employment on the Sabbath, for example, or against the defilement of the holy place with worldly and mercenary dealings. One story stands for a second story, one text for another one. The difference between this way of reading and modern interpretive methods is that the story stops here—there is no allegory behind the allegory, no third text to which the second text is allowed to refer. In this way, the Bible becomes a closed work.

## ORIGEN

Throughout this chapter I have stressed the attempts made by Augustine and Aquinas to promote a particular kind of interpretation. Their approach was based on the view of the world as univocal, as speaking with a single voice—that of God—about the eternal theme of God's creation and the coming of the redeeming Christ. According to this view, everything in the world, necessarily contained within Scripture since Scripture speaks of everything, tells this story, sometimes directly, but often veiled in metaphor, represented by symbols and allegories, narrated in figurative language.

But it is not the case that this view had always been espoused in the commentaries of writers within the church. We have already seen that it is possible to read the Augustinian-Thomist tradition as a reaction against the "too much" of free association. Such liberty would allow us to make associations of events related in Scripture with nonbiblical events and allow the Bible to have more than one voice, and this would be possible if Scripture were read *essentially* as allegory; that is, not as evidences of historical truths. This last idea is of course in direct opposition to Augustine and Aquinas, but it is precisely the view held by a much earlier church father, Origen (186–c. 254), who, it will come as no surprise, is the only church father not to have been canonized. He is probably the best-known representative of the Alexandrian school of interpretation, named after the Egyptian city in which it flourished. Here is an example of what Origen has to say on the Book of Genesis:

> Could any man of sound judgement suppose that the first, second and third days had an evening and a morning, when there was yet no sun or moon or stars? Could anyone be so unintelligent as to think that God made a Paradise somewhere in the east and planted it with trees like a farmer, or that in that Paradise he put a Tree of Life, a tree you could see

and know with your senses, a tree you could derive life from by eating its fruit with the teeth in your head? When the Bible says that God used to walk in Paradise in the evening or that Adam hid behind the tree, no-one, I think, will question that these are only fictions, stories of things that never actually happened, and that figuratively they refer to certain mysteries. (*Origen* 180)

Origen terms his method of interpretation "spiritual"; but he points out that Scripture employs "spirit" to mean "intellectual things, which we also term spiritual" in order to distinguish them from bodily things; that is, things of physical substance. He exemplifies his interpretive approach in a commentary on the Book of Moses:

The apostle, moreover, says, "Even unto this day, when Moses is read, the veil is upon their heart [i.e., the hearts of the hearers]: nevertheless, when [the heart] shall turn to the Lord, the veil shall be taken away: and where the Spirit of the Lord is, there is liberty." For so long as anyone is not converted to a spiritual understanding, a veil is placed over his heart, with which veil, i.e. a gross [i.e., erroneous] understanding, Scripture is said or thought to be covered: and this is the meaning of the statement that a veil was placed over the countenance of Moses when he spoke to the people, i.e. when the law was publicly read aloud. (*De principiis* 1)

The veil upon the hearts of those who hear the Book of Moses read aloud is the veil of ignorance, or "gross understanding"; and the same veil covers the whole of Scripture. Only if we apply a "spiritual" method of interpretation can this veil be lifted. It turns out then that, for Origen, "spiritual" equates to "intellectual": Scripture is not to be taken at face value, not to be read as historical truth, but treated as a collection of metaphors, symbols, and allegorical *fabliaux* that must be decoded by application of the intellect.

Apart from Origen's insistence on an allegorical reading of Scripture, it is this association of spirit with intellect that creates an unbridgeable gulf between his interpretive method and Augustine's. Origen begins by denying that God can be a "body," a physical being; God is, rather, an "intellectual thing" (*De principiis* 1); God is not worldly in the sense that human beings and the furniture of the physical universe are worldly things. Like the *fabliaux* of the Bible that tell, allegorically, of his works, God must be perceived "spiritually" by the intellect: he must be interpreted. There is in

36

Origen's approach a strong relationship between the intellectual and the nonworldly: spiritual things must be intellectually perceived. This is anathema to Augustine, for whom all worldly things must be explained and categorized according to fixed symbolic values, and for whom, though the events related in Scripture may sometimes be recognized as allegory, in which case they are to be interpreted according to set formulae, they are always to be read literally as well. He deals with the inevitable difficulties arising from such literal readings, as we have seen, by discussing their subject matter in terms of the parabolic sense, the secondary literal meaning, which allows us to read both "historically" and allegorically at the same time. For Augustine, to have allowed an "intellectual" reading of Scripture in Origen's sense would have allowed of too much potential freedom of interpretation—hence his insistence on the immutable symbolic values of physical signs. Indeed, he must claim that these values are what God, whom he surely saw as the real author of the Bible, actually intended.

The relevance of this discussion of patristic methods of interpretation (the methods of the church fathers) will now (I hope) be clear. On the one hand we can see in Origen a theorist who allows of something like a personal response by the reader, while Augustine is deeply concerned with *intentio auctoris,* the intentions of the author (or Author). As we know, this polarization of critical "schools" is still very much in evidence today; and though modern critical theorists are not fond of hearing it, even a cursory reading of early interpreters makes both poles look rather less than modern.

For the moment, though, we must leave Augustine and Thomas Aquinas in control of the debate (and indeed remember that parts of Origen's work came to be considered heretical). In many ways, the Augustinian-Thomist system is a beautiful one—self-sustaining, self-explanatory, symmetrical. Like the Ptolemaic understanding of the universe as geocentric, it can be seen as a reflection—but also a functioning one—of the desire to realize, to make apparent, the divine order and perfection that governed every aspect of human existence, and in this sense it is a very "medieval" system. But even during Aquinas's own lifetime this perception was being questioned, and the radical implications for textual interpretation inherent in this challenge were already becoming manifest.

# DANTE ALIGHIERI, HERMETISM,
# AND RENAISSANCE ITALY

### *DANTE*

The long tradition of scriptural interpretation from Augustine to Aquinas essentially appropriated the spiritual world for itself. We have seen that in this tradition it is only in a scriptural context that any spiritual interpretation is allowed: the "real" world is now officially devoid of mystic symbols. Umberto Eco points out that one of the effects of this is that it becomes "uncertain under the inspiration of whom (God, Love, or other) the poet unconsciously speaks" but that at the same time "the theological secularization of the natural world implemented by Aquinas . . . set free the mystical drives of the poetic activity" (*Limits* 17). In other words, poets began not only to seek justification within the tradition for seeing their work as conveying spiritual meaning but also to look beyond that tradition to other authorities. One of these was the Corpus Hermeticum, a collection of Gnostic writings produced in the late Hellenic period. We shall be looking at the Corpus in some detail in this chapter.

In the Augustinian-Thomist tradition, the poet, surely concerned with aspects of human existence that are also the concern of Scripture—love, God, metaphysical anxieties, death, for example—is in effect denied all scriptural and spiritual authority. At best he might claim that his writings speak parabolically of the spiritual. Though the Florentine poet Dante Alighieri (1265–1321) was not the first to question this limitation, he was the most famous poet to do so. His now-celebrated dedicatory letter to Cangrande della Scala, accompanying *Paradiso,* the final book of the *Divina Commedia,* discusses Psalm 114 in such a way as to make clear his conviction that his own poem is to be read as spiritual allegory. His comments on the psalm are in themselves orthodox and conventional—he follows

Aquinas in considering the four accepted allegorical "senses"—but at the same time the letter contradicts Aquinas's view of worldly poetry as having only a literal sense.

Dante begins discussion of his poem by pointing out that its sense is not simple: "rather, we should call it 'polysemous,' having many senses; the first being that which comes from the letter, the second that which is signified by the letter. The first sense is called the literal, the second, allegorical or moral or anagogical." He then goes on to discuss this method of reading his poem in the context of Psalm 114. In the King James Version, the psalm runs as follows:

> When Israel went out of Egypt, the house of Jacob from a people of
>     strange language;
> Judah was his sanctuary, and Israel his dominion.
> The sea saw it, and fled: Jordan was driven back.
> The mountains skipped like rams, and the little hills like rams.
> What ailed thee, O thou sea, that thou fleddest? thou Jordan that thou
>     wast driven back?
> Ye mountains, that ye skipped like rams; and ye little hills, like lambs?
> Tremble, thou earth, at the presence of the Lord, at the presence of the
>     God of Jacob;
> Which turned the rock into a standing water, the flint into a fountain
>     of waters.

Dante interprets the lines in this way:

> If we look at it in the literal sense, it means the exodus of the Children
> of Israel from Egypt at the time of Moses; the allegorical sense is our
> redemption through Christ; the moral sense is the conversion of the
> soul from the misery of sin to a state of grace; while the anagogical sense
> speaks of the departure of the sanctified spirit from the corruption of
> the flesh to the freedom of eternal glory. And though these mystical
> senses are given different names, all of them can be called allegorical,
> because they are different from the literal or historical sense.

Having distinguished between a literal sense and a generalized allegorical one, he begins to discuss his own poem in the same way. He states that the literal sense of the *Commedia* is the condition of the soul after our death, whereas the allegorical sense is the progress of man, "either gaining or losing merit" through the exercising of his free will, and his subsequent punishment or reward according to divine justice. It is clear that in all of this Dante interprets his own poem as spiritual allegory; furthermore, he goes on to discuss the linguistic devices of the *Commedia* not only in terms of the "poetic, fictive, descriptive, digressive, transumptive"—traditional terms of poetic discourse—but also in terms of the "definitive, divisive, probative, improbative, and the giving of examples," all of which are terms from theological or philosophical discourse. In other words, in accordance with his claim that there are two senses in which the *Commedia* is to be read, he himself talks about the poem as a literary construct, on the one hand, but as a theological or philosophical work, on the other. That he considers his work to have moral and spiritual purposes is clear from his statement that the poem is intended "to remove those living in this life from misery and to lead them into a state of bliss."

Even so, we should beware of thinking of Dante's approach to the interpretation of allegory as revolutionary. It is certainly true that he makes a number of comments that we can take to indicate a growing distance between what poets thought about their work and the official opinion of the theologians, but he also makes comments that seem to place him firmly in the Thomist tradition. His interpretation of Psalm 114 is unusual not because of what it says about its subject but because of the context in which he gives it; and he seems to think of the event he discusses, the exodus of the Jews from Egypt, as an example of *allegoria in factis,* rather than *allegoria in verbis:* that is to say, he does not imply a belief that the events described in the psalm are not historical fact. Moreover, the ideas he expresses are not always consistent with his other writings. In the *Convivio,* for example, he distinguishes between the allegory of secular poets and that recognized by theologians in Scripture, and again this distinction seems to realign him with Aquinas, since poetic allegory can be read as "parabolic" reality.

The *Convivio* (c. 1304) is essentially a lesson by Dante in how to read his own poems, and in fact begins by establishing itself as an allegorical representation of the poems and of the commentary it contains. He tells us that he intends to prepare us a banquet consisting of meat (the poems themselves) together with the bread (his own commentary) that always accompanies the main course: "Blessed are those few who sit at the table where the bread of Angels [i.e., wisdom] is eaten, and most unhappy are those who share the food of sheep! . . . Therefore . . . I offer to all men a banquet of what I have shown them [i.e., the poems] and of the bread which should accompany such food, and without which it could not be digested" (*Convivio* 1.1). This sounds rather precious; and indeed what Dante is saying is that his poems cannot be properly understood by the general reading public unless he himself offer a detailed explication of them. The poems in question here, the *canzoni* (literally, "songs"), were not well received initially; furthermore, in 1302 Dante had for political reasons been exiled from his native Florence and sentenced to death, and these combined factors are likely to be responsible for the sometimes bitter tone of the *Convivio*. But the point here is that this work contains a lengthy discourse on the function and interpretation of allegory in worldly poetry and is representative of a changing attitude to interpretation generally, not only of literary texts but of the natural world and everything in it.

Dante admits that it is quite possible to read the canzoni without his explication. In this case, however, "their beauty [will be] more pleasing than their goodness" (*Convivio* 1.1), by which he means that the cleverness of their physical structure, the sound of the words themselves, their musicality, will be appreciated for themselves rather than for any intellectual and moral meanings they convey.[1] He therefore sets out to deal with the poems, just as though he were a theologian elucidating a passage from Scripture, by first distinguishing the literal from the allegorical meaning and then discussing each in turn (insisting, by the way, on the relevance of authorial intentions in the process): "Since my real meaning was different from that which the previously mentioned *canzoni* superficially reveal, I shall explain these *canzoni* by means of an allegorical exposition, having first discussed the literal sense, so that both dishes will be tasted by those who have been invited to this dinner" (*Convivio* 1.1). At the same time, he is insistent that his explication is necessary for a full understanding of the canzoni, and tells us that he intends to show us the true meaning of his poems, which "nobody can perceive unless I myself reveal it, because it lies hidden beneath the figure of allegory" (*Convivio* 1.2). This last statement confirms Dante as a medieval writer who does not question the existence of an unalterably true meaning that can be discerned according to certain rules of interpretation. The rules he employs are the same as those formulated by Aquinas in his discussion of the four senses of scriptural allegory. He also, incidentally, shows himself to be a good Renaissance reader when in the same passage he goes on to echo Aristotle by saying that his explication "will not only delight the ear, but provide useful instruction concerning both this manner of speaking [i.e., the explication itself] and this way of understanding the writings of others."

All the same, Dante was certainly aware that what he was attempting in the *Convivio* was something new. Apart from the fact of his applying Aquinas's rules for scriptural interpretation to his own, worldly, poetry, he celebrates the Italian vernacular by employing it for a literary-scholarly work. This, too, was a new idea, so new in fact that Dante felt able to eulogize the *Convivio* as "a new sun to rise where the old shall set and to give light to those who find themselves in shadows and in darkness because the old sun no longer casts its rays upon them" (*Convivio* 1.13).

Much of the first chapter of the *Convivio* is taken up with Dante's reasons for using the vernacular rather than Latin, and it is only in the second that he begins the actual discussion of the first poem, the canzone beginning *Voi che 'ntendeno il terzo ciel movete*. Here he begins by exemplifying the four senses in which his poem is to be read: the literal, the sense that "does not go beyond the surface of the letter"; the allegorical, "the sense hidden beneath the cloak" of the literal; the moral, "the sense that teachers should assiduously seek in the Scriptures, both for their own profit and for their pupils'"; and the anagogical, which is what lies "beyond the senses." He describes the allegorical as "truth hidden beneath beautiful fiction" and gives as an example the story of Orpheus, who tamed wild animals and made rocks move toward him with the beautiful sound of his lyre (*Metamorphoses* 10.86–147). The truth behind this fiction is, Dante says, that with the instrument of his voice the wise man is able to make cruel hearts grow tender, and that those who have no rational life are "like stones." As an example of the moral significance of scriptural "fact," he tells us that when Christ ascended the mountain to be transfigured, he took only three of the apostles with him, which tells us that matters of great secrecy should be revealed to only a chosen few. Finally, to exemplify the anagogical sense he refers back to Psalm 114. Here he tells us that, although the psalm speaks of historical fact and should therefore be read in the literal sense, there is a spiritual sense that "signifies by means of the things signified" the higher things of the eternal glory of God (*Convivio* 2.1). To say that the spiritual sense signifies something by means of the things signified means that spiritual truth is revealed through the literal sense: the historical event is an *allegoria in factis* and is both true in itself and stands for something else.

But what does Dante mean when he says in the same chapter that the allegorical sense is understood differently by theologians and by poets? Perhaps his term "beautiful fiction" provides an answer. Aquinas insists that all four senses are true, but also that the truth of the three allegorical senses depends on the historical truth of the literal. In the example just cited from the *Convivio*, Dante clearly does not believe in the historical truth of the story of Orpheus—this is what he calls "beautiful fiction." In addition, in the case of a theological reading of the Old Testament as referring forward to the deeds of Christ on earth, the allegorical sense is clearly also referring to "historical truth." The distinction made by Dante seems, then, to lie in these two senses, the literal and the allegorical. Dante's point is that even if the literal sense does not equate to the truth, it is still possible for it to convey a valid spiritual message. In any case, the moral and the anagogical senses hold for both the theologians and the poets.

But now let us examine the canzone in question, the first two stanzas of which run as follows:

> You who with your thought the third sphere move,
> Now hear the words that lie within my heart,
> For so rare are they, whom else should I tell?
> The heaven that moves obedient to your power
> Draws me, O noble beings that you are,
> Into the state in which I find myself.
> Therefore it seems most fitting that these words
> About the life I lead should be addressed
> To you; and so I pray that you will hear
> While I tell of the strangeness in my heart,
> And of the tears of my unhappy soul,
> And how against her speaks a spirit now
> Descending on the beams of your own star.

The reading Dante gives is rather long-winded and involves, among various excursions, a quite technical discussion of astronomy. I shall cite the most relevant details here.

The sphere he refers to is the third from the earth in the medieval universe,[2] and in the beginning of the stanza he addresses "those Intelligences, or angels, as we usually call them, who preside over the heaven of Venus [i.e., the third sphere] as its movers." At this point we need to know (so Dante tells us) that after the death of his beloved Beatrice, "Venus' star had twice moved through her sphere" when he began turn to another love, only this time a spiritual and intellectual rather than a physical one: Dame Philosophy. Therefore, to excuse himself for this change of heart (since as a true lover he should of course have mourned Beatrice until the end of his days), he addresses the angels who move the sphere of Venus because Venus is the Latin name for Aphrodite, the Greek goddess of love, whose son is Cupid, or Amor, or Love with a capital *L*.

He deals with each line in the same way, explaining the literal meaning of each and the reason for its presence in his poem: we learn, then, that when he addresses those who move the sphere of Venus with their thought alone, and asks them to hear his words, he does not mean that they should really listen as humans do, for "they have no sense perception." These heavenly creatures "hear" by means of the intellect. He then goes on to explain that throughout this canzone, *heart* is meant allegorically as "the secret place within" from which his words come, and not literally as a part of the body (*Convivio* 2.6). The last point Dante makes here on the nature of *heart* is interesting because he discusses it in precisely the same way that Aquinas talks of God's arm, as something recognizable by its effect rather than by its physical presence, in order to give an example of the parabolic sense. Eco makes the same point when he says that Dante does not detach himself wholly from the Thomistic point of view and that "the allegorical sense of his poems still is a parabolic one because it represents what Dante intended it to mean" (*Limits* 16). But we need to remember, too, that so far Dante has discussed his poem only in the context of its literal-parabolic sense; he has not yet pointed to an allegorical significance of *heart*.

He tells us that he is justified in addressing these angels of Venus's sphere, firstly, because of his condition, which he claims to be unique and therefore unintelligible to other human beings; secondly, because "when a person receives either benefit or injury, he should first inform the one who has caused it." In other words, the sphere of Venus and its accompanying Intelligences are responsible for the benefit he has reaped from this new love, and he now wants to tell them about it. He very craftily sets out to charm these Intelligences into listening to him by assuring them that it is his intention to speak of "rare" things—the division of his soul caused by the memory of Beatrice, on the one hand, and his new love on the other—and "momentous" things—the influence of the star of Venus that they themselves govern. On the final three lines of this stanza, he says that the spirit who descends on the beams of Venus's own star is in fact a recurring desire "to praise and adorn this new lady" and that his "unhappy soul" is simply "another thought together with an act of assent, which, though in opposition to the former [thought], praises the memory of the glorious Beatrice." The star of Venus, Dante finally tells us, exercises enormous influence on our souls; and this, he says, is the literal exposition of the first stanza of his poem.

Book 2.12 of the *Convivio* begins by introducing the "allegorical and true" exposition of the poem. Here we are reminded of the distinction he made earlier between theological and poetic readings, for if the allegorical reading is the true one, this must mean that the literal reading is untrue, that it is a "beautiful fiction," like the tale of Orpheus. Nonetheless, it is clear that this literal untruth—the story of Dante's encounter with his new "love"—has been constructed specifically to lead us to a spiritual truth, and this is a very important point. It is important because it means that every thing and event in the literal poem ("heart," "spirit," "soul," and so on) must be read as a symbol standing for something else. Dante's symbols therefore lead to truth (or, at least, to "truth"), and this idea is essentially the same as that espoused centuries later by the French symbolist poets, who in turn influenced the way twentieth-century poets like T. S. Eliot and Ezra Pound thought about poetic symbols. For the moment, though, let us see what Dante has to say about the allegorical meaning of his poem.

He tells us that in his despair at the loss of Beatrice he turned to philosophy. This idea was suggested to him by "that book of Boethius"—that is, the *Consolation of Philosophy,* composed in 523 A.D. while its author was in prison: "So, in my search for solace, I found also . . . sciences, and books. Contemplating these, I realized that Philosophy . . . was a great thing. I imagined her as a gentle lady, and could see her only as full of compassion, so that the part of my mind that perceives truth gazed at her so willingly that I could scarcely turn it away from her" (*Convivio* 2.12). Dante falls in love with Dame Philosophy, and he does so (necessarily) according to the laws of Renaissance psychology and physiology, under which all the major organs and faculties are ruled by "spirits" or "essences." These were not insubstantial ideas but, like "humors," were tangible, physical phenomena distilled by physical processes of the human body. They worked as follows: when Dante fell under the spell of Beatrice, the spirit that governed his sight, the *spirito visivo,* was so enchanted by this beautiful apparition that it felt unable to remove itself from her presence. Certainly, though, it would have hurried off to tell the *spiriti* governing the other organs—the brain, liver, and heart. All of these spirits would then have crowded into the eyes to witness this beautiful creature. This explains why lovers' sight grows dim when they behold the object of their desire. In absolute awe, the spirits would then have hidden themselves away in a special chamber of the heart, where they would have trembled in ecstasy—hence the palpitations that begin at the appearance of the beloved.

But Dante's new love is no mere human being, and this is not erotic love, the physical love of one human being for another, for he feels himself "raised from the memory of that first love to the virtue of this one" (*Convivio* 2.12). The key word here is *raised,* and it tells us that Dante's attitude to this love is a Neoplatonic one. According to Plato, we can ascend a "heavenly ladder" toward God, leaving behind more and more of the worldly and ephemeral with each rung we pass. In this way, we can progress from earthly love, the love of one human being, to the (spiritual or idealistic) love of two, three, many, on so on. From the love of human beings we can then progress to the love of "institutions"—ideas such as the State, the Law, Philosophy. As we ascend, our soul feels the increasing nearness of God, and begins to sprout wings in its desire to reach him, thereby drawing us closer and closer to him. This, Dante tells us, is what is happening to him.

He now sets out to explain to us what he means by the "third heaven." His explanation is rather technical and very discursive, and again I cite only those passages most relevant to this study:

> It remains to be understood why the "third" heaven is mentioned, and here we can compare the order of the heavens with that of the sciences . . . the seven heavens nearest to us are those of the planets; next come two heavens above them, which are in motion, and one above them all, which is immobile. The first seven correspond to the seven sciences of the Trivium and the Quadrivium: Grammar, Dialectics, Rhetoric, Arithmetic, Music, Geometry, and Astrology.[3] To the eighth sphere [i.e., the sphere of the "fixed stars"] corresponds natural science, which is Physics, and the first science, which is Metaphysics; Moral Science corresponds to the ninth sphere, and Divine Science, or Theology, corresponds to the immobile heaven. . . . The heaven of Venus can be compared to Rhetoric because of two properties: one is the brightness of its aspect [i.e., "face," appearance], which is sweeter than that of any other star; and the other is its appearance both in the morning and in the evening. And these two properties are found also in Rhetoric, for Rhetoric is sweeter than all the other sciences . . . and it appears in the morning

when the rhetorician speaks directly to his listeners, and it appears in the evening . . . when the rhetorician speaks through writing . . . therefore, we can see that by the third heaven I mean Rhetoric. (*Convivio* 2.13–14)

Why is rhetoric "sweet"—sweeter indeed than "all the other sciences"? To answer this question we need to return to Dante's comments on the literal reading of his poem, to the point where he tells his readers that, even if they are unable to perceive the "true" meaning of the canzone, they can still appreciate its beauty, which is apparent in its composition, in "the order of its discourse," and in its rhythm and musicality (*Convivio* 2.11). Sweetness seems to mean the beauty inherent in "the order of [a poem's] discourse," not the same thing as its syntax (the concern of grammarians) or its rhythm. In this case, "order of discourse" seems to refer to classical notions about the construction of arguments, which emphasized the logical progress from one point to another. As we have seen in Dante's literal explication, he is certainly concerned to emphasize the same aspect of his poem, insisting that the progress from one idea to the next is both logical and necessary. Moreover, this quality of rhetoric is apparent not only when the rhetorician addresses his audience by speaking to them, but also, as is the case here with Dante, when he addresses them by means of the written word. We can say, though, that he orally addresses those "whose thought the third sphere moves" in that the poem opens with a plea for an audience. Like Augustine in *De doctrina christiana,* what Dante produces in the opening lines is something very like the request for the assistance of a Muse typically employed by classical poets, especially in epic poetry. Here, though, it ultimately turns out from his own allegorical reading that he addresses historical figures whose circumstances he felt comparable to his own: Boethius and Tully,[4] who "guided me with the sweetness of their discourse" toward "this most gentle Dame Philosophy." Once this is understood, he tells us, we can understand the true meaning of the first stanza of the canzone "by means of the fictive and literal exposition" (*Convivio* 2.15).[5]

How far are we really justified in seeing Dante's interpretive methods as new? If we begin with his own assessment of the *Convivio* as "a new sun" designed to give light where the old sun sets, to illuminate with a new kind of knowledge "those in shadows and in darkness," we can agree with him (perhaps in slightly less rhapsodic terms) that a seriously analytical work of literary criticism written in his own widely comprehensible vernacular, rather than in Latin, is indeed a new thing. Whether we see Dante's decision to write in Italian as the result of democratic instincts or of his belief in the expressive possibilities of his native language (an agenda that became important to English Renaissance theorists), or simply of his sense of national pride, it is certainly true that in doing so he set an example for future critics. And it is also certainly true, as we have seen, that he set a further example by applying to worldly poetry the rules for allegorical interpretation laid down by Augustine and Aquinas for the study of Scripture. On the other hand, he still clearly believed in poems as closed texts: they were interpretable within fixed limits, and these limits depended on the intention of the author—this he makes perfectly clear in the discussion of his own poetic intentions in the *Convivio*. Furthermore he accepts the *form* of the limits as laid down by Aquinas—the four senses; and even in opening up interpretive possibilities by constructing relationships between the "spheres" of the planets and the sciences, he is limiting them at the same time by labeling, defining, and attributing fixed symbolic meanings.

But Eco (*Limits* 17) makes the point that Dante also saw poets as "prophets" continuing in a way the work of the authors of the Scriptures:

> In the *Comedy* Statius says of Virgil that he was to him "as the one who proceeds in the night and bears a light, not for himself but for those who follow him" (*Purgatory* 22.67–69). This means that—according to Dante—Virgil was a seer: his poetry, and pagan poetry in general, conveyed spiritual senses of which the authors *were not aware*. Thus for Dante poets are continuing the work of the Holy Scriptures, and his poem is a new instance of prophetic writing. His poem is endowed with spiritual senses in the same way as the Scriptures were, and the poet is divinely inspired. If the poet is the one that writes what love inspires in him, his text can be submitted to the same allegorical reading as the Holy Scriptures, and the poet is right in inviting his reader to guess what lies hidden "sotto il velame delli versi strani" (under the veil of strange verses).

Eco sees this as indicating the advent of a new mystical approach to the poetic text (encouraged, ironically, by the very theological authorities who sought to demystify worldly poetry); and, as we shall see, he is right when he suggests that this new way of reading has survived, through various lines of descent, until the present day.

## *NEOPLATONISM AND THE CORPUS HERMETICUM*

The whole idea of a European Renaissance is inextricably bound up with Neoplatonism. We all know that the Renaissance in Italy "meant" the rediscovery and renewed study of texts produced by classical Greek and Latin authors, but this alone tells us nothing. It will help us to understand the changes in theories of knowledge (epistemological changes) that occurred during this period in Italy if we know something about what people read and how they responded to what they read. First of all, what do we mean by *Neoplatonism*?

Dante was writing in an already existent Neoplatonic tradition influenced by Augustine: a tradition that saw God as sole, all-inclusive, and ultimately incomprehensible creator of the universe. What Augustine had been anxious to achieve was the limitation of interpretive possibilities that this all-inclusive and incomprehensible nature necessarily entailed. The problem with thinking of God as all-inclusive—as containing the Platonic Idea or Form of everything—is that he seems to become self-contradictory. As discussed above, if God contains love, he must also contain its opposite, hatred, and so on. How then can we possibly speak of him? One way would be to call him, for example,

> a flashing darkness which is neither body nor figure nor shape, which has no quantity, no quality, no weight, which is not in a place and does not see, has no sensitivity, is neither soul nor mind, has no imagination or opinion, is neither number nor order nor greatness, is not a substance, not eternity, not time. (After *On Mystical Theology;* quoted by Eco in *Limits* 9–10)

This is how the monk Pseudo Dionysius, or Dionysius the Areopagite (fl. c. 500), wrote of a God, an original One, who because of his apparently self-contradictory nature was impossible to describe except by opposites and negations. His work *On Mystical Theology,* from which this attempt to describe God is taken, deals with prayer and meditation as ways of rejecting the senses, the physical world and its phenomena—an essential aspect of Platonic philosophy—in order to experience the "light from the divine darkness" and spiritual union with God. His notion of "triads" is related to the great chain of being, an idea systematized by the Roman Neoplatonist philosopher Plotinus (A.D. 205–70). It is a hierarchical system that comprises the whole of existence, and its insistence on a tripartite structure can be seen as a symbolic reflection of the Holy Trinity. Dionysius's writings were instrumental in establishing a Neoplatonic trend, especially in the western church, and especially in the interpretation of Scripture. Scripture, and indeed God himself, are for Dionysius open texts, for their symbols cannot be translated without the interpreter arriving at contrasting and even contradictory meanings. In this sense, God is unknowable. However, even if God was unknowable, Dionysius certainly did not believe that he was in himself really self-contradictory. The contradictoriness lay not in the nature of God but in the inability of humans to perfectly comprehend him and the inability of human language to perfectly express him. It is this point that distinguishes the Christian Neoplatonism—from Augustine and Dionysius to Aquinas—from the Renaissance Neoplatonism developed, under the influence of hermetic writings, by Italian philosophers like Marsilio Ficino (1433–99) and Pico della Mirandola (1463–94).

Hermetic writings (or hermetica) are a collection of texts, revelationary in tone, on astrology and occult "sciences" as well as on theology and philosophy. They were attributed to the Egyptian god Thoth, who in Greek mythology becomes the god Hermes Trismegistos, the "thrice-greatest Hermes." To Thoth was attributed the invention of written language, and he therefore became the patron of the literary arts. Written in the form of Platonic dialogues, the hermetica date from about the first three centuries A.D., and the chief work of this genre, the Corpus Hermeticum, presents a fusion of eastern religious elements with Platonic and other Greek philosophies. Ficino translated the Corpus, as well as all of Plato's writings, into Latin, and in fact developed his own theory of Christian hermetism that was further developed by Pico della Mirandola.

Like the Bible, the Corpus Hermeticum begins with an account of creation, only here the story is narrated through a dialogue between God ("Man-shepherd") and a human who questions him on the nature of the universe. The briefest reading of this first book of the Corpus, "Poemandres, the Shepherd of Men," shows its similarity to Genesis (and other creation myths) and to Revelation, as well as its insistence, absent in Genesis, on God's limitlessness and incomprehensibility. It begins with a waking dream:

Methought a Being more than vast, in size beyond all bounds, called out my name and saith: What wouldst thou hear and see, and what hast thou in mind to learn and know?

And I do say: Who art thou?

He saith: I am Man-Shepherd, Mind of all-masterhood; I know what thou desirest and am with thee everywhere.

. . . and I see a Vision limitless, all things turned into light—sweet, joyous. And I became transported as I gazed. But in a little while Darkness came settling down on part [of the light], awesome, and gloomy, coiling in sinuous folds, so that methought it like unto a snake. And then the Darkness changed into some sort of a Moist Nature tossed about beyond all power of words, belching out smoke as from a fire, and groaning forth a wailing sound that beggars all description. And after that an outcry inarticulate came forth from it, as though it were a Voice of Fire.

There[up]on out of the Light a holy Word descended on that Nature. And upwards to the height from the Moist Nature leaped forth pure Fire. . . . The Air, too, being light, followed after the Fire; from out of the Earth-and-Water rising up to Fire so that it seemed to hang therefrom. But Earth-and-Water stayed so mingled with each other, that Earth from Water no one could discern. Yet were they moved to hear by reason of the Spirit-Word pervading them.

Then saith to me Man-Shepherd: Didst thou understand this Vision what it means?

Nay; that shall I know, said I.

That Light, He said, am I, thy God, Mind, prior to Moist Nature which appeared from Darkness; the Light-Word from Mind is Son of God. (Corp. Herm. 1. 1–6)

Here we are introduced to a creating god with a finely developed sense of the theatrical and a love of special effects. He uses these to create the four elements, fire, earth, air, and water, that various pre-Socratic philosophers considered to be the essences of all things. These are brought about "from Will of God" by Nature, who "received the Word" and turned herself into a cosmos "by means of her own elements and by the births of souls" (Corp. Herm. 1.7). There then followed seven "Rulers" who enclose the cosmos and whose ruling we know as Fate. The third of these Rulers later turns out to be the "literal" addressee of Dante's canzone; and in the "Light-Word," or "Spirit-Word," *Son of God*, we recognize the divine Word,

*Logos,* from the beginning of the Gospel according to John. In the Corpus, too, God and Son of God are inseparable:

> The Light-Word from Mind is Son of God. . . .
> Know that what sees in thee and hears is the Lord's Word; but Mind is the Father-God. Not separate are they the one from other; just in their union is it that Life consists.

Above all, the Corpus lays emphasis on the idea of an essential harmony and kinship between all things, a kind of oneness that links the constituent parts of the cosmos together, and to everything in it. God is "male and female both"; Logos is "at-oned" and "co-essential" with the cosmos, and with "the Formative Mind," which in turn is "at-oned" with Reason, who surrounds the spheres and sets them in motion. Those creatures (apart from humans) created to inhabit the earth—animals, fish, birds, and so on—lack reason because they were formed from "downward," earthly elements; but humans rule the animals, and the animals recognize the divine spark in humans. Man is "mingled" with Nature—indeed they become lovers; and he reflects the contradictoriness of the hermetic God: he is "mortal because of body, but because of essential man immortal"; "deathless and possessed of sway o'er all, yet doth he suffer as a mortal doth, subject to Fate." Man is "male-female, as from a Father male-female" (Corp. Herm. 1.14–16).

This system can be called Neoplatonic because of the way it reflects the idea of the great chain of being. The term refers to an interpretation of the universe based on three specific characteristics: continuity, plenitude, and linear gradation. The principle of continuity states that the universe consists of an infinite series of essential forms, each of which is related to its neighbors in that it shares with them at least one attribute. This principle is connected to that of linear gradation, which sees the series of forms as a hierarchy leading from the basest and least spiritual to the *ens perfectissimum,* the most perfect being, or God. The principle of plenitude states that the universe is "full" in the sense that the maximum possible quantity of kinds of forms is already in existence. As far as interpretive theories are concerned, the principle of continuity is highly important since by a series of progressions it allows everything to be related to everything else. We have already seen that problems can arise if we attempt to put this theory into practice—it is possible, but only as long as we ignore any syntagmatic, contextual framework that might exist.

Such universal kinship, where every thing is related to every other, means that each creature or object may be understood as a symbol. But here there are no limitations as to what may be signified, since everything potentially symbolizes everything else. Unlike Augustine or Aquinas, unlike Dante, the hermetic writer—and reader—can, in Sidney's words, truly "range freely within the zodiac of his own wit." Perhaps we should rethink the meaning of *Renaissance* and begin to see the concept not only as a revival of interest in classical texts but also as a radical change in the understanding of symbols and in the methodology of interpretation.

This kind of Neoplatonism views symbols as signs that refer to something unknowable. We begin at the summit of the great chain of being with God, the ultimate unknowable: a reality but a self-contradictory one since in God are contained all contradictions and he can never be defined, only described and symbolized. Moreover, descriptions of him, since they are necessarily symbolic, must always refer to other ideas—God = Lion, Light, Fire, and so forth. But because these ideas themselves contain at least one attribute of their neighbors in the great chain, they can also be taken to symbolize them; and so on, ad infinitum. We are led into a world of apparently free symbolic association that can be limited only by the personal experience of the interpreter (aleatory conditions): interpretation in this case depends on the reader's own intuition and imagination. Nor can we fail to recognize another "kinship" here in the similarities between hermetic Neoplatonism and some modern interpretive theories.

For humanist philosophers like Marsilio Ficino, this idea of kinship was interpretable in terms of Christian love. He, too, was attracted by the theory of the great chain of being, but saw the human soul as central to its hierarchy. He was able to do so because he held an idealistic belief in the innate goodness of man, claiming that man's natural tendency was toward religion and godliness. It was this tendency that formed the essential distinction between humans and other animals. Since the human soul was central to the great chain, it could function as a link between the highest and the lowest beings. In this way it became possible to view man's position as pivotal and essential, with the rest of creation wheeling about him in the same way as the rest of the universe rotated about the earth in the pre-Copernican system—a humanist idea, indeed. But his views on religion are recognizably hermetic, for he sees them all as partially true: they are all related in the same way as all things are related in hermetic thought.

For the younger Pico della Mirandola, the important point was not man's position in the great chain of being—for surely, he says in the *Oration on the Dignity of Man,* even if we are indeed only a little below the angels, the angels are nonetheless higher and should therefore be admired more than we admire ourselves. The real reason that humans are the most fortunate beings in creation is that they might become whatever they wish: they are neither heavenly nor earthly, neither mortal nor immortal, so that by exercising their free will they may choose their own destiny. Through the human intellect and reason, we may attain the highest forms, the divine. This can happen only if we concentrate all our energy on relinquishing the worldly, however. Indeed, free will makes it equally possible for us to become "animals and senseless beasts."

With its underlying message that humans can achieve the spiritual state of the highest order of angels, this view of human capabilities is remarkably optimistic, more so even than Ficino's *Platonic Theology* or *On Love.* In the context of our study, we can see all of these works, with their constant references to Platonic philosophy and hermetic writings, as well as Dante's more tentative *Convivio,* as expressions of a desire to break away from theological constraints (as well as, increasingly, scientific ones) on the interpretation of the visible universe.

# ENGLAND IN THE LATE MIDDLE AGES
# AND THE RENAISSANCE

## LANGLAND, CHAUCER, AND THE BIBLE IN ENGLISH

There has been a tendency for critical commentary on the English poetry of the fourteenth century to concentrate on the authors' individual rather than their common characteristics. Chaucer, Gower, Langland, and the *Gawain* poet (or poets) do not "belong together" in the way that the Victorians, the Romantics, or the Elizabethans are thought to, so that the term *fourteenth-century* refers to chronology rather than to genre (Burrow 1–10). The temptations to think in this way are powerful. Most obviously, *Gawain* and *Troilus and Criseyde, Piers Plowman,* and *The Canterbury Tales* do not speak the same dialect. Then there is the fact that Langland and the *Gawain* poet wrote alliterative verse, while Chaucer and Gower did not. When we discuss the Renaissance, it is common to think in terms of a unified "age," of having "arrived" and become something quite distinct from the immediate past, which Renaissance writers seem to have been careful to foster. The term *Dark Ages* is a Renaissance invention. This, too, is an idea not usually associated with England in the fourteenth century, at least as far as the study of its literature is concerned.

Nonetheless, though geographically remote and relatively provincial, England was still a part of the Holy Roman Empire and of the western (Roman) Catholic world. The teachings of the church fathers were as valid in England as they were in Florence or in Paris, and the mystical and Neoplatonic responses to their authority did not leave England untouched. We might therefore reasonably expect the texts produced in England during the fourteenth century to reflect in some way the ideas and concerns discussed in the preceding chapters of this book. Here, though, we run into another problem: fourteenth-century critical commentary on poetry in

English is practically nonexistent. As far as the interpretation of symbol and allegory are concerned, the "official" versions were the same for Chaucer as they were for Dante: the writings of Augustine, Aquinas, and the other commentators on Scripture. But Chaucer produced no *Convivio* or *Oration on the Dignity of Man* that would offer us a ready formulated interpretive method through which we could approach his own work and that of his contemporaries. He did, though, fortunately, produce *Troilus and Criseyde, The Canterbury Tales,* and other literary works, and it is to these that we can turn to see in what ways—if at all—they respond to the theories of allegory and symbolism that were current, and changing, during Chaucer's lifetime; and the same applies of course to the work of Gower, Langland, and the *Gawain* poet.

How far were the poets we are concerned with aware of the intellectual debates current in Renaissance Italy? We know that Chaucer read Dante and Boccaccio; we know that he read at least some of the Latin authors, Ovid especially. The case of William Langland is different. We know far less about him generally, but we do know that his education was interrupted:

> As for theology and the writings of the Fathers, Langland knows enough to whet his appetite but not enough to satisfy it. . . . Most of his knowledge, including his non-biblical and non-liturgical Latin tags, was probably picked up from the collections from Patristic writings which were widespread, in a variety of forms, in the Middle Ages. . . . The intensity of his interest in intellectual and theological matters is often that of a man who has not been to university . . . but wishes he had. It should not be thought that this is a defect in Langland as a poet: it might be argued, without straining the paradox, that one of the hidden strengths of the poem is that its author is only partly-educated (in terms of a university education, that is), and that he is able to communicate the restless urgency of his search for truth because he is not liable to bury every question as it arises under a mountain of Patristic authorities. . . . His knowledge of devotional and contemplative writing is revealed at several points, but he makes his own use of what he knows; he rejects unworldly and élitist spirituality. (Pearsall 19)

This seems to suggest that we cannot, or should not, read *Piers Plowman* in the same way as we have read Dante (though making personal use of what they knew is a quality they certainly shared). We know that Dante was familiar with the official interpretive theory of the four senses and that he intended his poems to be read in accordance with it: he tells us precisely this in the *Convivio*. We cannot say the same of Langland, about whose own reading we know comparatively little. What we can most definitely say, though, is that *Piers Plowman* is self-evidently allegorical, and that, in spite of the difficulties involved in talking about the intentions of its author, the poem, equally self-evidently, conveys spiritual meaning. Moreover, it does this so obviously that it is impossible to imagine Langland intending anything else.

Of course, we know that in the real world we can read *Piers Plowman* in any way we like, according to any ancient or modern interpretive approach. But at the moment we are, in one sense, not in the real world (or at least not only in the real world) for apart from being wherever we happen to be at the moment of reading these lines, we are also trying to represent to ourselves a very different place and time—the fourteenth-century England in which Langland wrote his poem. Some modern theorists hold this task to be an ultimately impossible and therefore pointless one: perhaps they are right. If they are, there is a strong case for claiming that the only sensible way of reading *Piers Plowman* would be to approach it through reader-response theories. All the same, we cannot now un-know what we already know; namely, that in Europe in the late Middle Ages there were certain theories in circulation on the interpretation of symbols and allegory and that at least one writer of symbolic and allegorical poetry made a point of telling us that his work could be interpreted according to at least one of them.

Of course, Dante might have been lying in the *Convivio*. He might also have been temporarily insane, or drunk, or experiencing a drug-induced hallucination that led him to believe that he could put his work on a spiritual par with the Bible. I have no ready way of disproving any of these possible interpretations. But they are extremely uneconomical, in the same way as employing the associative chain *dog—animal—human—philosopher—Augustine of Hippo* is uneconomical: we would have to make too many assumptions if we really wanted to deduce *Augustine of Hippo* as the intended message of *dog*. In order to justify such assumptions as the rather extreme examples above, we should anyway have to attempt the same, perhaps impossible, task of historical reconstruction just mentioned. We could of course attempt to exclude all historical reference from our reading; but let us for the moment see how economical an interpretation we can arrive at by using the evidence we have. We can justify this by saying that we want to find out whether what Langland seems to have thought about allegory was in any way related to Dante's (or Augustine's or Aquinas's) ideas—a reasonable assumption since these ideas were part of contemporary European thought processes.

That Langland's poem is allegorical is abundantly clear from the prologue "The Fair Field Full of Folk":

> In a somur sesoun whan softe was the sonne
> Y shope me into shroudes as y a shep were;[a]
> In abite as an heremite,[b] vnholy of werkes,[c]
> Wente forth in the world wondres to here,
> And say many sellies and selkouthe thynges.[d]
> Ac[e] on a May mornyng on Maluerne hulles[f]
> Me bifel for to slepe, for werynesse of-walked;[g]
> And in a launde[h] as y lay, lened[i] y and slepte,
> And merueylousliche me mette,[j] as y may telle.
> Al the welthe of the world and the wo[k] bothe
> Wynkyng,[l] as hit were, witterliche y sigh hit;[m]
> Of treuthe and tricherye, tresoun and gyle,
> Al y say slepynge, as y shal telle.
> Estward y beheld aftir[n] the sonne
> And say a tour—as y trowed,[o] Treuthe was there-ynne.
> Westward y waytede[p] in a while aftir
> And say a depe dale—Dethe, as y leue,[q]
> Woned in the wones,[r] and wikkede spiritus.
> A fair feld ful of folk fond y ther bytwene
> Of alle manere men, the mene and the pore,[s]
> Worchyng and wandryng as this world ascuth.[t]
> Somme potte hem to the plogh, playde ful selde,[u]
> In settynge[v] and in sowynge swonken[w] ful harde

a. "dressed myself as a shepherd" (or "sheep," with connotations of following as a disciple); b. in the clothes of a hermit; c. i.e., "without holy works to my credit," and not "a performer of unholy deeds"; d. saw many marvels and strange things; e. but; f. i.e., Malvern Hills, in the English Midlands; g. weary from walking; h. meadow; i. rested; j. something wonderful happened to me; k. woe, or ill; l. dozing, or sleeping; m. truly I saw it; n. in the direction of; o. I saw a tower, as it seemed to me; p. looked; q. as I believed; r. dwelt in the houses; s. lowly or common people; t. demands. u. some worked the plow, seldom complaining; v. planting; w. worked

And wonne that these wastors with glotony destrueth.[x]
And summe putte hem to pruyde and parayled hem ther-aftir[y]
In continance[z] of clothyng in many kyne gyse.[aa]
In preiers and penaunces potten hem mony,[bb]
Al for loue of oure lord lyueden swythe harde[cc]
In hope to haue a good ende and heuenriche[dd] blisse
As ankeres and eremites that holdeth hem in here selles,[ee]
Coueyten no in contreys to cayren aboute[ff]
For no likerous liflode here lycame to plese.[gg]

    And summe chesen chaffare—thei cheueth the bettre,[hh]
As it semeth to oure sighte that suche men ythryueth;[ii]
And summe murthes to make as mynstrels conneth,[jj]
Wolleth neyther swynke ne swete,[kk] bote sweren grete othes,
Fyndeth out foule fantasyes and foles hem maketh[ll]
And hath wytt at wille to worche yf thei wolde.[mm]
That Poule prechede of hem preue hit y myhte;[nn]
*Qui turpiloquium loquitur*[oo] is Luciferes knaue.

    Bidders and beggars fast aboute gede[pp]
Til here bagge and here bely was bretful[qq] ycrammed,
Fayteden for here fode and foughten at the ale.[rr]
In glotonye then gomus[ss] goth thei to bedde
And ryseth with rybaudrye then Robardus knaues;[tt]
Slep and also slewthe sueth suche euer.[uu]

    Pilgrymes and palmers plighten hem togyderes[vv]
To seke seynt Iame[ww] and seyntes of Rome,

x. that which these wasters destroy by their gluttony (*Winner and Waste* is another allegorical poem dealing with the condition of England in the 1350s); y. some devoted themselves to vanity and dressed accordingly; z. display; aa. of many kinds; bb. many devoted themselves to prayer; cc. led so hard a life; dd. heavenly; ee. like anchorites who keep to their (monastic) cells (anchorites were hermits who followed a strictly regulated lifestyle); ff. cared not to travel abroad; gg. i.e., they did not choose to lead worldly or luxurious lives; hh. some chose trade—and made therein the better choice; ii. thrive; jj. know how to make merry; kk. do not want to work and sweat; ll. invent licentious tales and make fools of themselves; mm. could work well enough if they wanted to; nn. I could prove that Saint Paul preached this (a reference to 2 Thess. 3.10: "If any man will not work, neither let him eat"); oo. *He who speaks filth;* pp. went about everywhere; qq. full to the brim; rr. posed as beggars to obtain food, and brawled in the alehouse; ss. those men; tt. Robert's men—a colloquialism used to signify robbers; uu. such are always attended by sleep and laziness; vv. joined together, traveled together; ww. i.e., the shrine of Santiago de Compostela in Galicia, Spain

> Wenten forth on here way with many wyse tales
> And hadde leue to lye aftir, al hir lyf-tyme.
> Eremites on an hep[xx] with hokede staues
> Wenten to Walsyngham, and here wenches aftir;[yy]
> Grete lobies and longe[zz] that loth were to swynke
> Clothed hem in copis[aaa] to be knowe fram othere
> And made hemself heremites, here ese to haue.[bbb]

In Dante's sense, the "fictive," literal meaning is that the speaker of the poem received a dream vision of a tower, which he recognized as symbolizing Truth; then of a valley, which he recognized as a symbol for Death. Between these two, he saw gathered together various groups of people representing corresponding groups from contemporary society.

We can recognize the allegorical mode in the choice offered between life—Truth and God—and spiritual Death. Making the right choice leads to redemption and salvation—the point that Dante makes in his allegorical explication of Psalm 114 (though Aquinas would call this sense parabolic and see it as an extension or subdivision of the literal sense). Further, just as we are presented with the choice between allegorical life and death, the poem also offers us the same choice in the physical world. Spiritual life and death, two possible states of the soul, are symbolized by two worldly states: we can choose between plowman and pseudobeggar. In other words, if we read the lines in Dante's moral sense, we can see the plowman's uncomplaining patience, fortitude, and humility, and his work of tilling the soil, planting, and sowing as preparations for "heauenriche blisse." The pseudobeggars and minstrels, on the other hand, while they undoubtedly have a much better time of it on earth, are in for an unpleasant surprise in the afterlife. Finally, we can recognize the mystical sense in the promise of the soul's departure, if we are good plowmen, from its state of corruption in the world of toil and "swete" to one of grace and "blisse."

It seems, then, that we can conduct a Dantesque reading of these lines according to the four interpretive senses without imposing too many conditions on the poem and without subjecting reason to too many assumptions. We need not worry about the question of whether the Tower of

---

xx. in great numbers;  yy. i.e., they went to the shrine of Our Lady of Walsingham, in Norfolk, and their women went them (Walsingham was then a famous English place of pilgrimage);  zz. great tall louts;  aaa. hooded cloaks (like those of friars); bbb. i.e., to have an easy life.

Truth and the Dale of Death are *allegoria in factis* or *allegoria in verbis*, because we have already been told that the lines refer to visions received in a dream. However, the distinction does become important when we come to discuss the "bidders and beggars" of lines 42 ff. since we can (very economically) assume that these characters not only represent other, real human beings seen by Langland but are also symbols for the condition of England, or for one aspect of it, during Langland's lifetime. In this way, the beggars' function can be described as parabolic: their allegorical sense is, in the Augustinian-Thomist view, an extension of the literal one, and it is also very close to it.

And indeed, given that *Piers Plowman* is generally a conservative poem in that it comments with regret on the changes taking place in English society, and in that it looks back to an ideal and idealized past, we would perhaps be more justified in reading Langland's allegory according to the understanding of the church fathers than according to Renaissance developments of their theories of symbols. The world of the poem is a troubled one, but it is still univocal. Its symbols speak of God's creation and of redemption through Christ and his teachings. It is a troubled world because of the increasing intervention of human affairs—in particular the effects of money, trade, and commerce—in the life of the spirit, and one of the ways the poem works is by setting up a very clear opposition of symbols denoting these two conflicting worlds: plowman against false friar, patient agricultural toil against idleness and sensuality, the promise of future unity with God against the immediate gratification of worldly desires. In this sense, the poem's symbolism is a very "medieval" one, and it becomes even more so with the introduction of characters such as Conscience, Reason, Repentance, and Lady Meed, who represents corruption through money. It is medieval also because there still seems to be no distinction between symbol and allegory: we know that characters like Conscience, Reason, and Repentance are to be read in a Christian context, and we know that representations of evil, or of wrong behavior, mean evil and wrong in the same Christian context.

There is no real freedom here to interpret Conscience or Repentance outside their scriptural relevance. Even Aquinas would have found it hard to deny this relevance to Langland's poem. He could only have done so by claiming that its spiritual sense was the parabolic one. He would surely have been forced to admit, however, that the Tower of Truth and the Dale of Death were not objects in the physical world and therefore not true or literal. This would have caused a problem because the parabolic sense was defined as an extension of the literal, and clearly where there is no really literal sense there cannot under the terms of this definition be a parabolic one. To read the "Fair Field" passage in Aquinas's sense we would have had to claim that the dream itself really occurred and that the *visions* of the Tower of Truth and the Dale of Death can in this way be regarded as literal, and therefore interpreted spiritually in a parabolic sense.

There remain, though, the "bidders and beggars." According to our model of interpretation, they can be read as symbols denoting a way of life held to be wrong according to a particular system of ethics and religious belief. In this way their function is moral-educational: they teach by negative example. But they are also representatives of a real social class in the physical world and in this way symbolize one of the socioeconomic ills of fourteenth-century England. Langland may well have seen these ills as the result of a general spiritual decline, but even if he did, it was the physical phenomena of widespread beggary and vagrancy that he himself witnessed and interpreted that led him to recognize them as ills in the first place. We can therefore reasonably and economically interpret these false mendicants as doubly symbolic—as literal characters in the physical world having both moral (spiritual) and political significations.

It is tempting to think of "social" poetry as modern, but satire is of course a very old form; nor does Langland's poem in fact reflect a new kind of symbolism. It makes us aware of social change, but does so from the point of view of a Christian traditionalist who, it turns out, is just as much concerned to limit the interpretive possibilities of the symbols he employs as Augustine was concerned to limit those of the symbols of Scripture. Indeed, so obvious is this concern throughout *Piers Plowman* that it is difficult to talk of an interpretation in a modern sense: we "know" what the characters in the poem represent because we know—or we can turn to other texts such as those of Augustine and Aquinas to find out—what repentance, truth, and conscience mean, or meant, in an orthodox medieval Catholic context.

What is the student to do? If we really are faced with a situation in which all we have to do is unlock a poem and discover what it "means," then the act of reading becomes a transparent and self-negating one, for once a poem has been unlocked we need never read it again. Of course, modern theories of interpretation have different methods of reading from those recommended by Augustine (though not so different as some critics like to think), but what we are trying to do in this study is to understand the attitude toward symbol and allegory that underlies a particular poetic genre. It seems that *Piers Plowman* uses symbols and allegory in such a way that we can reasonably read the poem in the context of Augustine's rules for interpretation, but this does not mean that Langland's poem is merely a historical curiosity. Twentieth-century interpretive theories, which we shall discuss in the final chapter of this book, will offer us different ways of reading the symbolism of the past (and the present). We shall understand those ways better if we can see how they have been arrived at.

The point of interest here, then, is not what is signified by any particular symbol, but what medieval theorists of language called the *modus significandi*—the *manner* of signifying. Burrow contended that the prevailing fourteenth-century mode in England was not allegorical at all. But Burrow does not make the medieval distinction between *allegoria in factis* and *allegoria in verbis;* nor does he discuss the medieval idea of the parabolic sense. He writes, instead, of the medieval preference for exemplification:

> If it be granted that the prevailing *modus significandi* in Ricardian narrative is not allegorical but literal, it remains to define this literal mode more exactly. . . . Their favored mode is exemplification. A story, for them, is pre-eminently an example which illustrates some truth or concept concerning human life and conduct. Their stories exhibit more than the general representative significance which, admittedly, attaches to any literary fiction whatsoever. They are designed to exemplify some specific idea. Often this idea is stated quite explicitly . . . but even where it is not so stated, it generally proves to be susceptible of precise, even formal, definition. (Burrow 82)

In the context of our examples from *Piers Plowman,* Burrow is probably right about the possibility of "precise, even formal, definition." But such a definition leads us directly back to the rules for interpretation formulated by the church fathers, who, as we have seen , were very careful to distinguish two basic allegorical modes—*in factis* and *in verbis.* Furthermore, they had a lot to say about the literal sense of texts, allowing in particular that the literal may be accompanied by a parabolic sense.

If a poem is "pre-eminently an example which illustrates some truth or concept," and if that illustration is not a dogmatic formula such as *Thou shalt not kill* or *Charity is a virtue* but, on the contrary, takes the form of a literary text through which we can assume we are intended to see, however simply and clearly, those same truths and concepts, then there is no escaping the fact that that text is written in the allegorical mode. The "precise" and "formal" definition of the "specific idea" signified, or "illustrated," by the literal sense is the parabolic sense recognized by Aquinas as its possible extension. And if Burrow is right in his claim (82) that the age that produced the "The Parson's Tale" was one in which poets naturally exercised strict control over the moral bearings of their work, then those poets can also be said to have made no real distinction between symbol and allegory. In the same way, like Dante in the *Convivio,* they can be said to have done their best to limit, at least in the context of their own lifetimes, the interpretive possibilities of the poems they wrote.

The case of Chaucer is not so straightforward, for *The Canterbury Tales* invite interpretation in a way that *Piers Plowman* does not. "The Nun's Priest's Tale" is a good example. In this tale, an empirical author whom we agree to call Chaucer writes of a narrator who reports (so he tells us) what was told by the nun's priest, who in turn tells us of the words improbably spoken by a rooster named Chauntecleer and his favorite hen, Pertelote. Furthermore, what Chauntecleer has to say concerns events that occurred in dreams, or that were reported in other fables by other empirical narrators. There seem to be various authors at work here, each of whom, as it turns out, is very interested in the idea of *modus significandi.*

The nun's priest's tale is lighthearted in tone—he has been urged to make it so after the company of Canterbury pilgrims has just been forced to listen to a monk's rather depressing narrative. Perhaps the monastic life is not conducive to jollity since the monk tells them that he has "no lust to pleye" and sulkily suggests that someone else should take over the storytelling. How, then, does the nun's priest respond to the host's request to "Telle us swich thyng as may oure hertes glade"? Certainly the beginning of his tale is not promising, for we are immediately introduced to a poor, aged widow who lives in a small, soot-blackened cottage and who has next to nothing to eat. However, it soon becomes apparent that she is not in fact important to the content of the tale—the main characters are the rooster Chauntecleer and the hen Pertelote—but she fulfils two important poetic functions. Firstly, the nun's priest uses her to symbolize, albeit in a lighthearted, even ironic way, the same Christian virtues of hard work, patience, and humility recommended by Langland in *Piers Plowman,* for we learn that she "foond no lak" in her diet of brown bread, milk, broiled bacon, and an occasional egg or two: "Attempree diete was al hir phisik, / And exercise, and hertes suffisaunce." Simultaneously, though, she is used as an ironic comment on those who lead very different lives: "Repleccioun ne made hire nevere sik. . . . The goute lette hire nothyng for to daunce] / N'apoplexie shente nat hir heed" (i.e., she was never sick from overeating, the gout never prevented her from dancing, and she never suffered from apoplexy).

All of this clearly carries moral significance, as well as a Moral, but it is equally obvious that it is meant to be humorous: we are supposed to laugh. But at what? Is the nun's priest inviting us to find comical the plight of the poor widow? Is he himself perhaps meant to stand for the callous cynicism of a well-fed clergy? Certainly he delivers his tale in a consistently mock-heroic style—from his description of the cottage, with its references to the "bour" and the "hall" associated with a lord's mansion, to his description of Chauntecleer, whose instinctive crowing at dawn is, we are told, due to an ability to measure "ech ascensioun / Of the equinoxial," an ability proven by the fact that "whan degrees fiftene weren ascended, / Thanne crew he"; and to the learned discourse on dreams conducted between Chauntecleer and Pertelote, during which there are references to the fall of Troy, at least one philosopher of classical Rome, the Bible, Ptolemaic astronomy, the *Chanson de Roland,* Saint Augustine, Boethius, a medieval Latin bestiary, the *Aeneid,* the medicinal powers of various herbs, medieval physiology and psychology, the story of Sir Lancelot, and a fifth-century commentary on Cicero. Chauntecleer is obviously an educated rooster. We should not, though, be surprised at his loquacity, since the nun's priest has already told us that his tale is set in a distant past, in days when "Beestes and briddes koude speke and synge."

Chaucer, Chauntecleer, and the nun's priest all employ the same *modus significandi:* unless we believe that Chaucer's pilgrims are actual, particular pilgrims who embarked on this particular, actual journey to Canterbury; that they spoke the words that Chaucer, by an astonishing feat of memory, retained and wrote down; that this particular nun's priest addressed this particular company in precisely this way; and that roosters and hens, together with all other beasts and birds, had at one time the gift of speech (and in Chauntecleer's case considerable erudition)—we must surely accept that the *Tales* are written in the allegorical mode and that the literal sense is not meant to be taken literally.

On the other hand, we can easily accept that the literary pilgrims of the

*Tales* represent types—that there are real people in the real world who demonstrate varying degrees of similarity of character to their literary counterparts (it would be impossible to read the *Tales* if there were not). But we are by no means constrained to believe that *this* pilgrimage to Canterbury ever occurred. This may be obvious, but it is also important because it explains something about the way the *Tales* work—about their *modus significandi*. Langland's dream-vision, his "Fair Field Full of Folk," is a world limited by moral imperatives: there is a stark choice between spiritual life and death, and we are shown very clearly the paths leading to each. It is an allegorical landscape, but one whose features are easily recognizable, and, ironically, one in which it is difficult to get lost. We may or may not believe that a man named Langland had a dream during which a vision occurred as described in the "Field" and that this vision was a prophetic comment on the possible futures of human souls. Some of his contemporaries may well have believed precisely that. I confess to finding it impossible to believe that anyone would make the same claim about Chaucer's contemporaries and their responses to the *Tales*. On the contrary, I find it very easy to believe not only that his contemporaries understood the *Tales* to be literary fabrication, but also that they knew it did not matter. It is partly because of this understanding that we are able to laugh at the mock-heroic description of the widow's cottage and at Chauntecleer's erudition. We can also refer back to what Aristotle said about representation in the *Poetics:* that "we delight in looking at the most detailed images of things which in themselves we see with pain." Most of us would not laugh at the real poverty of a real widow, but we do find it possible to be amused by a certain kind of representation. (I am aware, by the way, that this is a delicate point and that some readers may here deduce a claim that representations of, say, violence on television are harmless. One response would be to point out that the representation of violence is not the same thing as actual violence and that the same people would not see Langland's "bidders and beggars" as an inducement to fraudulence.)

There is a literariness, a purely literary use of the allegorical mode, to "The Nun's Priest's Tale," and to the *Tales* generally, that is absent from Langland's "Fair Field." It is an absence reflected by others, for most conspicuously absent from this "Fair Field Full of Folk" are the Folk themselves. There are two kinds of inhabitants of Langland's allegorical landscape: the good and the evil, the devout and the heretic, the morally strong and the morally weak. Whatever human characteristic the text describes is immediately attributable to one or the other of these categories. "Folk" are absent from the "Fair Field," just as interpretive possibilities—outside carefully proscribed limits—are ultimately absent from medieval exegetical writings on Scripture from Augustine to Aquinas, and to the same effect: the text becomes a closed one. In what sense, then, can this field be called "full"? One answer is that, in terms recognized by the authorities just mentioned, full is precisely what it is, for in the sense of the devout medieval Christian it contains everything. It is full insofar as we can say that all there is (i.e., plenitude) is a right and a wrong way to live, a succession of deeds and actions representing moral choices that human beings must make. We can live, the text of the "Fair Field" tells us, according to God's laws or outside them; we can live in God, patiently preparing a spiritual acre for the growth of the soul in "blisse," or we can wander with the "bidders and beggars" in spiritual desolation. All of these choices—or, rather, the same choice put repeatedly and variously—are contained in the space between the "tour of Treuthe" and the "depe dale of Dethe" that mark the limits of spiritual but also of physical existence: life is the space between light and dark.

In this way, the world of the "Fair Field" is a univocal one. It speaks of one thing, of one choice, one possibility of salvation; and, like the encyclopedias and bestiaries that attempted to ensure the "right" interpretation of the physical universe, everything in it speaks of the work and word (or Word) of one God. We would soon run into difficulties if we tried to read the *Tales* in the same way. The *Tales,* for one thing, are indeed "full of folk" (as well as talking roosters, hens, and foxes) and if these folk are sometimes recognizable as types, they are also recognizable as human beings we might actually meet in the real world: they contradict themselves and each other, they are capable of both bawdy humor and high seriousness, they have prejudices, they change their minds. They are far from being mere symbols for, say, "vice," "greed," "virtue," "death"—a quality shared by the inhabitants of the "Fair Field" and the characters of medieval morality plays such as *Everyman*. The *Tales* contain the gray areas necessarily omitted from Langland's text, and it is these gray areas, among other qualities, that constitute what I have just called their literariness. The world they speak of is not univocal because it frequently demands interpretation in a modern sense, where the text of the "Fair Field" seems intent on making us interpret in one sense only. Any attempt to make the *Tales* fit the kind of reading demanded by Langland's text would be extremely uneconomical because in order to do so the reader would have to make too many assumptions: we would have to attribute symbolic meanings to each of the *Tales'* characters, insisting, at the same time, that each symbol speaks of the same thing, in order to create a single, unalterable context, a final "truth." In other words, we would have to read the *Tales* in the same way as Augustine read Scripture.

The question of a text's "literariness" (or of its semiotic possibilities) is central to this study, and, of course lies at the heart of all debate on literary interpretation. I have just distinguished (I hope) between two kinds of literary text, between two kinds of allegorical representation: a "closed," univocal *Piers Plowman* and an "open," polysemous *Canterbury Tales*. To support my readings I have used what to me seem logical arguments, based on the criterion of economy and, I have claimed, justifiable by the texts themselves. But I cannot escape the fact that in every act of interpretation there is an element of choice, a personal preference for one approach to a text over another: at some point I have made a more or less conscious decision to read two literary texts in a particular way. In this example the decision has resulted in my seeing *The Canterbury Tales* as more "literary," more open to interpretation, than *Piers Plowman*. Of course, I believe that the arguments I have listed justify my distinction between the two, but I am also perfectly aware that another reader may well bring other, equally justifiable, arguments, based on different criteria, for reading the two texts in precisely the opposite way (even though I think it unlikely).

Why is it important to be aware of this element of personal choice? I believe the answer can best be illustrated by returning to a question we have already discussed: why was it important for Augustine and Aquinas to limit the interpretive possibilities of Scripture? If we accept that a text's openness is one of the qualities that constitute its literariness, it follows that a reading that attempts to close it also attempts to make it less literary. Each time someone says "This is not art," what they are also saying is: "This need not be interpreted." This should not be taken to mean that everything that demands interpretation must be understood as art; we attempt to interpret the cosmos, for example, but even though we can easily think of the cosmos as beautiful, it would be difficult to support the claim that it has artistic merit. But the attempt to limit a text's interpretive possibilities is beyond any doubt whatsoever an admission that to do the opposite—to think of that text as, say, poetry—would be to allow the validity of a potentially indefinite number of parallel interpretations. We can see the history of literary interpretation, and perhaps of all interpretation, as synonymous with the history of attempts to limit it, as the struggle between those who have tried to close texts and those who have insisted on opening them. We should remember that many of this latter group paid for their approach to interpretation by being burned at the stake.

The relevance of this point here is that England was beginning to witness an intensification of this struggle, and its outward sign was a series of translations, and therefore interpretations, of the Bible—either banned or officially sanctioned. It would be a serious mistake to think of this as a purely academic issue, for its repercussions affected the lives of everyone in the country and were inextricably bound up with both the idea and the fact of what we now know as the Reformation. We must therefore take time to consider the conflicting approaches to the one book of which everyone could at least quote paraphrases.

To talk of the meaning of Scripture as "hidden" is not merely to use language figuratively. The Bible read out loud by parish priests, the words of the Mass, were written down in Latin. It is no surprise to find rural, medieval congregations (or indeed any congregations anywhere) ignorant of Latin; but the fact is that the majority of the English clergy were in the same position, unable to understand the meaning of the words they spoke to their faithful. If priests, the nominally learned, could not understand this book of books, the work perceived as most central and most crucial to the idea of a culture and its faith, surely, the argument ran, the populace was even less in a position to do so. And if this sounds like a convincing argument in favor of an English translation of the Bible, we need only remember that translation necessarily entails—is even synonymous with—interpretation, and interpretation was jealously guarded by the clergy. Lawton (52) points out that the King James Version of 1611

> comes at the end of more than 500 years of debate on who should be allowed to read the Bible, about what extracts from the Bible, in what reworked form, should be divulged to the common or "illiterate" people [i.e., those who could not read Latin]. Throughout that period of 500 years, one biblical phrase appears again and again to summarize the reaction of the learned to giving vernacular scriptures to the common people: the phrase is "casting pearls before swine."

One such caster of pearls may have been John Wycliff, an Oxford academic who wrote theological treatises in Latin and who was, perhaps, involved in vernacular Bible translation. He was condemned for heresy in
1384. It has been claimed that the translation of 1382—the first complete
Bible in English—was Wycliffe's work, but this is by no means certain.
What is known is that in the 1380s and 1390s, the Lollards produced two
complete translations, the second of which is considered the better work
because it is less painstakingly faithful to the Latin Vulgate and consequently more natural a work of English prose. It is also more radically
Protestant in its explanatory glosses. Wycliff's followers, the so-called Lollards, were with good reason seen by the authorities as a political threat,
and they were therefore outlawed when in 1401 a statute was passed to
the effect that Lollardry was a form of heresy and that those convicted of
it should be burned at the stake. Possession of the Wycliffite translation
was taken as proof of guilt. About ten years earlier, however, Richard II's
queen, Anne of Bohemia, seems to have enjoyed personal use of a Wycliffite Bible—this moreover with the approval of Archbishop Arundel,
the man personally responsible for conducting the persecution of the Lollards. It would be a mistake, therefore, to see the medieval debate on interpretation as a contained, learned discussion of the finer points of Christian doctrine. It extended far beyond these to embrace fundamental social
and political issues that were already changing the face of English society.

Lawton (53 ff.) discusses the growing pressure for a vernacular Bible in
England in the context of this social change:

> What seems to have mattered is not what was read (the Lollard Bible),
> but who read it. In the period before 1401 many of Wycliff's support-
> ers were gentlefolk, courtiers, clerics or renegade academics, and the
> support of many of these was no longer so evident after the Statute of
> 1401. In any case, by 1401 it was clear that the Lollards were gaining
> popular support among shopkeepers, tradesmen and artisans; and there
> developed a serious revolt in 1413. It would be a mistake to overem-
> phasize the difference between the learned and the unlearned arms of
> English Lollardry. But political circumstances vary, and with them atti-
> tudes to Bible translation. . . . In the Reformation what was the con-
> nection between Bible translation . . . and political revolt? It is probably
> wise to think of Protestantism as reaction against an international estab-
> lishment, the Church, which lays down the law in Latin, and which
> claims, in Latin, to be the ultimate authority—spiritual, moral, political

and intellectual. . . . Revolt against such an all-encompassing authority, and soon revolt against any authority at all (such as a king), will stress whatever may be used as counter-authority, and is at the same time open to individual interpretation. What more natural rallying point for such political opposition than the call for a vernacular Bible? . . . The pressure for Bible translation occurs like most radical political movements at times of prosperity and upward social mobility. It is by no means accidental that the late fourteenth-century English Bible translation happens at a time when the English language and literature are also undergoing a great revival: some of Chaucer's best friends were Lollards. An upwardly mobile middle class wanted a greater political say and a quality literature in their own language, both secular (Chaucer, and many other fine poets of the late fourteenth century) and religious: an English Bible.

I have quoted at some length here because Lawton very clearly demonstrates the relation between the conflicting forces at work on late-medieval English society. Latin was the language of the universities, and anyone wishing to study had to take minor orders. The church concentrated and consolidated its power by excluding all but a minority, essentially a social and intellectual elite, from access to its language—the language of its mysteries, of the Bible, of official "truth": language and power are thus synonymous. A Bible in English would obviously diminish that power. Opposed to this hegemony, an increasingly prosperous middle class could afford a sense of individualism that the landless and unpropertied poor could not, and began to turn against what today we would call big, centralized government. In Lawton's words, they wanted "a bigger say," and having a bigger say in intellectual life necessarily entailed access to Scripture.

In spite of the dangers involved, there must have been a steady manuscript production of the Wycliffite version. More than two hundred manuscripts still exist today, most produced during the fifteenth century—precisely, in other words, during the period that saw the severest persecution of mainly poor people for owning a copy. It seems, then, that those of a certain social standing were able to persuade or bribe the authorities to ignore at least one heresy. Nonetheless, the demand for an English Bible that was actually available in England (rather than in Geneva or in Luther's Germany, the spiritual homes of reformist translators such as Tyndale) would not be met until the mid-1530s, when, no longer able (or perhaps no longer willing) to resist the demand for a vernacular Bible, the Convocation of Canterbury—the official English church itself, in other words—petitioned for an English translation. Tyndale's translation of 1525–26 was something new in English, based on the Hebrew and Greek texts rather than on the Latin Vulgate, and written in an English prose directed toward ordinary lay readers. It was immediately suppressed, and Tyndale himself was executed by strangulation and burning on the order of the Roman Catholic emperor Charles V. His death occurred in 1535—one year after the Convocation of Canterbury had petitioned for an official translation.

This is not a history of Bible translation, but I hope it is now clear that there are crucial connections between interpretation, translation, Reformation politics, and what I have described as literariness. The question of how far this term can be applied to Scripture is important because certain parts of the Bible have traditionally been thought of as poetry, especially the Old Testament books Job, Psalms, Proverbs, Ecclesiastes, and the Song of Solomon. Also according to tradition, if we are told that a particular text is poetry, or at least poetical, we tend to read it differently from the way we read prose: we expect different things. The idea of the Bible as poetry has recently been challenged, and the view put forward that we have come to think of, say, the psalms as metrical because Philo of Alexandria, who exerted a profound influence on Origen, discussed Hebrew writings in the terminology used to discuss Greek meters. Both Philo and Origen saw the Bible as allegory, not as historical narrative. In other words, in Lawton's words again (70) "the desire to find poetry in the Bible is associated with the desire for interpretative openness." If we think of this desire for openness in the context of the demand for a Bible in English, we can understand that for an individual to insist on the individual's right to interpret the Bible is to insist that the Bible *is* interpretable by the individual. This is clearly a move toward Protestantism. But it is also a move toward seeing the Bible as a work of literature, which no two individuals will read in quite the same way. Obviously, such an approach can only undermine the authority of the church, not only in terms of its official interpretation but also in terms of its temporal power: an open Bible is a secular Bible—and who would have read a Wycliffite Bible if not millers, cooks, men of law, wives of Bath, merchants, franklins, physicians, shipmen, sergeants-at-law, haberdashers, carpenters, and weavers?

A closed text does not want to be interpreted; or, rather, it tries to ensure that it can be interpreted in one way only. It does this by establishing for itself a context that, as far as possible, will not be mistaken for another one. For this to happen, there needs to be an agreement between text and reader. Under the terms of this agreement, the text makes its conditions clear and the reader accepts them: he or she agrees to read the text in the way the text wants to be read. An open text cannot be treated in the same way because what constitutes its openness is the impossibility of deciding what its terms are. With open texts, any agreement between text and reader can be at best provisional, for different ways of reading it (different possible contexts) will always be discovered. We can say that the model reader of an open text is one who does not try to read it as though it were a closed one. Of course, no one is obliged to accept the terms. But if, for example, we decide to treat a closed text as an open one, we run into the problems raised by the criterion of economy: an open text is not the same thing as an interpretive free-for-all. The same applies if we try to turn an open text into a closed one: to do this we must either ignore evidence of its literariness or impose upon it a context within which it can be argued to be closed. As we have seen, this is precisely what Augustine does with those passages in the Bible that are clearly allegorical.

Because it makes its terms so clear, I have described *Piers Plowman* as less literary—that is, less open—than *The Canterbury Tales*. It happens that the appearance of a very open work, the *Tales,* coincides with a growing demand for an English Bible. I know we can just as easily say that the appearance of *Piers Plowman* coincides with the church's insistence on its own authority, but this is a rather less interesting statement in that for the medieval church to insist on its own interpretation of Scripture can hardly be called remarkable. From the point of view of this book, it would be convenient if, after *The Canterbury Tales,* English poetry became more and more open: we should be able to construct a theory of how the Middle Ages became the Renaissance. But this is not the case—fortunately, too, because if poetry had indeed been growing progressively open since 1400, it would by now be completely incomprehensible. What is interesting, though, is that when English Renaissance critics begin to discuss medieval poetry, which they generally regard as not worth the trouble of reading, they are unanimous in singling out Chaucer for praise and almost unanimous in not mentioning Langland. We need, then, to find out whether the Renaissance in England is distinguished not only by the interest in the literatures of classical Greece and Rome with which it is always associated, but by a particular appreciation of textual openness. In other words, we need to ask what Renaissance critics thought about symbol and allegory.

## *THE SIXTEENTH CENTURY*

One of the most memorable, and saddest, acts carried out in the name of English Puritanism was the destruction of around 90 percent of English art. In particular, this destruction was directed against two kinds of sign, both of which were to be found inside churches: the effigies of saints and of the Holy Family and the rood screens separating the congregation from the high altar and the crucifix behind it. The destruction of rood screens can be readily understood as a rejection of the church's authority: what better sign of the division between the institution of the church and the people and of the gulf between comprehension of the holy mysteries, on the one hand, and the congregation, on the other, than an actual, physical barrier? Authority, understanding, access to God, all lay behind the intricate latticework of the rood screen, in the domain of the priests; and if this physical barrier was designed to inspire and maintain religious awe, it also served to protect what lay in the forbidden zone beyond it: both mystery and priestly authority, where the interpretation of mystery was concerned. Crossing that barrier is an irrevocable act of revolution.

The symbolic value of barriers goes back a long way. In *Interpretation and Over-interpretation,* (27 ff.), Eco discusses the sacrilegious significance of crossing them. In ancient Rome, bridges were sacrilegious because they spanned the *sulcus,* the moat that formed the city boundary, and for this reason they were to be built only under the strictest priestly supervision. Also: "If the time ever comes when there is no longer a clear definition of boundaries, and the barbarians (nomads who have abandoned their original territory and who move about on any territory as if it were their own, ready to abandon that too) succeed in imposing their nomadic view, then Rome will be finished and the capital of the empire could just as well be anywhere else." The analogies will be clear: for the "barbarians"—the "swine" before whom the pearls of interpretive understanding must not be cast—to succeed in crossing the barrier between congregation and priest, whose domain they can then treat "as if it were their own," will mean an end to traditional authority: authority will then rest somewhere else.

The destruction of religious effigies, or, where this proved impossible, their quite literal defacement, the scratching out of all features that might make them recognizable, can be related to the Old Testament commandment against idolatry; and we have seen that Augustine repeatedly warned against attaching more importance to signs than to that which they are intended to signify. These two acts of destructive zeal, however, share a common idea: both can be seen as directed against representation. We can begin to understand how an apparently democratic, progressive approach to interpretation, as promised by the Wycliffite and Tyndale Bible translations, becomes a Puritan attack on art in general. Art does not tell the truth; it is representation, a collection of signs; we are in constant danger of mistaking the sign for the signified, thereby attaching greater importance to it; art can lead us away from the truth and into error; art leads us into sin. If the argument again sounds familiar, this is because, in a different religious context, it is precisely the one used by Plato to justify the banishment of all artists from his ideal republic. Naturally, the Puritan poet-whippers also quote, or misquote, biblical and exegetical authorities in an attempt to give their moral argument historical justification.

The first response against the Puritan attack was a succession of "Defenses" or "Apologies" for poetry, of which Sidney's is, today at least, the best known, and that generally quote, or misquote, the same classical, biblical, and exegetical authorities to prove the opposite point (a fact that very well exemplifies the kind of problems we encounter if we try to deal with open texts as if they were closed). For the Puritans, suspicious of representation, the past was a time in which actions of any value were performed rather than written about. This is how Sidney puts it in his *Apology for Poetry:* "They alledge heere-with, that before Poets beganne to be in price our Nation hath set their harts delight vpon action, and not vpon imagination: rather doing things worthy to be written, then writing things fitte to be done" (Gregory Smith 1:187). In other words, just as the idol, the religious icon, the pietà, all distract us from what they signify and should therefore be eradicated, poetry distracts the reader from the virtue and noble deeds it purports to describe: actions speak louder than words. Sidney's response to this claim is dismissive: "What that before tyme was, I thinke scarcely *Sphinx* can tell: Sith no memory is so auncient that hath the precedence of Poetrie." Poetry's defense is here that it has always been around and is therefore the oldest authority. Moreover, it is the oldest authority for all nations, including, according to George Puttenham (*Of Poets and Poesy* [1589]: Gregory Smith 2:11), "strange peoples wild and sauage, affirming that the American, the Perusine, and the very Caniball do sing their highest and holiest matters in certaine riming versicles" (Gregory Smith 2:11).

This "historical" side of the debate is unedifying and, not infrequently, descends to the level of personal slander. The apologists' responses to the charge that poetry is morally corrupting, however, constitute the first serious attempts by early modern critics to formulate a theory of poetry. The whole debate on the value of poetry in many ways echoes that between Plato and Aristotle. Firstly, poetry is claimed by its defenders to be of divine origin—in Plato a negative criticism since it means that poetry is not *technē;* but in England in the 1500s divine means scriptural and, therefore, of the highest possible authority. Accordingly, in the *Apology* Sidney cites the Old Testament as an example of the divine, and especially the prophetic nature of poetry:

> And may I not presume a little further, to shew the reasonableness of this worde *Vates* [seer; prophet]? And say that the holy *Dauids* Psalmes are a diuine Poem? If I doo, I shall not do it without the testimonie of great learned men, both auncient and moderne: but euen the name Psalmes will speake for mee, which, being interpreted [i.e., translated], is nothing but songes. Then that it is fully written in meeter, all the learned Hebricians agree, although the rules be not yet fully found. Lastly and principally, his handeling [of] his prophecy, which is meerely [i.e., wholly and purely] poetical. For what els is the meaning of [the metaphor of] awakening his musicall intruments; the often and free changing of persons; his notable Prosopopeias [the introduction of a pretended speaker or narrative voice] when he maketh you, as it were, see God comming in his Maiestie; his telling of the Beastes ioyfulnes, and hills leaping, but a heauenlie poesie, wherein almost hee sheweth himselfe a passionate louer of that vnspeakable and euerlasting beautie to be seene by the eyes of the minde, onely cleered by fayth? (Gregory Smith 1:154–55)

If Sidney makes a strong case for poetry by quoting the psalms, Thomas Lodge could hardly have made a better one by citing, in his *Defence of Poetry* of 1579, the Song of Solomon, repeating Origen's claim that it is written in classical meter. After all, which exegete would dare suggest that the Song of Solomon, cited by Lodge above, were anything but allegorical? I here reproduce chapter 5, following the King James Version's division into verses, as an illustration:

> 1. I am come into my garden, my sister, my spouse: I have gathered my myrrh with my spice; I have eaten my honeycomb with my honey:

I have drunk my wine with my milk: eat, O friends: drink, yea, drink abundantly, O beloved.

2. I sleep, but my heart waketh: it is the voice of my beloved that knocketh, saying, Open to me, my sister, my love, my dove, my undefiled: for my head is filled with dew, and my locks with the drops of the night.

3. I have put off my coat: how shall I put it on? I have washed my feet. How shall I defile them?

4. My love put in his hand by the hole of the door, and my bowels were moved for him.

5. I rose up to open to my beloved: and my hands dropped with myrrh, and my fingers with sweet smelling myrrh, upon the handles of the lock.

6. I opened to my beloved: but my beloved had withdrawn himself, and was gone: my soul failed when he spake: I sought him but I could not find him: I called him but he gave me no answer.

7. The watchmen that went about the city found me, they smote me, they wounded me: the keepers of the walls took away my veil from me.

8. I charge you, O daughters of Jerusalem, if ye find my beloved, that if ye find my beloved, that ye tell him, that I am sick of love.

9. What is thy beloved more than another beloved, O thou fairest among women? what is thy beloved more than another beloved, that thou dost so charge us?

10. My beloved is white and ruddy, the chiefest among ten thousand

11. His head is as the most fine gold, his locks are bushy, and black as a raven.

12. His eyes are as the eyes of doves by the rivers of waters, washed with milk, and fitly set.

13. His cheeks are as a bed of spices, as sweet flowers: his lips are like lillies, dropping sweet smelling myrrh.

14. His hands are as gold rings set with the beryl: his belly is as bright as ivory overlaid with sapphires.

15. His legs are as pillars of marble, set upon sockets of fine gold: his countenance is as Lebanon, excellent as the cedars.

16. His mouth is most sweet: yea, he is altogether lovely. This is my beloved, and this is my friend, O daughters of Jerusalem.


Apart from biblical witnesses for the defense of poetry, the apologists never tired of calling on classical authorities, and the one they quoted most frequently was Aristotle on representation. We have seen how, for

Plato, the idea of mimesis was wholly negative since he equated it with mere imitation. Because of this, art became a mere copy of physical realities, or of ideas, and therefore one step further from "truth" than the copied original. For Aristotle, however, mimesis was representation rather than imitation, and therefore a good thing because people can learn from representations since they are attracted to them (i.e., they derive aesthetic pleasure from them). A representation is certainly not the same thing as a copy: if we represent the idea "love" by referring to it as a rose, no one can say that we are copying nature: a rose is not really "love," but we have come to accept the analogy as an artistic commonplace, and everyone understands that when Robert Burns tells us his love is "like a red, red rose," he does not wish us to infer that she has a long green neck and petals for a head.

For the sixteenth-century English apologists, poetic representation, and in particular its use of allegory, is, or can be, morally instructive. That it should not be seen as synonymous with mere copying is the first point made by Roger Ascham in his discussion of "Imitatio" in *The Scholemaster* (1570): "*Imitation* is a facultie to expresse liuelie and perfitelie that example which ye go about to folow. And of it selfe it is large and wide: for all the workes of nature in a maner be examples for art to folow" (*The Scholemaster*: Gregory Smith 1:5). The general rule, then, is that we can choose from "all the workes of nature" to create, as "liuelie and perfitlie" as our own poetic abilities allow us, an artistic representation of any particular idea. This is not the same as saying that art imitates nature: indeed, according to Elizabethan theory, it lies within the capabilities of the good poet to "improve" upon nature. How could nature, God's work, be improved upon by humans? And how could such a belief be expressed, let alone held, in a now officially Puritan England and in a period when nonattendance at church was a punishable offence? The answer to these questions forms the basis of Elizabethan theories of allegory.

In the dedicatory introduction to his translation of the first four books of Virgil's *Aeneid* (1582), Richard Stanyhurst argues that the virtue of allegorical writing is twofold. Firstly, it can be used as a way of revealing the truths of human existence—in other words, the poet is again *Vates,* the seer, whose language, like the language of the Bible, must be figurative in order to express the otherwise inexpressible. Secondly, and on a rather more mundane level, those readers not equipped to see the truth beneath the surface of the poetry may still derive some pleasure from reading it—

the point made by Dante in the *Convivio*. Here, in Stanyhurst's rather eccentric orthography and very lively imagery, are the first few lines of his introduction:

> What deepe and rare poynctes of hydden secrets *Virgil* hath sealde up in his twelue bookes of Aeneis may easelye appeere too such reaching wyts as bend theyre endewours too thee vnfolding thereof, not onlye by gnibling vpon the outward ryne of a supposed historie, but also by groaping thee pyth that is shrind vp wythin thee barck and bodye of so exquisit and singular a discourse, For where as thee chiefe prayse of a wryter consisteth in thee enterlacing of pleasure wyth profit, oure author hath so wiselye alayed thee one wyth thee oother as thee shallow reader may bee delighted wyth a smooth tale, and thee diuing searcher may bee aduantaged by sowning a pretiouse treatise.

Moreover, Virgil

> dooth laboure, in telling as yt were a *Cantorburye tale,* too ferret owt the secretes of *Nature,* with woordes so fitlye coucht, wyth verses so smoothlye slyckte, with sentences so featlye orderd, with orations so neatlie burnisht, with similitudes so aptly applyed, with each *decorum* so duely obserued, as in truth hee hath in right purchased too hym selfe thee name of a surpassing poët, the fame of an od oratoure, and the admiration of a profound philosopher. (Gregory Smith 1:136–7)

Only very recently has criticism suggested that it is not in fact the purpose of art to hide truths, nor the task of the reader to discover them. We can understand Stanyhurst's insistence on this function of poetry, however, in the context of the attacks made against it: that is has no moral value, that it corrupts the reader, that it is frivolous, that it pretends to learning where it has none.

By mentioning Chaucer in the same breath as Virgil—one of the darlings of cultivated Elizabethan readers—Stanyhurst does two things. Firstly he makes a contribution to the debate on the value of the English language itself. English vernacular was held by many theorists, especially in the universities, to be unfit for learned or artistic discourses. Rather, it was Latin, respectable because it was one of the "original" languages of the Bible and because of its antiquity, that was seen as the proper medium for all serious debate. Almost all of the Elizabethan critics feel obliged to defend not only poetry but poetry in English. But Stanyhurst's comparison of the *Aeneid* with the *Tales* also makes an important case for allegory. Virgil is respectable: he is antique and wrote in Latin; the *Aeneid* is a great work, more than mere "supposed historie"—in fact, it is crucial that it be "supposed," for if it is, then it must be read allegorically rather than as historical narrative. It is no accident that so many of the Elizabethan apologists quote the *Aeneid*. They do so largely in order to point out that allegory can teach virtue: "euen in the most excellent determination of goodnes, what Philosophers counsel," asks Sidney, "can so redily direct a Prince . . . as *Aeneas* in *Virgill*?" Or who "readeth of Aeneas carrying olde Anchises on his back [in their escape from the burning Troy] that wishes not it were his fortune to perfourme so excellent an acte?" In this way, by describing virtuous deeds, allegorical writing inspires virtue; and if it describes evil, then its purpose must be to make us shun evil. Also, if it causes us aesthetic pleasure into the bargain, so much the better, since, according to this view, it is the function of poetry both to instruct and to please. Even poets know that humans are not all as noble-minded as Aeneas, but since it is their professed aim to instill noble-mindedness, they have the license, as Sidney explains in the *Apology,* to represent an improved version of human nature in their writing: they can speak, allegorically, of what Aristotle called "possibilities":

> Onely the Poet . . . lifted vp with the vigor of his owne inuention, dooth growe in effect another nature, in making things either better then Nature bringeth forth, or, quite a newe, formes such as neuer were in Nature, as the *Heroes, Demigods, Cyclops, Chimeras, Furies,* and such like: so as hee goeth hand in hand with Nature, not inclosed within the narrow warrant of her guifts, but freely ranging onely within the Zodiack of his owne wit. . . . Nature neuer set forth the earth in so rich tapistry as diuers Poets haue done, neither with plesant riuers, fruitful trees. sweet smelling flowers, nor whatsoeuer els may make the too much loued earth more louely. Her world is brasen, the Poets onely deliuer a golden (Gregory Smith 1:156–58).

In a world inhabited by Furies, Heroes, and Demigods, there is room for Chauntecleer and Pertelote, just as there is also room for Faerie Queenes and Redcrosse Knights.

But does virtue need allegorizing in the first place? Do the Puritan critics, and Plato, not have a case in that, if the sign is too attractive, people will prefer it to the signified? The usual reply to this charge—so usual in fact that it is an Elizabethan commonplace—is interesting because it seems to contradict the humanist idealism that believes in our natural tendency toward good. The reply is that allegory is the sugarcoating on the bitter pill. This gives poetry its raison d'être: the allegory is there because the pill is necessary. But it also makes a poor case for the pill in question, for (unless we are Puritans of the very grimmest variety) if we experience our doses of moral education as bitter, we can hardly be said to have a natural tendency toward virtue. For this reason it is wise to think of the apologists' claims for the moral value of poetry in terms of a necessary response to the threat of official censure as well as thinking of them as a serious theoretical approach.

At any rate, the apologists' point is that allegory—poetry—contains truth, and the reader can pursue this truth at will. If the poem is a good one, if it fulfils its task to delight, we will be drawn toward discovering the truth, and the second task, to teach, will thus also be fulfilled. It is interesting, too, that here there is an informal acknowledgement that there must be an agreement in place between text and reader in order for the text to function. Renaissance theorists did not talk about an *intentio operis*, an intention of the text, but they do frequently talk about allegory, rather than about the writer of the allegory.

Sir John Harrington's *Brief Apology for Poetry* (1591) returns us to the point at which Dante suggested that the rules for reading allegory could be applied to secular poetry. Harrington enlarges on Dante's comments and takes an example from classical poetry—the tale of Perseus and the Gorgon from Ovid's *Metamorphoses*—rather than from the Bible. I quote the passage that contains Harrington's explication of the various senses in which allegory can be read:

> *Perseus* sonne of *Iupiter* is fained by the Poets to haue slaine *Gorgon,* and, after that conquest atchieued, to haue flown vp to heauen. The Historicall sense is this, *Perseus* the sonne of *Iupiter,* by the participation of *Iupiters* vertues which were in him, or rather comming of the stock of one of the kings of Creet, or Athens so called, slew *Gorgon,* a tyrant in that countrey (*Gorgon* in Greeke signifieth earth), and was for his vertuous parts exalted by men vp vnto heauen. Morally it signifieth this much: *Perseus* a wise man, sonne of Iupiter, endewed with vertue from aboue, slayeth sinne and vice, a thing base and earthly signified by Gorgon, and so mounteth vp to the skie of vertue. It signifies in one kind of

Allegory thus much: the mind of man being gotten by God, and so the childe of God killing and vanquishing he earthlinesse of this Gorgoni-call nature, ascendeth vp to the vnderstanding of heauenly things, of high things, of eternal things, in which contemplacion consisteth the perfection of man: this is the natural allegory, because man [is] one of the chiefe works of nature. It hath also a more high and heauenly Alle-gorie, that the heauenly nature, daughter of Iupiter, procuring with her continuall motion corruption and mortality in the inferiour bodies, seuered it selfe at last from these earthly bodies, and flew vp on high, and there remaineth for euer. It hath also another Theological Allegorie: that the angelicall nature, daughter of the most high God the creator of all things, killing & ouercomming all bodily substance, signified by *Gor-gon,* ascended into heauen. The like infinite Allegories I could pike out of other Poeticall fictions, saue that I would auoid tediousnes. (Gregory Smith 2:202–3)

What Harrington says about the possibility of infinite allegorical readings is certainly tantalizing, and we might wish that this 1590s author had been less concerned to "auoid tediousnes" and had given further examples of what sounds rather like the modern concept of indefinitely deferred mean-ing. However, we must be careful of attributing twentieth-century ideas to sixteenth-century theorists. Even Sidney's memorable phrase "freely ranging onely within the Zodiack of his owne wit," attractive though it is, cannot be taken as a plea for what a poet of our own times would under-stand as artistic license (though it is safe to say that it can be seen as a step in that direction). The phrase was written in the context of a defense against quite specific attacks, and if the *Apology* speaks of the aesthetic pleasure poetry can give, it necessarily points to the other function of poetry: poetry must both "teach and delight," and what it must teach is moral correctness. The only way this theory can work is by making a distinction between "proper" poetry and "vulgar," popular verse—the apologists are, after all, courtiers or scholars. All of them are careful to concede the moral point to the extent of admitting that certain kinds of poetry—that is, bad poetry (not their own)—can indeed be regarded as worthless or even pernicious, but they are just as careful to point out that good poetry is different—another reason for their insistence on the poetry of the Bible and on its fre-quent use of poetic devices, allegory in particular. It is only the true poet who is *Vates* and therefore allowed to "range freely" as far as his own wit, his powers of association and invention, will allow, for the work of the true poet will necessarily be interpretable as moral allegory. In the twentieth century, the poet Robert Graves said almost precisely the same thing. I shall have occasion to discuss Graves's work at some length in the final chapter of this book.

It must be said that, because these apologies were produced for a specific purpose, it is impossible to decide how far their authors were writing down ideas they believed were applicable outside the context of the puritan attack on poetry. We have no way of knowing whether they believed the moral issue important at all or whether they merely felt obliged to discuss it in order to help support a more general case for poetry. What we can say is that they frequently establish an association between reading poetry *solely* for "delight" and the uneducated "common" people. Harrington, for example, writes in his *Brief Apology* that

> the weaker capacities will feede themselues with the pleasantnes of the historie and sweetnes of the verse, some that haue stronger stomackes will as it were take a further taste of the Morall sence, a third sort, more high conceited than they, will digest the Allegorie: so as indeed it hath bene thought by men of verie good iudgement, such manner of Poeticall writing was an excellent way to preserue all kinde of learning from that corruption which now it is come to since they left that mysticall writing of verse. (Gregory Smith 2:203)

We gather from this that allegorical writing will be appreciated only by a select group, while the majority of readers (or listeners) will content themselves with mere pleasure. This becomes even more apparent when, a few lines later, Harrington discusses the way in which the necessary musicality of "proper" poetry can render an unpleasant topic agreeable. Here we might expect, for example, another description of the horrors of the fall of Troy. What we are in fact presented with is this:

> for myne owne part I was neuer yet so good a husbandman to take any delight to heare one of my ploughmen tell how an acre of wheat must be fallowd and twyfallowd, and how cold land should be burned, and fruitfull land must be well harrowed; but when I heare one read *Virgill*, where he saith,
>
> > *Saepe etiam steriles incendere profuit agros,*
> > *Atque leuem stipulam crepitanibus vrere flammis.*
> > *Siue inde vires & pabula terrae*

> *Pinguia concipiunt: siue illis omne per ignem*
> *Excoquitur vitium, atque exsudat inutilis humor,* &c.,

and after,

> *Multum adeo, rastris glebas qui frangit inertes,*
> *Vimineasque trahit crates iuuat arua;*[1]

with many other lessons of homly husbandry, but deliuered in so good Verse that me thinkes all that while I could find in my hert to driue the plough. (Gregory Smith 2:207)

One is tempted to find that the instructive power of verse must be great indeed if it is able to make Harrington consider dirtying his hands.

We discover, then, that we have to be very much on our guard when the sixteenth-century apologists use the word *allegory,* or even the word *poetry.* If they no longer agree with the medieval exegetes that moral or spiritual allegory are to be found only in Scripture, they seem to claim that, even where they do exist in secular poetry, that poetry will be fully appreciated and will probably have been written only by themselves and people like them. What was once reserved for the Roman Catholic Church is now, it appears, reserved for the secular social and intellectual elite. Again we are reminded of pearls and swine. In this way, the English apologists' claim for the value of allegory can in fact be seen as a step backwards from Dante's position. He, too, maintained that it was possible to read his *Commedia* either for its allegorical (moral, spiritual) content or for its musicality and "sweetness." He does not, however, use his theory of allegorical interpretation to underline social divisions or imply that interpretation is the prerogative of a particular class. If for Harrington allegorical texts are open, they are open to only a very small minority of readers.

Since the nature of their criticism is so exclusive, it is unsurprising that when the apologists refer to contemporary writing they quote each other, though in the case of Thomas Nash and Gabriel Harvey, reference and debate descend to the level of publicly ridiculing each other. Here is an example taken from Nash's *Strange Newes* (1592):

But ah! what newes do you heare of that good Gabriel huffe snuffe, Knowne to the world for a foole, and clapt in the Fleete [i.e., prison] for a Rimer? . . . You will neuer leaue your olde trickes of drawing M. *Spenser* into euerie pybald thing you do. If euer he praisd thee, it was because he pickt a fine vaine foole out of thee, and he would keepe thee still by flattring thee, til such time as he had brought thee into that extreame loue with thy selfe, that thou shouldst run mad with the conceit, and so be scorned of all men. (Gregory Smith 2:241)

This had been prompted by, and itself prompted, criticism composed in the manner of the following attack on Nash taken from Harvey's *Pierces Supererogation* (1593):

Would God, or could the Diuell, giue him that vnmeasurable allowance of witt and Arte that he extreamely affecteth, and infinitely wanteth, there were no encounter but of admiration and honour. . . . But out vpon ranke and lothsome ribaldry that putrifieth where it should purify, and presumeth to deflowre the moste florishinge wittes with whom it consorteth, wyther in familiarity or by favour! . . . One Ouid was too much for Roome, and one Greene too much for London,[2] but one Nashe more intollerable then both, not bicause his witt is anye thinge comparable, but bicause his will is more outragious . . . I will not heere decipher thy vnprinted packet of bawdye and filthy Rymes in the nastiest kind: there is a fitter place for that discouery of thy foulest shame, & the whole ruffianism of thy brothell Muse, if she still prostitute her obscene ballats, and will needes be a younge Curtisan of olde knauery. (*Pierces Supererogation*: Gregory Smith 2:252 ff.)

It is Edmund Spenser, mentioned by Nash above, who comes in for more or less consistent praise, both for the *Shepheardes Calender* and for the *Faerie Queene*. But when they discuss Spenser (having perhaps dealt with the moral issue to their satisfaction), the apologists concentrate on that quality that Harrington found so attractive in Virgil's *Georgics*. Harvey, always ready to compliment Spenser (as Nash was quite correct in stating) asks his readers whether "Spenser in his braue Faery Queene [is not] the Virginall of the diuinest Muses and gentlest Graces?" while Francis Meres feels able to claim, "I knowe not what more excellent or exquisite Poem may be written"; and in *The Returne from Parnassus,* performed in 1601 (i.e., two years after Spenser's death) at Saint John's College, Cambridge, the characters Iudicio and Ingenioso have this to say:

> Iud. Nay, hearers hong vpon his melting tong,
> While sweetly of his Faiery Queene he song,
> While to the waters fall he tun'd her fame,

> And in each barke engrau'd Elizaes name.
> And yet, for all this, vnregarding soile
> Vnlac't the line of his desired life,
> Denying mayntenance for his deare reliefe;
> Carelesse ere to preuent his exequy,
> Scarce deigning to shut up his dying eye.
> Ing. Pity it is that gentler witts should breed,
> Where thick skin chuffes laugh at a scholar's need.

There is no mention of moral virtue or of allegory in any of this praise: Spenser is a musical instrument to be played upon by the Muses and Graces, his poem is "exquisite," a sweet song; it is felt to be tragic that the rebels in Ireland (selfishly attempting to reclaim their own land) deprived him of his home and property and forced him to return impoverished to England; and it is "pity" that such noble spirits should be forced to breathe the same air as unrefined, common folk.

Spenser himself, however, takes infinite care to discuss the allegorical reading of his poem. The frontispiece of the 1596 edition tells us that it is "Disposed into twelue bookes, Fashioning XII. Morall vertues," and the dedication to Elizabeth expresses the hope that "these his labovrs [will] live with the eternity of her fame." The edition of 1590 included a letter to Sir Walter Raleigh, which was not reproduced in 1596, "expounding [Spenser's] whole intention in the course of this worke: which for that it giveth great light to the reader, for the better understanding is hereunto annexed." Such prefatory letters to poems or to collections of poems were commonplace in England and in Italy: Dante's letter to Can Grande della Scala is only one example of many. Spenser's is of interest to us because of what it says about a particular understanding of allegorical writing and its functions. It begins by announcing what is in effect an attempt to limit interpretation.

> Sir, knowing how doubtfully all Allegories may be construed, and this booke of mine, which I have entituled the Faery Queene, being a continued Allegory, or darke conceit, I have thought good aswell for avoyding of gealous opinions and misconstructions, as also for your better light in reading thereof, (being so by you commanded,) to discover unto you the general intention and meaning, which in the whole course thereof I have fashioned, without expressing of any particular purposes or by-accidents therein occasioned.

*Darkness* and *light* are traditional exegetical terms: spiritual ignorance is darkness; darkness is the place where all things are hidden, and it is dispelled by the light of understanding. It seems strange that a poet should go to the trouble of hiding things in a "continued . . . darke conceit" only to shed light upon them himself before the reader has reached even the first line. To do so is surely to rob that reader of some of the pleasure of reading and to render the poet's efforts futile. Why then should he or she do so? In the case of the Faerie Queene, there is one obvious, political reason that Spenser himself mentions: he does not want any "gealous opinions and misconstructions," by which he means that he wishes to avoid the possibility of willful misinterpretation of the poem in the context of contemporary politics. But there are further designs:

> The generall end therefore of all the book is to fashion a gentleman or noble person in vertuous and gentle discipline: Which for that I conceived shoulde be most plausible and pleasing, being coloured with an historicall fiction, the which the most part of men delight to read, rather for variety of matter, then [i.e., than] for profit of the ensample: I chose the historye of king Arthure, as most fitte for the excellency of his person, being made famous by many mens former workes, and also furthest from the daunger of envy, and suspition of present time.

Choosing the figure of King Arthur was an astute precaution because the Tudors were well known for their fondness for rather fancifully tracing their ancestry back to him, and no one, therefore, could reasonably call the poem a treasonable text if its preface contained such obvious flattery of a reigning Tudor monarch. More interesting for our study is the claim that most people read such works more for their entertainment value than for moral instruction: in other words, to be delighted rather than taught. What is a Renaissance poet, a member of the social elite and highly respected by his contemporaries, doing pandering to the tastes of the masses? Does this not contradict a crucial point in the defense against Puritan criticism of poetry? On the one hand, we could respond to the question by reminding ourselves that the poem announces itself as a representation of twelve moral virtues. On the other hand, the apologists, in their theoretical writings, always seek to distance themselves from the kind of poetry that is perceived as aimed principally at those "weaker capacities [who] will feede themselues with the pleasantnes of the historie." The letter explains this seemingly paradoxical situation by acknowledging that some readers will dislike the poem precisely because it is allegorical: they, it is claimed, "had rather have good discipline delivered plainly in view of precepts, or sermoned at large, then [i.e., than] thus clowdily enwrapped in Allegoricall devises." They should, however, "be satisfide with the use of these dayes, seeing all things accounted by their showes, and nothing esteemed of, that is not delightfull and pleasing to commune sence." This is rather different from arguing that it is the *purpose* of poetry to teach and to delight. On the contrary, what this seems to be saying is that for poetry to be morally instructive is all well and good, but if it is not entertaining into the bargain, nobody will read it.

The letter supports this claim by comparing the writings of Plato with those of Xenophon: "[Plato] in the exquisite depth of his judgement, formed a Commune welth such as it should be, but [Xenophon] in the person of Cyrus and the Persians fashioned a government such as might best be. So much more profitable and gratious is doctrine by ensample then by rule." The letter might well have quoted Aristotle, too: "Representation is natural to human beings from childhood . . . everyone delights in representations." The rule seems to be that it was the fact that the poem is allegorical, rather than what it allegorizes, that found favor with the its earliest critics. A hundred years later, critics were still saying the same thing. John Hughes, in his *Remarks on The Faerie Queene and The Shepheardes Calender* (1715), found that the poem's chief merit "consists in that surprizing Vein of Invention, which runs thro it, end enriches it every where with Imagery and Descriptions more than we meet with in any other modern Poem. The Author seems to be possess'd of a kind of Poetical Magick; and the figures he calls up to our View rise so thick upon us, that we are at once pleased and distracted by the exhaustless Variety of them" (Maclean and Prescott 661ff). There is no mention here of the poem's moral value as a "chief merit." Indeed, it is tempting to suppose that what Spenser's "Poetical Magick" distracts us from is what to many modern tastes is the poem's overbearing moral direction. I suspect that it is the obviousness of the allegory—its resistance to openness—that many students today find difficult to deal with:

> A gentle Knight was pricking on the plaine,
>   Y cladd in mightie armes and silver shielde,
>   Wherein old dints of deepe wounds did remaine,

. . . . . . . . . . . . . . . . . . . .
But on his brest a bloudie Crosse he bore,
. . . . . . . . . . . . . . . . . . . .
A lovely Ladie rode him faire beside,
    Upon a lowly Asse more white than snow,
    Yet she much whiter, but the same did hide
    Under a vele, that wimpled was full low . . .

And by her in a line, a milke white lambe she lad . . .

So pure and innocent, as that same lambe,
    She was in life and every vertuous lore.

                                        (1.i.1–5)

Interestingly, the equally obvious allegory of postmodern fantasy and science fiction, especially in the cinema—*BladeRunner* the pseudohistorical settings of the *Conan* movies; and the uncomplicated symbolism of *Rocky* and *Rambo*—continue to find popular resonance. They are all more or less closed texts, reducible to a few very old "virtues": notions of honor; faith (in God or in a god, in oneself, in a cause); justice. These in turn are represented by the struggle between good and evil; the fight of the oppressed against the oppressor; the hero-outcast; the superhuman protector of the threatened. These last two figures appear only at the right moment—that is, at the last moment and in answer to a "prayer."

Not all sixteenth-century allegory is as closed as the *Faerie Queene,* with characters quickly identifiable (on the author's direction) as representations of particular concepts or of historical figures. An example of a very open poem, written between 1519 and 1521, is John Skelton's remarkable "Speke, Parrot," The first five stanzas of this remarkable poem are here reproduced.

    My name ys Parott, a byrde of Paradyse,
    By Nature devysed of a wonderowus kynde,
    Deyntely dyeted with dyvers delycate spyce,
    Tyll Eufrates, that flodde, dryvethe me into Ynde,
    Where men of that contre by fortune me fynde,       5
    And send me to greate ladyes of estate;
    Then Parot moste have an almon or a date.

    A cage curyowsly carven, with sylver pynne,
    Properly paynted to be my coverture;

A myrrour of glasse, that I may tote therin;                                  10
These maydens full meryly with many a dyvers flowur
Fresshely the dresse and make swete my bowur,
With, "Speke, Parott, I pray yow," full curteslye they sey,
"Parott ys a goodlye byrde and a pratye popagay."

Wythe my beke bent, and my lytell wanton iye,                                 15
My feathyrs fresshe as ys the emerawde grene,
Abowte my necke a cerculett lyke the ryche rubye,
My lytell legges, my fete bothe fete and clene,
I am a mynyon to wayte apon a quene;
"My propyr Parott, my lytell pratye fole."                                    20
With ladies I lerne and goe with them to scole.

"Heghe, ha, ha, Parott, ye can lawghe pratylye!"
"Parott hathe not dyned of all this long day";
"Lyke owur pus catt Parott can mewte and crye."
Yn Latyn, in Ebrue, and in Caldee,                                           25
In Greke tong Parott can bothe speke and sey,
As Percius, that poete, dothe reporte of me,
Quis expeduit psitaco suum Chyre?[3]

Dowche Frenshe of Paris Parot can lerne,
Pronownsyng my purpose after my properte,                                    30
With, "Parlez byen, Parott, ow parles ryen."
With Dowche, with Spaynyshe, my tong can agree;
In Englysshe to God Parott can supple:
"Cryste save Kyng Herry the viiith, owur royall kyng,
The red rose in honour to flowrysshe and sprynge!"                           35

In these opening stanzas, most of what Parrot says concerns saying: he
talks about language, or, more precisely, about kinds of language: about
ways of saying things. He is certainly polyglot, an expert in classical and
modern languages, as well as being able to "mewte and crye" like a cat. But
his use of language is also strictly controlled: he is ordered to speak "byen
. . . ow parles ryen"—that is, to speak well, or properly, or else not at all;
his tongue can "agree" with Dutch or Spanish, which may mean simply
that he can speak these languages but may also, especially in the context of
the command to speak well or not at all, be taken as a sarcastic comment

on the futility of language in the position he finds himself in—all he is allowed to do is agree with what is said by those around him. Besides, parrots do not really speak: they imitate sounds. They can learn to repeat, for example, "Cryste save Kyng Herry the viiith, owur royall kyng." Probably they know from experience that when they reproduce this and similar formulas they will be rewarded with "an almon or a date."

We know that Skelton was both a priest and a court poet—*the* court poet, in fact: "Skelton Laureat," as occasional references in his poems remind us—and we know that he had been tutor to the young man who became Henry VIII. We know, too, that he managed to make an enemy, at least temporarily, of Cardinal Wolsey, the most powerful statesman in England. (Not without a sense of irony, Wolsey seems to have banished Skelton, also temporarily, to the rectory at Diss in Norfolk: Dis is Hades, the classical underworld or hell.) We can use this information from outside the text to support a reading of Parrot as a representation of the court poet, a semiofficial commentator forbidden to comment and reduced to the role of decorative curiosity; rather exotic perhaps; an entertainer—the sort of educated servant monarchs were supposed to have around them but not supposed to take too seriously. In this view we can see what Parrot has to say about his own linguistic abilities as a sarcastic comment on the restrictions placed on them by the political environment in which he finds himself. He must, for his personal safety, speak (and write) allegorically, since a closed text (i.e., one in which his criticism of the court was immediately understood) would surely result in punishment.

There are other, very different readings of the poem. One critic, for example, has seen Parrot both as mad and as a parodic representation of the Holy Ghost who uses his madness, demonstrated by what this critic sees as his "verbiage" as a "homeopathic remedy" for the madness of Wolsey's rule.[4] In either case, the irony of Parrot's situation is that he uses obscure language (in my reading, allegory) in order to speak plainly. This is supported by the following stanzas on Wolsey from the conclusion of the poem, in which Parrot (or Skelton) speaks plainly indeed:

> So many moral matters, and so little used;
>> So much new making, and so mad time spent;
> So much translation into English confused;
>> So much noble preaching, and so little amendment;
>> So much consultation, almost to none intent;            5

So much provision, and so little wit at need—
Since Deucalion's flood there can no clerkes rede.

. . . . . . . . . . . . . . . . . . . . . . . . . . . .

So many truces taken, and so little perfite troth;                                45
   So much belly-joy, and so wasteful banqueting;
So pinching and sparing, and so little profit grow'th;
   So many hugy houses building, and so small householding;
   Such statutes upon diets, such pilling and polling;
So is all thing wrought wilfully withoute reason and skill—              50
Since Deucalion's flood the world was never so ill.


So much ragged right of a rammes horn;
   So rigorous revelling in a prelate specially;
So bold and so bragging, and was so basely born;
   So lordly in his looks and so disdainously;
   So fat a maggot, bred of a fleshe-fly;
Was never such a filthy Gorgon, nor such an epicure,
Since Deucalion's flood, I make thee fast and sure.[5]

Sadly, perhaps, Skelton is not representative of his age. The apologists we have seen did not quite know what to make of him, but generally regarded his lack of "polish" as suspect: "*Skelton* (I wot not for what great worthines) surnamed the Poet *Laureat* . . . a sharpe Satirist, but with more rayling and scoffery than became a Poet Lawreat . . . in deed but a rude rayling rimer & all his doings ridiculous . . . pleasing only the popular eare" (Puttenham, *Art of English Poesy*: Gregory Smith 2:1–193); "As Sotades Maronites, the Iambicke Poet, gaue himself to write impure and lasciuious things: so Skelton (I know not for what great worthines surnamed the Poet Laureat) applied his wit to scurrilities and ridiculous matters" (Francis Meres, *Palladis Tamia* [1598]: Gregory Smith 2:308–24); though William Webbe had found that he could "wyth good ryght yeelde him the title of a Poet: hee was doubtles a pleasant conceyted fellowe, and of a very sharpe wytte, exceeding bolde, and would nyppe to the very quicke where he once sette holde" (*Discourse of English Poetrie* [1586]: Gregory Smith 230–302).

In this way, the moral question again becomes important, for the courtly poet is also the upholder of a system of behavior that separates him, and by extension his readers (or at least his model readers), from the rest of society. A poet such as Skelton, who not only attacks court hypocrisy but writes allegories in a style likely to please "the popular eare," is unlikely to find favor among critics increasingly obsessed with notions of elegance, polish, wit, decorum, and "conceits." The apologists' idea of "proper" poetry is of a form that is definitely not for the masses, who, in turn, should not be invited (by people like Skelton) to scoff at courtly excesses. For them, decorum in style and subject matter is essential, the appropriateness of the speeches given to characters in epic poetry, for example, or in verse drama. This is the point raised by Plato in his argument against having the gods portrayed in poetry as saying and doing ridiculous—that is, ungod-like—things. Princes and courtiers must, in the view of the apologists, be represented in art as princely and courteous. Allegory, because it is by defi-nition a representation of things *allos,* other than as they appear in the real physical world, always runs the risk of subverting such attempts to ideal-ize the proposed subject matter of poetry—hence, the need regularly felt by those in a position of authority to limit its interpretive possibilities by imposing rules to govern the way we read it, and, in this case as in the case of Scripture, to govern when it can be considered a valid form.

In all of the critical writings we have so far seen, from Aristotle's com-ments on the social value of poetry, through the exegetical theses of the church fathers, to the beginnings of formal literary criticism in England, the debate has been concerned not only with the function of art but with the question of who it is for. If this second question seems remote and no longer relevant to a readership used to free access to the whole of litera-ture, we need only remember the censorship of art and the suppression of particular artists by certain regimes to realize that this is not everywhere the case.

## THE "ALLEGORY OF LOVE"

The heading here (minus the quotation marks) is also the title of a book by C. S. Lewis on the idea of courtly love. The book first appeared in 1936 and exercised considerable influence up to about the middle, or just after the middle, of the twentieth century. Lewis had a definite religious agenda, and I reproduce words from the title of his work here not because I agree with his general critical approach (I do not) but because it is indeed pos-sible to think of the efflorescence of courtly English love poetry in the late sixteenth century, and especially in the 1590s, toward the end of Eliza-beth's reign, as a sustained exercise in allegorical writing. Nonetheless, all readings are, to a greater or lesser extent, agendas — manifestos, even — and represent quite specific beliefs about the nature of literature, about the purpose of criticism, about politics, and about wider social issues. Furthermore, Lewis's book constitutes a serious theory proposed by a serious scholar and cannot be ignored in what claims to be a serious study of allegorical interpretations.

According to Lewis, courtly love poetry appeared suddenly in what is now the Languedoc region of southern France around the end of the eleventh century. In this poetry, the beloved is necessarily distant and forever unattainable. If we are to worship we must also idealize because, so the argument runs, we can no longer worship something if it becomes a commonplace: adoration depends upon the impossibility of ever reaching the object of desire. Typically, this is either the lady, left alone with her courtiers and household servants while the lord, her husband, to whom she remains sexually faithful, is off crusading in the Holy Land; or it is one of her ladies-in-waiting. Her utter and unquestionable (if theoretical) fidelity does not prevent her accepting, and even encouraging, the stylized attempts at seduction of her poet-courtiers. It is in fact necessary that she should encourage so that she may ultimately reject and in this way both maintain her own status as object of worship and, at the same time, prolong the agony of unfulfilled passion. It all seems like a rather genteel game of flirtation. For Lewis it was more of a sophisticated joke — a joke, moreover, that was completely misunderstood by poets of the Renaissance in Italy. Lewis saw the Languedoc poets as quite deliberately taking over the devotional language of Scripture — the hyperbole of the Song of Solomon, for example — and using it to describe earthly rather than spiritual passion. The beloved therefore becomes angel, saint, heavenly, divine. Lewis's point is that Renaissance poets such as Petrarch did not get the joke: they took it seriously and were therefore faced with the difficulty of writing about sexuality in terms of divinity without treating the whole idea as a joke. The response is the spiritualization of sexuality, or, rather, the division of love into the spiritual and the sexual, with a subsequent insistence on the spiritual quality of the passion they express.

But Renaissance poets were also able to help themselves to a different vocabulary: that of classical Greek and Latin poetry. This is important because it gave them the opportunity to idealize sexuality in terms that would not offend religious sensibilities, at least not as far as their choice of allegory was concerned. They were able, in other words, to use a language and a system of symbols that would be immediately recognized as devotional because of associations with the gods and goddesses of classical mythology, but that, for the same reason, could not be interpreted as profane or sacrilegious in Christian terms. They could spiritualize by talking of saints and angels, but concentrate on physical beauty and sexual pleasure by referring to nymphs (and the natural world generally), Aphrodite, and Diana. The following two stanzas from a poem by Bewe (c. 1578) is an example of English Renaissance use of the popular Diana and Actaeon story:

> I would I were Actaeon, whom Diana did disguise,
> To walk the woods unknown whereas my lady lies;
> A hart of pleasant hue I wish that I were so,
> So that my lady knew alone me and no mo;
>
> To follow thick and plain, by hill and dale alow,
> To drink the water fain and feed me with the sloe.
> I would not fear the frost, to lie upon the ground,
> Delight should quite the cost, what pain so that I found.

The poetic symbols related to the natural world are very familiar: cheeks and lips are roses, or roses bloom in or on them; or, with emphasis on a different kind of value perhaps, they are rubies, as eyes may be sapphires; necks and breasts are snowy-white like swans' (there are implied social distinctions here: a suntan means life outdoors, which in turn means agricultural labor);[6] the beloved is mild as the spring or warm and glorious as the summer; the rejected lover lives in a personal winter of despair, with both the fire of passion and the ice of refusal forever failing to cancel each other out.

Because of the familiarity of these symbols, and because so much has in recent years been written on the Renaissance allegorization of love, I shall concentrate here on attempts made by some Renaissance poets in England to modify and, finally, reject its terms. Firstly, there is a sonnet by Spenser (no. 21 of the *Amoretti,* published 1595) that seems to question the very purpose of the kind of poem it represents:

> Was it the worke of nature or of Art,
> Which tempred so the feature of her face,
> That pride and meeknesse mixt by equall part,

Doe both appeare t'adorne her beauties grace?
For with mild pleasance, which doth pride displace,
She to her love doth lookers eyes allure:
And with sterne countenance back again doth chace
Their looser lookes that stir up lustes impure.
With such strange termes her eyes she doth inure,
That with one looke she doth my life dismay:
And with another doth it streight recure,
Her smile me drawes, her frowne me drives away.
Thus doth she traine and teach me with her lookes,
Such art of eyes I never read in bookes.

The Renaissance beloved—rather, Beloved—has by the 1590s become a convention, an artistic commonplace; an allegorical patchwork created by (male) poets out of elements drawn from classical mythologies, Christian ideals, Platonic notions of love, and the natural world; a symbol for the idea that art creates a better nature than the original. If this Frankenstein's monster of virtue does not exist in nature, the only place left for her is within the poems themselves: she cannot exist outside the text. This makes Spenser's poem a very interesting one indeed because it does two surprising things: it questions the reality of its addressee and it implies that this "she"—as a representative of all addressees of this kind of poem—shares the responsibility for her own creation in art. One of the effects of this is that the poem itself seriously questions the validity of the form in which it is written. How does this work?

For one thing, the poem employs very typical Renaissance devices, but it does so in such a way as to make it perfectly obvious that that is precisely what they are. The first quatrain forms a question that can be read (very economically) as referring to both the addressee and the poem itself. The poetic commonplace is there: the exact balance between "pride and meeknesse" essential in the Beloved ensures that she will first allow the lover to approach and then (to maintain propriety and to sustain the image of herself as ultimately untouchable—and therefore worthy of continued adoration) send him packing. Also, the equal mixture of these two qualities can be seen as symbolizing immortality according to the theory, dating back to pre-Socratic philosophers, that (physical) death is brought about by a disbalance between the constituent elements of a living organism. This disbalance can be rectified in poetry—an example of art improving upon nature—and, in my reading, the point of the opening question is to draw the reader's attention to this fact. Is the Beloved a real creature in the natural world or merely a work of art, an allegory telling us the story of Aristotle's "possibilities," in Plato's sense a mere representation of an idea?

The word *art* occurs twice in the poem—once, capitalized, in the first line, and again, this time not capitalized, in the last. I am going to assume that the capitalization in the first line is not the result of a printer's error or of a personal whim on the part of the original typesetter (this may in fact not be a very safe assumption: English printing in the sixteenth century was hardly exemplary). But I want to make a distinction between the "Art" of the first quatrain and the "art" of the last line; and every edition of Spenser's poems I have seen makes the same one. I suspect that the "Art" of the first line is Spenser's own, the art of poetry, because it is this art that makes possible the existence of the wholly idealized Beloved in the first place. In accordance with this ideal, there follows, throughout the second and third quatrains, the usual sequence of encouragement and rejection, the conventional mutability that must always lead to the lover's conventional despair, with the moral instruction to avoid "lustes impure" into the bargain. It has also been pointed out (Maclean and Prescott 995) that the poem's use of legal terminology—"termes" (negotiable conditions) and "inure" (to put into legal effect) indicates that it discusses love in the language of public life. This supports the idea that the kind of love the poem describes can be seen as a sophisticated game played out before an aristocratic audience, a ritual of courtship performed within the close confines of a court where privacy as we would understand it was more or less impossible. In this view, the final couplet sounds like an ironic comment on the situation: "I had no idea that eyes could do all this." It is as though Renaissance courts suddenly got the joke that Lewis believed he saw, but realized that it was no longer funny.

As court poetry shows signs of losing interest in this stylization, the same reaction can found in Shakespeare. Particularly in the plays, but also in the sonnets, there are frequent rejections of the allegorized lover. In the plays, it is usually the male character who is forced to understand, through a more or less painful learning process instigated by a woman, that human love exists in the real world only and that idealizations belong to the world of poetry. The Orsino of the beginning of *Twelfth Night* is an obvious example. The only sensible response to his "If music be the food of love, play on" is: But it isn't—love requires something rather more substantial. Perhaps the most famous first line in English poetry makes the same point:

"Shall I compare thee to a summer's day?" (*Sonnet* 18) is a very serious question, and when we read the next line, "Thou art more lovely and more temperate," we understand that the question is really: *Why* should I compare you to a summer's day? The point is made even more clearly in this other famous sonnet:

> My mistress' eyes are nothing like the sun;
> Coral is far more red than her lips' red;
> If snow be white, why then her breasts are dun;
> If hairs be wires, black wires grow on her head.
> I have seen roses damasked, red and white,
> But no such roses see I in her cheeks,
> And in some perfumes is there more delight
> Than in the breath that from my mistress reeks.
> I love to hear her speak, yet well I know
> That music hath a far more pleasing sound.
> I grant I never saw a goddess go;
> My mistress when she walks treads on the ground.
>    And yet, by heaven, I think my love as rare
>    As any she belied with false compare.
>
>                          (*Sonnet* 130)

Convention after convention is rejected, love is demystified and made real by the dismantling of the allegorical beloved: here the mistress becomes a human being again. Just as the final couplet serves to underline the rejection of poetic commonplaces as ultimately worthless, so they themselves, examined throughout the three quatrains, serve to reinforce the impact of the last two lines. Like the other two poems just mentioned above, this is as much about the function of poetry as about love. It is also a move toward a more personal poetic expression than the formulaic stylizations of court poetry can allow.

# PHILOSOPHY AND REPRESENTATION
# IN THE SEVENTEENTH CENTURY

## TROPES AND FIGURES: BACON, HOBBES, AND COWLEY

Sixteenth-century criticism focused largely on defending poetry against those who questioned its moral value. These attacks were no doubt partly related to the anti-Catholic position whose supporters found an easy target in what they thought of as italianate styles of writing: the Pope was in Rome, Italy represented decadence, license, and moral turpitude; the "italianate Englishman" was the devil incarnate whose aim was to corrupt English youth by means of subversive texts. Toward the end of the century, however, criticism began to grow more detached and more analytical in a sense that we would recognize as such today. Francis Bacon's *Advancement of Learning* (1605), for example, divides poetry into various categories that he then discusses in terms of what we would call the psychology of the imagination.

There are a few scattered references to poetry in Bacon's *Essays* of 1597—he claims, for example, that the study of poetry makes us "witty" (*On Studies*), that is, teaches us about our associative faculty—but most of what he has to say on the theme is in the *Advancement*. Some of his comments here are familiar—he echoes his predecessors in finding that the parables of Scripture are "divine poesy"—but the following extracts will make clear that Bacon was attempting something on a much larger scale. First of all, he makes use of the widely held theory that the brain was divisible into three functions of memory, imagination, and reason:

The parts of humane learning haue reference to the three partes of Mans vnderstanding, which is the seate of Learning: History to his Memory,

Poesie to his Imagination, and Philosophie to his Reason. Diuine learning receiueth the same distribution, for the Spirit of Man is the same, though the Reuelation of Oracle and Sense be diuerse: so as Theologie consisteth also of Historie of the Church, of Parables, which is diuine *Poesie,* and of holie Doctrine or *Precept.* For as for that part which seemeth supernumerarie, which is *Prophecie,* it is but Diuine History, which hath that prerogatiue over humane as the Narration may bee before the fact aswell as after. (*Advancement* 2: Spingarn 1:4)

Before Bacon, nobody seems to have used this theory in order to classify knowledge; and his idea that not only actual doctrine but also the history of the church itself forms a part of theology is a fascinating one in that it creates a picture of faith as the result of centuries of interpretation and reinterpretation, "For it is not Saint *Augustines* nor Saint *Ambrose* workes that will make so wise a Diuine as Ecclesiasticall Historie thoroughly read and obserued" (Spingarn 1:5).

Poetry, then, is a product of the part of the brain that governs imagination. But the imagination was suspect to many seventeenth-century thinkers since it was frequently perceived as a potential source of the disruption affecting poet, madman, and lover (hence, love is a disease, *amor vulgaris*). For Bacon, the imagination is not a negative force that leads to abnormal states, but a creative one, and its product, poetry, is good and should be the subject of serious analysis. In the following rather lengthy passage from the *Advancement,* Bacon discusses different kinds of poetry and explains how each works.

Poesie is a part of Learning in measure of words for the most part restrained, but in all other points extreamely licensed, and doth truly referre to the Imagination, which, beeing not tyed to the Lawes of Matter, may at pleasure ioyne that which Nature hath seuered, & seuer that which nature hath ioyned, and so make vnlawfull Matches and diuorses of things: *Pictoribus atque Poetis &c.* [The quote is from Horace's *Ars Poetica:* "Painters and poets (have always been allowed to take whatever liberties they wished)."] It is taken in two senses in respect of Wordes or Matter. In the first sense it is but a *Character* of stile, and belongeth to the Arts of speeche, and is not pertinent for the present. In the latter, it is, as hath beene saide, one of the principall Portions of learning, and is nothing else but Fained History, which may be stiled as well in Prose as in Verse.

The vse of this Fained Historie hath beene to giue some shadowe of satisfaction to the minde of Man in those points wherein the Nature of things doth denie it, the world being in proportion inferiour to the soule; by reason whereof there is agreeable to the spirit of Man a more ample Greatnesse, a more exact Goodnesse, and a more absolute varietie then can bee found in the Nature of things. Therefore, because the Acts or Euents of *true Historie* haue not that Magnitude which satisfieth the minde of Man, Poseie faineth Acts and Euents Greater and more Heroicall; because *true Historie* propoundeth the successes and issues of actions not so agreable to the merits of Vertue and Vice, therefore *Poesie* faines them more iust in Retribution and more according to Reuealed Prouidence; because *true Historie* representeth Actions and Euents more ordinarie and lesse interchanged, therefore *Poesie* endueth them with more Rarenesse and more vnexpected and alternatiue Variations: So as it appeareth that *Poesie* serueth and conferreth to Magnanimitie, Moralitie, and to delectation. And therefore it was euer thought to haue some participation of diuinesse, because it doth raise and erect the Minde, by submitting the shewes of things to the desires of the Mind, whereas reason doth buckle and bowe the Mind vnto the Nature of things. And we see that by these insinuations and congruities with mans Nature and pleasure, ioyned also with the agreement and consort it hath with Musicke, it hath had accesse and estimation in rude times and barbarous Regions, where other learning stoode excluded.

The diuision of Poesie which is aptest in the proprietie therof (besides those diuisions which are common vnto it with history, as fained Chronicles, fained liues, & the Appendices of History, as fained Epistles, fained Orations, and the rest) is into Poesie Narrative, Representative, and Allusive. The Narrative is a meere imitation of History with the excesses before remembered, Choosing for subiect commonly Warrs and Loue, rarely State, and sometimes Pleasure or Mirth. Representative is as a visible History, and is an Image of Actions as if they were present, as History is of actions in nature as they are, that is past; Allusive, or Parabolicall, is a Narration applied onely to expresse some speciall purpose or conceit: Which later kind of Parabolicall wisedome was much more in vse in the ancient times, as by the Fables of Aesope, and the briefe sentences of the seuen,[1] and the vse of *Hieroglyphikes* may appeare. And the cause was for that it was then of necessitie to expresse any point of reason which was more sharpe or subtile then the vulgar in that maner, because men in those times wanted [i.e., lacked] both varietie of examples and subtiltie of conceit: And as Hieroglyphikes were before Letters, so parables were before arguments: And neuerthelesse now and at all times they doe retaine much life and vigor, because reason cannot bee so sensible, nor examples so fit. (Spingarn 1:5–7)

If, as we are told in the first paragraph of this passage, poetry can "join" and "sever" at will in order to make "unlawful" matches, then it can make associations of things not normally or logically associated: it can associate the idea "rose" with the idea "love," for example. Poetry is allowed to do this because imagination, which creates these associations, is "not tied to the laws of matter." In other words, the poet can move "within the zodiac of his own wit."

Sidney felt obliged to qualify his claim for poetic license by various moral caveats—poetry will teach virtue if it is good poetry; it is the *function* of poetry to teach; and so on—but Bacon seems to feel less constrained by such an obligation. He is therefore freer to talk about the psychological processes involved in reading and writing poetry without having to bother so much with moral justifications. At the same time, if Bacon's approach is applied, it follows that, without a moral obligation (in the apologists' sense), and since the imagination is not constrained by physical laws, a poet may or may not be concerned to impart to readers an appreciation of a particular virtue; he or she need not in fact discuss moral issues at all. What kind of poem would this poet produce, and how are we to respond to it? Suppose, for example, we come across this anonymous poem, written in the sixteenth century but not published until 1790:

> Western wind, when will thou blow,
>     The small rain down can rain?
> Christ, if my love were in my arms
>     And I in my bed again!

We might choose to follow the apologists and dismiss this as poetry for the "masses," the "wrong" kind of poetry: it has no obvious moral content; its form is simple, it employs no conceit—it may have been a popular song; it is easy to see how it might, by an Elizabethan Puritan at any rate, be read as licentious and corrupting, probably blasphemous; nor— importantly—is there any immediately obvious connection between the western wind and the pain of separation from the person one loves. But we cannot escape the fact that this poem has lasted for about four hundred years. Why? There is nothing new about missing one's lover. In England, rain is hardly a novelty. The first two lines might be spoken by a farmer lamenting a field of wilting corn; the last two by anyone at all. What is surprising is that the four lines should appear *together*, and it is this "unlawful match" of ideas that engages the reader. There is no way out: we have to ask ourselves what the connection might be between the first and the last two lines—or, rather, we are forced to make that connection ourselves.

This process, whereby the reader can be said to become involved in the act of creating the text he or she reads, seems to have been very important for Bacon—it is certainly very important indeed for modern reader-response theorists—and though he echoes what Sidney had to say about art's ability to improve upon nature, his theory of what happens when we read is presented in altogether more analytical terms and constitutes a serious attempt to explore the psychology of aesthetic responses. His memorable description of epic poetry and tragedy (i.e., of "fained historie") as giving "some shadowe of satisfaction to the minde of Man" can be read as a comment not only on the function of poetry, but on the reasons we read and write it in the first place. If there exist "points wherein the Nature of things doth denie" this satisfaction to us, and if as Bacon claims this is because the physical world, the world of "lawful" relationships between things and ideas, is "inferiour to the soule," this must mean that there is at least one kind of satisfaction, somewhere, that can be experienced *only* by the soul (the psyche) and not by the senses responding to things in logical contexts and in logical relation to each other.

Bacon tells us that the human mind and the human soul need more than nature can provide: historical events "haue not that Magnitude which satisfieth the minde of Man," and the spirit requires "a more absolute varietie then can bee found in the Nature of things." But how are we to take this? Has God perhaps created an insufficient world? Surely not: the point is that humans themselves are imperfect. But they can be led toward the recognition of perfection by poetry, because poetry "doth raise and erect the Minde, by submitting the shewes of things to the desires of the Mind, whereas reason doth buckle and bowe the Mind vnto the Nature of things." In other words, poetry inspires ("erects") the mind by allowing it to perceive things differently from the way they actually appear in nature, while reason forces the mind to perceive reality. This is especially true of what

Bacon calls "parabolicall" or "allusive" poetry, which he sees as functioning not only to "expresse some speciall purpose or conceit," but also to hide it: "parabolicall" poetry "tendeth to demonstrate and illustrate that which is taught or deliuered" but may also "retire and obscure it: That is, when the Secrets and Misteries of Religion, Pollicy, or Philosophy, are inuolued in Fables or Parables. Of this in diuine Poesie wee see the vse is authorised." Here Bacon brings us back to biblical allegory in order to exemplify one use of "parabolicall" poetry—the deliberate obscuring of religious or philosophical "truths." Presumably the church fathers had thought the same as Bacon, and it is easy to see why they had been so anxious to assert that allegorical readings could be applied only to Scripture: only Scripture could contain truth.

Bacon echoes their argument that allegory can convey truths to the "simple" by demonstration and illustration. But he also seems to be telling us that the deliberate obfuscation of truth, or of certain kinds of truth, is necessary to what he calls the satisfaction of our minds. We make "unlawful matches" between things and ideas because

> the mind of man is far from the nature of a clear and equal glass, wherein the beams of things should reflect according to their true incidence; nay, it is rather like an enchanted glass, full of superstition and imposture, if it be not delivered and reduced. . . . Hence it cometh, that the mathematicians cannot satisfy themselves, except they reduce the motions of the celestial bodies to perfect circles, rejecting spiral lines, and labouring to be discharged of eccentrics. Hence it cometh, that whereas there are many things in nature as it were *monodica*, "sui juris," [i.e., unique and governed by their own laws] yet the cogitations of man do feign unto them relatives, parallels and conjugates, whereas no such thing is. (Vickers 226–27)

It seems even mathematicians are not free of a basic human need to allegorize and idealize the natural world. The ideal—the ideal world, the ideal system, that affords "some shadowe of satisfaction to the minde of Man"— seems to be best approachable or best comprehensible through the imagination and the "unlawful matches" it creates.

Here it is very tempting to read into Bacon's theory of the imagination a foreshadowing of Mallarmé and the French symbolists' claim that there is an ideal world attainable *à travers la poésie*, through the medium of poetry; and we could go on to point to the apparent similarities between their view of symbolism as a comparison of the abstract with the concrete and Bacon's distinction between imagination and reason. But we must be realistic and again beware of attributing views formulated in the intellectual atmosphere of late-nineteenth-century France to a man thinking and writing in early-seventeenth-century England. Having said this, Bacon's acceptance of "unlawful matches" as the positive products of the imagination can be seen quite reasonably as a step in the direction of Romantic idealism and the high value it places on the aesthetic responses of the individual. If "unlawful matches" are acceptable, one of them is seeing human nature reflected in the natural world.

Not all critics were so enthusiastic about the imagination. In his *Answer to Davenant* (1650), Thomas Hobbes continues Bacon's analytical approach and in doing so sets up a kind of division of labor between reason and imagination, which he terms Judgement and Fancy:

Time and Education begets experience; Experience begets memory; Memory begets Judgement and Fancy: Judgement begets the strength and structure, and Fancy begets the ornaments of a Poem. The Ancients therefore fabled not absurdly in making memory the Mother of the Muses.[2] For memory is the World (though not really, yet so as in a looking glass) in which the Judgement, the severer sister, busieth her self in a grave and rigid examination of all the parts of Nature, and in registring by Letters their order, causes, uses, differences, and resemblances; Whereby the Fancy, when any work of Art is to be performed, findes her materials at a hand and prepared for use, and needs no more than a swift motion over them, that what she wants, and is there to be had, may not lie too long unespied. So that when she seemeth to fly from one *Indies* to the other, and from Heaven to Earth, and to penetrate into the hardest matter and obscurest places, into the future and into her self, and all this is a point of time, the voyage is not very great, her self being all she seeks; and her wonderful celerity consisteth not so much in motion as in copious Imagery discreetly ordered & perfectly registred in the memory, which most men under the name of Philosophy have a glimpse of, and is pretended to by many that, grosly mistaking her, embrace contention in her place. But so far forth as the Fancy of man has traced the ways of true Philosophy, so far it hath produced very marvellous effects to the benefit of mankinde. All that is beautiful or defensible in building, or marvellous in Engines and Instruments of motion, whatsoever commodity men receive from the observations of the Heavens, from the description of the Earth, from the account of Time, from walking on the seas, and whatsoever distinguisheth the civility of *Europe* from the Barbarity of the *American* savages, is the workmanship of Fancy but guided by the Precept of true Philosophy. But where these precepts fail, as they have hitherto failed in the doctrine of Moral vertue, there the Architect, Fancy, must take the Philosophers part upon her self. (Spingarn 2:59–60)

Here, both Judgement and Fancy are the results of memory, which in turn is the natural product of Time and Experience. By "strength" and "structure," attributable to Judgement, Hobbes seems to mean intellectual content and physical form; while "ornament" seems to be the product of what Bacon discussed in terms of wit, the associative faculty that enables the poet to make "unlawful matches" or poetic conceits. But while Fancy has positive effects on the appearance of the physical world and on the world of ideas—visible in the beauty of buildings and machines, and in the results of the sciences of navigation and astronomy—these effects can only come about if Fancy works in conjunction with "true Philosophy," which is the concern of Judgement. (Furthermore, Fancy is subordinate to a materialistic world view which assesses all sciences in terms of their physical benefits to human beings.)

So far, though, Hobbes has, at least in theory, given the imagination a respectable and necessary role to play in intellectual and artistic life. The only condition he seems to make is that there be a balance between imagination and reason. Such a balance is bound to have an effect on our understanding of how unlawful an unlawful match may be. But trying to decide this is like trying to answer the question, How slow is an iceberg? Hobbes addresses this problem in pretty much the same way as Augustine and Aquinas by attempting to define how far "Poeticall Liberty" and, therefore, interpretation can go:

There are some that are not pleased with fiction, unless it be bold, not onely to exceed the *work,* but also the *possibility* of nature: they would have impenetrable Armors, Inchanted Castles, invulnerable bodies, Iron Men, flying Horses, and a thousand other such things, which are easily feigned by them that dare. Against such I defend [Davenant's poem *Gondibert*] (without assenting to those that condemn either *Homer* or

*Virgil*) by dissenting onely from those that think the Beauty of a Poem consisteth in the exorbitancy of the fiction. For as truth is the bound of Historical, so the Resemblance of truth is the utmost limit of Poeticall Liberty. . . . Beyond the actual works of nature a poet may now go; but beyond the conceived possibility of nature, never. I can allow a Geographer to make in the Sea a Fish or a Ship which by the scale of his Mapp would be two or three hundred mile long, and think it done for ornament, because it is done without the precincts of his undertaking; but when he paints an *Elephant* so, I presently apprehend it as ignorance, and a plain confession of *Terra incognita*. (Spingarn 2:60)

From this it becomes clear that, for Hobbes, Ornament, the product of Fancy, is acceptable so long as it is recognizable as such—that is, so long as it does not presume to function within "the precincts of the poet's undertaking": it must not become the main focus of the poem.

Presented in this way, this is no bad argument: it is easy to criticize a poem that appears full of style but empty of intellectual content. But is that what Hobbes means? When he disparages "impenetrable Armors, Inchanted Castles," and "invulnerable bodies" as lying beyond "the utmost limit of Poeticall Liberty," he is denying the possibility, or at least the value, of an allegorical reading of a poem such as the *Faerie Queene,* and ultimately of course of the poem itself. Why does Hobbes find a three-hundred-mile-long fish more acceptable? The only answer to this must be that he sees the dragons and magicians and enchanted castles in the *Faerie Queene* as the poem's main focus and therefore denies them any allegorical significance. But this is very hard to believe, especially since Hobbes presumably read not only the poem but also the explanatory preface on its author's use of allegory. It may be that Hobbes does not see Spenser's poem as "the description of Great Men and Great Actions," which he thinks should be "the constant designe of a Poet" (Spingarn 2:62). The examples he gives of such men and actions come from Virgil: the funeral games of Anchises and the duel between Aeneas and Turnus—"worthy circumstances" (Spingarn 2:62) in which men (not women) engage in physical rather than spiritual combat (without the intervention of witches or dragons) for worldly, rather than heavenly, reward. It seems Hobbes is prepared to read Virgil allegorically; and he does so in a way rather like Augustine's method of reading scriptural allegory.

As we have seen, it was essential for Augustine that the events described in Scripture not only stood for something else, but actually happened in the real world. Now even though Hobbes does not claim that the duel between Aeneas and Turnus or the funeral games for Anchises actually took place, he could not unreasonably claim that they may well have done: both events are easily seen as "the Resemblance of truth" lying well within "the utmost limit of Poeticall Liberty." Hobbes knows very well, however, that the fabulous monsters and witches and impenetrable shields of Spenser's poem never existed because (again, let us be realistic) there is no such thing as magic or Faerie Land. Hobbes wants us to be *reasonable,* to subordinate Fancy to Judgement, to reject all those products of the imagination which can exist only beyond the limitations imposed by the natural world. The mythologies of classical Greece and Rome, on the other hand, are acceptable material for poetry because they concern religious doctrine, and even "wrong" doctrine, so long as it is not Roman Catholic doctrine, must be respected: "amongst the Heathen such strange fictions and Metamorphoses were not so remote from the articles of Faith as they are now from ours, and therefore were not so unpleasant" (Spingarn 2:62).

Hobbes has a lot to say on the natural world, and particularly on human nature. In his view, the poet must make this his business above all things, for "the subject of a Poem is the manners of men, not natural causes" (Spingarn 2:56), and again he echoes the church fathers when he insists that knowledge of natural phenomena is essential: "For in him that professes the imitation of Nature, as all Poets do, what greater fault can there be then [i.e., than] to bewray an ignorance of nature in his Poem" (Spingarn 2:62–63). The poet must demonstrate his understanding of nature in two ways: he must know "well," and know "much": "A signe of the first is perspicuity, property, and decency, which delight all sorts of men, either by instructing the ignorant or soothing the learned in their knowledge. A signe of the latter is novelty of expression, and pleaseth by excitation of the minde; for novelty causeth admiration, and admiration curiosity, which is a delightful appetite of knowledge." It seems from this as though we are back with Sidney's "teaching and delighting," but Hobbes is not so enthusiastic about novelty of expression that he is unaware of its inherent dangers: many words, he says, "have no sense at all, and so many others . . . lost their meaning by being ill coupled. . . . To this palpable darkness I may also add the ambitious obscurity of expressing more then is perfectly conceived, or perfect conception in fewer words then it requires." And in what seems to be an attack directed specifically toward

John Donne, he adds that such expressions, "though they have had the honor to be called strong lines, are indeed no better then Riddles, and, not onely to the Reader but also after a little time to the Writer himself, dark and troublesome" (Spingarn 2:63).

Poetic ornament, wit, "Fancy," imagination, are here all acceptable so long as they remain secondary, but attract censure as soon as they can be suspected of assuming a more dominant role. This approach to symbols and extended metaphor ("riddles") can be called Puritan in that it disparages the view of signs as more important than the signified. Throughout Hobbes's criticism there is an appeal for what we would call a down-to-earth, commonsense view of art that is impatient of obscurity and the ornate, and he criticizes these qualities not only where he perceives them in poetic language but also where they form a poem's physical structure: "In a Epigram or a Sonnet a man may vary his measures, and seek glory from a needlesse difficulty, as he that contrived Verses into the formes of an Organ, a Hatchet, an Egg, an Altar, and a paire of Wings."

Students today will probably be familiar with the following examples from George Herbert's collection *The Temple* (1633). The first is "The Altar":

> A broken ALTAR, Lord, thy servant rears,
> Made of a heart, and cemented with tears:
>      Whose parts are as thy hand did frame;
>      No workman's tool hath touched the same.
>                A   HEART   alone
>                Is  such  a  stone,
>                As   nothing   but
>                Thy pow'r doth cut.
>                Wherefore each part
>                Of my hard heart
>                Meets in this frame,
>                To praise thy name.
>      That, if I chance to hold my peace
>      These stones to praise thee may not cease.
> O let thy blessed SACRIFICE be  mine,
> And  sanctify  this  ALTAR  to  be  thine.

The second example is the very well known "Easter Wings":

Lord, who createdst man in wealth and store,
Though foolishly he lost the same,
Decaying more and more,
Till he became
Most poor:
With thee
O let me rise
As larks, harmoniously,
And sing this day thy victories:
Then shall the fall further the flight in me.

My tender age in sorrow did begin:
And still with sickness and shame
Thou didst so punish sin,
That I became
Most thin.
With thee
Let me combine,
And feel this day thy victory:
For, if I imp my wing on thine,
Affliction shall advance the flight in me.

These poems are certainly ornate physically, but pose no problems as far as their use of symbol is concerned; or, rather, there is a very obvious relation between subject matter and physical appearance, for in the case of "The Altar," what at first looks like a symbol—the shape of the poem printed on the page—is in fact something altogether different. A symbol is a sign that is understood to stand for something else—a rose used for love; a sapphire for fidelity; and so on. "The Altar," however, is a poem, printed in such a way as to remind us of an altar, that seems to be about altars, or interpretations of the idea "altar." In this way, if we insist that the altar-shape of the poem is a sign, then it must be a redundant one—an altar signifying an altar. And a sign that signifies itself is not only beyond "the utmost limit of Poeticall Liberty" but beyond the utmost limit of logic as well.

Why is Hobbes unwilling to accept this altar-shape as mere ornament? It may be that he sees it as something pretending to be a sign, pretending in other words to be significant. (Perhaps he resented being tricked by initial impressions.) I believe (employing the criterion of economy) that his own answer to the question would be something like this: "This altar-shape adds nothing to our understanding of the poem. I will not accept it as ornament because for ornament to be good it must be produced not by Fancy alone but by Fancy in conjunction with Judgement, and it must result in a complement to or enhancement of the poem's overall perfection. But perfection is inseparable from usefulness, as can be readily seen from the observation of God's creations, and the purpose, or usefulness, of a poem lies in its ability to make us understand more clearly the noble actions or thoughts or moral virtues that it is its duty to discuss—for (as I have said elsewhere) it is the manners of men that should be the subject of a poem. The altar-shape of this poem does not have this effect on our understanding and is therefore ultimately pointless."

"Easter Wings" is slightly less open to this criticism because of the relation between its physical form and its subject-matter—it is not a poem about wings in the same way as "The Altar" is "about" altars. All the same, though the physical widening and narrowing of the lines corresponds roughly with the poem's descriptions of spiritual opening and closing, or life and death, or awakening and ignorance, and though the X shape of the poem is an obvious reminder of the Crucifixion, Hobbes would again be justified in claiming that the physical appearance of "Easter Wings" does nothing to aid our understanding of Herbert's lines. Both of these poems are closed texts in that the context in which we are supposed to read them—here the Anglican Church and its doctrine—is immediately clear. Once this context has been recognized we can rely on the rules that necessarily accompany and define it when we read. The poems are not "riddles" in the modern sense of puzzles that must be deciphered, and their physical forms are illustrative, rather than allegorical or symbolic.

There are poems by Herbert that do make use of allegory. They are not difficult poems because, as in the two examples above, the context and subject matter is always immediately recognizable; but they speak of one thing as though it were something else and, in this technical sense, must be called allegorical. "The British Church," also from *The Temple,* is a good example of this kind of poem:

> I joy, dear Mother, when I view
> Thy perfect lineaments and hue
>         Both sweet and bright.

Beauty in thee takes up her place,
and dates her letters from thy face,
When she doth write.

A fine aspect in fit array,
Neither too mean, nor yet too gay,
Shows who is best.

Outlandish looks may not compare:
For all they either painted are
Or else undrest.

She on the hills, which wantonly
Allureth all in hope to be
By her preferred,

Hath kissed so long her painted shrines,
That ev'n her face by kissing shines,
For her reward.

She in the valley is so shy
Of dressing, that her hair doth lie
About her ears:

While she avoids her neighbour's pride,
She wholly goes on th'other side,
And nothing wears.

But dearest Mother, (what those miss)
The mean thy praise and glory is,
And long may be.

Blessed be God, whose love it was
To double-moat thee with his grace,
And none but thee.

Once Herbert has decided to use the common epithet *mother* for the church, he is free to give her other human and specifically female attributes and to write as though he were describing the physical appearance of a beautiful woman whom he compares with her too-gaudy Roman and too-plain Puritan counterparts. Of course *mother* has other associations: with nurturing, with birth, with educating and instructing, with protecting— all of which terms can be understood in both literal and spiritual senses; and from Herbert's doctrinal standpoint, the moral (or, at least, moralizing) sense of the poem is the clear superiority of his own church. We end up with something like Dante's, or Augustine's, reading of allegory, except that the literal sense is missing—the church is not literally a woman, though parabolically it may be considered so.

In the preface to his *Poems* (1656), Abraham Cowley expresses similar attitudes toward imagination as those formulated by Hobbes. On the one hand, "The *Soul* must be filled with bright and delightful *Ideas,* when it undertakes to communicate delight to others, which is the main end of *Poesie*"; at the same time, though, he finds that "*Doctor Donnes Sun Dyal in a grave* is not more useless and ridiculous then *Poetry* would be in that *retirement*" (preface, Spingarn 2:81–82). Again, Fancy, novelty of expression, is a good thing and is able to "communicate delight to others," but it must be tempered and restrained by reason. But in the same preface, almost parenthetically, he makes a comment on the nature of poetic representation that constitutes something quite new in literary theory. A poem, he says, "is not the *Picture* of the *Poet,* but of *things* and *persones* imagined by him." Firstly, the poet here becomes a kind of Platonic god, in whose imagination there exist ideas of things and persons which are then given artistic representation in the form of words written down on paper in a particular way. Secondly, Cowley's remark leads immediately to the vexed question of the sincerity or "truth" of poetry: how true is something that exists in the imagination? What if this thing (an idea, an imagined event or person) exists in the imagination of one person only? Finally, if the thing imagined is not "true" in the physical world, can (or must) poetry ever tell the truth at all? This is a very modern question in that it continues to be the topic of heated debate, and Cowley has much to say on it. What he says, however, makes obvious that the question of truth and untruth in poetry is still a religious one, and that it is religion that must decide the rightness and wrongness of what the imagination creates.

The following extracts from the final paragraph of Cowley's preface offer a clear illustration of his views on metaphor and allegory:

It is not without grief and indignation that I behold that *Divine Science* [i.e., poetry] employing all her inexhaustible riches of *Wit* and *Elo-*

*quence,* either in the wicked and beggarly *Flattery* of great persons, or the unmanly *Idolizing* of *Foolish Women,* or the wretched affectation of scurril *Laughter,* or at best on the confused antiquated *Dreams* of senseless *Fables* and *Metamorphoses.* . . . There is not so great a *Lye* to be found in any *Poet* as the vulgar conceit of men that *Lying* is *Essential* to good *Poetry.* . . . I do not at all wonder that the old Poets made some rich crops out of these grounds [i.e., wrote so much poetry based on mythology]; the heart of the *Soil* was not then wrought out with continual *Tillage.* But what can we expect now, who come a *Gleaning,* not after the first *Reapers,* but after the very *Beggars?* Besides, though those mad stories of the *Gods* and *Heroes* seem in themselves so ridiculous, yet they were then the *whole Body* (or rather *Chaos*) of the *Theologie* of those times. . . . There was no other *Religion,* and therefore *that* was better then *none at all.* But to us who have no need of them, to us who deride their *folly* and are wearied with their *impertinencies,* they ought to appear no better arguments for *Verse* then those of their worthy *Successors,* the *Knights Errant.* What can we imagine more proper for the ornaments of *Wit* or *Learning* in the story of *Deucalion* then in that of *Noah?* Why will not the actions of *Sampson* afford as plentiful matter as the *Labors* of *Hercules?* . . . Can all the *Transformations* of the *Gods* give such copious hints to flourish and expatiate on as the true *Miracles* of *Christ,* or of his *Prophets* and *Apostles?* Why do I instance in these few particulars? All the *Books* of the *Bible* are either already most admirable and exalted pieces of Poesie, or are the best *Materials* in the world for it. (Spingarn 2:88–90)

It is surely difficult for a modern reader to feel much sympathy for Cowley's attitude, which can be summed up as the insistence that imagination will produce good "ornament" only if it is trained to the contemplation of Scripture. It is not the purpose of this study, however, to elicit sympathy (or, for that matter, antipathy), but to try to find out what poets and critics have thought about poetry and its use of specific devices. Cowley formulates an approach to allegory that is limiting in the extreme, and in fact it is as though he were attempting to impose Augustine in reverse: the father of the church tells us that spiritual allegory can be found only in scriptural poetry; Cowley informs us that poetry should draw its metaphors only from Scripture. Putting his approach into effect would lead to the same results as Augustine's: poetry would have only one context, all texts would be closed, and the world would once again be a univocal one.

Both Hobbes and Cowley, far from allowing the poet the freedom of "the zodiac of his own wit," view imagination as a potentially destructive force that must be strictly controlled. For Thomas Sprat its effects can be positively dangerous. In his *History of the Royal Society* (1667) he discusses the ill use into which metaphor and "eloquence" has fallen:

> The ill effects of this superfluity of talking have already overwhelm'd most other *Arts* and *Professions,* insomuch that when I consider the means of *happy living* and the causes of their corruption, I can hardly forbear . . . concluding that *eloquence* ought to be banish'd out of all *civil Societies,* as a thing fatal to Peace and good Manners. To this opinion I should wholly incline, if I did not find that it is a Weapon which may be as easily procur'd by *bad* men as *good,* and that, if these should onely cast it away, and those retain it, the *naked Innocence* of vertue would be upon all occasions expos'd to the *armed Malice* of the wicked. This is the chief reason that should now keep up the Ornaments of speaking in any request, since they are so much degenerated from their original useful-ness. They were at first, no doubt, an admirable Instrument in the hands of *Wise Men,* when they were onely employ'd to describe *Goodness, Hon-esty, Obedience,* in larger, fairer and more moving Images; to represent *Truth,* cloth'd with Bodies; and to bring *Knowledg* back again to our very senses, from whence it was at first deriv'd to our understandings. But now they are generally chang'd to worse uses: They make the *Fancy* dis-gust the best things . . . they are in open defiance against *Reason,* pro-fessing not to hold much corespondence with that, but with its Slaves, *the Passions;* they give the mind a motion too changeable and bewitch-ing to consist with *right practice.* Who can behold without indignation how many mists and uncertainties these specious *Tropes* and *Figures* have brought on our knowledg? . . . I dare say that, of all the Studies of men, nothing may be sooner obtain'd than this vicious abundance of *Phrase,* this trick of *Metaphors.* (Spingarn 2:116–17)

Sprat thinks metaphor is bad because it leads us away from truth; tropes and rhetorical figures are unhealthily and dangerously allied to the pas-sions and opposed to reason; eloquence corrupts, and the imagination "disgusts." We have come a long way (at least, a lot has happened) in the seventy years or so since Sidney and his contemporaries were formulating their panegyrics on wit, metaphor, allegory, and conceits. The imagina-tion, and what it produces, is now highly suspect, and it must therefore be the task of the Royal Society to exercise the strictest control on language. This it will achieve through its resolution

115

to reject all amplifications, digressions, and swellings of style; to return back to the primitive purity and shortness, when men deliver'd so many *things* almost in an equal number of *words*. [The Royal Society] have exacted from their members a close, naked, natural way of speaking, positive expressions, clear senses, a native easiness, bringing all things as near the Mathematical plainness as they can, and preferring the language of Artizans, Countrymen, and Merchants, before that of Wits or Scholars. (Spingarn 2:118)

It is probably fitting that a Puritan age should desire what it perceives as purity of language, a kind of linguistic one-man-one-vote situation in which each thing or idea would be represented by a single word. It is not difficult to see the relation between this ideal and the Puritan zeal for ridding the world of symbols. These, too—the images of the saints, the rood screens, the statues, and the paintings—were "digressions," unnecessary "amplifications," too attractive in themselves, perhaps, to allow the eye, and the mind, to see beyond them and find the ideas they sought to signify. As for equating linguistic purity with the language of artisans and countrymen, it would not be long before this demand was reformulated, in a very different context, with the appearance of a literary manifesto that called for poetry written "in the language of men."

## JOHN MILTON

For a Puritan, allegory must always be approached with considerable caution. It can be instructive, as in the case of Jesus' parables, and it can reveal divine providence; but it is also, always, potentially misleading since it demands interpretation, and interpretation is a human affair. Ironically, this means that a Puritan understanding of allegorical texts necessarily relates to the Augustinian—that is, Roman Catholic—interpretive tradition in that it needs to limit interpretive possibilities very strictly. If the "simple" learn more easily through parables, they can do so only if those parables are provided with a ready-made key. This made the task that John Milton set himself a very difficult one. He decided to write an epic poem—in seventeenth-century tradition the noblest poetic form he could think of—and needed a suitably noble and inspiring theme.

For a deeply learned, widely read poet who also happened to be a Puritan, the Old Testament provided a number of possibilities. His choice of the Fall of Adam and Eve and their subsequent banishment from the Garden of Eden enabled him to discuss several themes dear to the Puritan heart: sin and disobedience, human frailty (and therefore the human need for God's guidance), divine justice, the perpetual need to strive toward moral goodness in order to earn redemption—from the Puritan standpoint, the whole human condition. But he had to be careful: the story had, after all, been told already, written down by men inspired by God to produce the true history of humanity (we must not forget that Milton, and his readers, read the Bible as history). Even if the Bible was history, however, Adam and Eve could be seen not only as individuals but as representing humans generally, and in this case they are not only themselves but something else as well. In other words, they are allegorical figures: real, physical human beings, but also parabolical ones, extensions of the literal individuals whose creation by God is described in Genesis, and everything that happens to them happens to us, either literally or allegorically—we are banished from Paradise and must work hard (in more senses than one) to sustain and redeem ourselves; we are constantly subject to temptation of various kinds.

Nonetheless, there is no critical agreement on just how much of an allegory *Paradise Lost* is, or even on whether it can be called an allegory at all. There is no agreement, for example, on whether the characters who take part in the war between heaven and hell are meant to represent historical figures who took part in the war between royalist forces and those fighting for Cromwell. On the other hand, we do know from Milton's own notes that he intended specific allegorical abstractions: Michael represents the *idea* of justice, for example; and the outlines for the poem mention representations of Heavenly Love and Famine. But the game of hunt-the-allegorization is not necessarily rewarding and soon grows tedious. For the purpose of this study, the point is that in *Paradise Lost* we are presented with a poem in many ways like the *Divina Commedia*. Milton, like Dante (much admired by Milton) clearly believed that his poem could be read in a spiritual sense. And if we pose ourselves the question: How do we know Milton believed this? we can respond by asking: In view of what we know of Milton's own religious beliefs, and in view of the subject matter of his poem, how likely is it that he did *not* believe it?

Let us now see whether a Dantesque reading of *Paradise Lost* according to the four traditional senses is a feasible idea. The literal sense is the story of Adam and Eve, and here there is a problem, because, as his first readers were quick to point out, Milton takes certain liberties with the story as it appears in Genesis. For one thing, it is obviously much longer in Milton's version, and all the detail, much of which involves classical rather than Christian mythology, and all the extended monologues and dialogues, are Milton's own additions to or developments of Genesis. Are we then justified in claiming a literal sense for *Paradise Lost*? One response that immediately comes to mind is that if Dante is allowed to claim a literal sense to a poem that tells the story of a journey through the underworld in the company of Virgil's ghost, it is hardly fair to deny the same to Milton for a work generally accepted, by his contemporaries at least, as being rather closer to the truth. A more academic approach would be to point out that, in spite of its "poetic license," Milton's version contains the essential details of the Genesis story—Adam and Eve as God's creations, their state of innocence in the Garden of Eden, the temptation of Eve and her subsequent temptation of Adam, their expulsion and loss of grace—and therefore conveys the same truth as Genesis. If we think of *Paradise Lost* as an interpretation of the Genesis story, we can read it (though Milton would not be altogether pleased) in the light of what Augustine writes about the allegorical interpretation of Scripture: that we can interpret in any way we like, so long as our interpretation leads, ultimately, to the truth, which of necessity includes the literal sense of Scripture. We might also point out that the Bible went through numerous translations, each version necessarily different from the preceding one, and that the biblical canon itself underwent a tough editing process by church authorities before it reached its present form, or, rather, forms, for there are several versions currently in regular use—the King James, the Revised Standard, the Catholic Bible, and the Jewish Bible, to name only four, each of which can claim, with equal justification, the title of Bible.

We can see an allegorical sense firstly in the way that Adam and Eve can be said to stand for all humans and in the way that their tragedy—which, we must not forget, contains the idea of *felix culpa,* the "happy fall" that makes possible the desire to strive toward goodness and God—can be said to represent the basic human condition. But there are also more straightforward allegorizations: Michael for justice; Satan for sin in general and pride in particular; his companions in perpetual banishment for various other kinds of sin; the Son for mercy.

We can see a moral sense in (I believe) two ways, firstly by a reversal of the process described by Dante in his reading of Psalm 114. In that context, Dante sees the moral sense in the conversion of the soul from a state of sin to a state of grace. This of course is the precise opposite of what happens to Adam and Eve in Genesis and *Paradise Lost,* but if the moral sense concerns the process of change as a whole rather than change in one direction only—that is, from sin to grace—then there is certainly a moral sense to the Fall in Milton's poem. Secondly, the transformation of the soul in the opposite direction, from sin back to grace, is held out as a possibility: unlike Satan and his angels, who corrupted themselves, Adam and Eve were led into sin and can therefore be forgiven and earn redemption. In the same way, the mystical or anagogical sense can also be seen in a possible future, since what Dante describes as "the departure of the sanctified spirit from the slavery of this corruption to the freedom of eternal glory," the final voyage of the soul from the body to God and bliss, will be the result of redemption.

This seems to work well enough in theory. I admit that in practice the example I have chosen is not the best. Dante based his discussion of allegorical readings on Psalm 114, not on a poem he had written *about* Psalm 114 (though the exodus of the Jews from Egyptian captivity would certainly have made a good epic poem). The point is that in order to discuss *Paradise Lost* as allegory, I have had to cheat—I have had to discuss Genesis as well. Am I then really justified in claiming that an allegorical reading of Milton's poem is possible? Should I not in fact make clear that it is Genesis that can be read as allegory, and that Milton simply used Genesis?

There are a number of connected responses to this question and they all have to do with the history of reading literary texts (and therefore quite logically with the history of writing them). Firstly, there is the question of literary influence. Talking about the influences on any particular poet can be very useful, but it also forces us to think of literary production, and therefore of history, and of time, as linear—an arrow whose point is always now and along whose shaft there are notches representing "periods," "movements," and "great poems." If we hold this view, we must also hold that, for example, Milton could never have written *Lycidas* if there had never been any pastoral poetry before him. And if we believe this, we must ask ourselves what could possibly have influenced whoever it was who wrote the first pastoral poem. Now, I know very well that there is no such thing as "the first pastoral poem," but I also know that this fact is very good evidence in the case I want to make against placing too much importance on the idea of influence. Literature (or art, or culture) does not grow in straight lines. Once again, the Bible (if I can be forgiven for doing a metaphor to death) is a good example of something growing sideways: Hebrew, Greek, Latin, Luther's beautiful German, and a rush of versions in various other European languages, some officially sanctioned and some suppressed. Which of these influenced which? And after all, how much of a straight line—the shortest distance between two points—is an allegory? If art does not move in straight lines, it is because *people* do not. If we did, it is unlikely we would have produced any art at all. In this sense at least, we can think of *Paradise Lost* as growing in the same way as the Bible itself, as a version of the Adam and Eve story along with all the others.

Milton makes extremely liberal use of classical and biblical imagery, poetic conventions, and mythological landscapes and events, all of which can be read, and certainly have been read, as open to interpretation as spiritual allegory. The point here is that if Dante's theory still works in the context of *Paradise Lost,* it would seem either not yet to have been replaced by any other theory or to have existed alongside one or more other theories. I shall discuss this point at the end of the present chapter; for the moment, what follows is an example, taken from the beginning of book 11 of Milton's poem, of the way in which he draws simultaneously from classical, natural, and biblical imagery to produce what I believe can very economically be read as spiritual allegory. The lines describe the condition of Adam and Eve after the Fall and the Son's intercession for them in heaven.

> Thus they in lowliest plight repentant stood
> Praying, for from the Mercie-seat above
> Prevenient Grace descending had remov'd
> The stonie from their hearts, & made new flesh
> Regenerate grow instead, that sighs now breath'd
> Unutterable, which the Spirit of prayer
> Inspir'd, and wing'd for Heav'n with speedier flight
> Then loudest Oratorie: yet thir port
> Not of mean suiters, nor important less
> Seem'd thir Petition, then when th'ancient Pair
> In Fables old, less ancient yet then these,
> *Deucalion* and chaste *Pyrrha* to restore
> The race of Mankind drowned, before the Shrine
> Of *Themis* stood devout. To Heav'n thir prayers
> Flew up, nor missed the way, by envious windes

Blow'n vagabond or frustrate: in they passd
Dimensionless through Heav'nly dores; then clad
With incense, where the Golden Altar fum'd,
By their great Intercessor, came in sight
Before the Father's Throne: Them the glad Son
Presenting, thus to intercede began.
     See Father, what first fruits on Earth are sprung
From thy implanted Grace in Man, these Sighs
And Prayers, which in this Golden Censer, mixt
With incense, I thy Priest before thee bring,
Fruits of more pleasing savour from thy seed
Sow'n with contrition in his heart, then those
Which his own hand manuring all the Trees
Of Paradise could have produc't, ere fall'n
From innocence. Now therefore bend thine eare
To supplication, heare his sighs though mute;
Unskilful with what words to pray, let mee
Interpret for him, mee his Advocate
And propitiation, all his works on mee
Good or not good ingraft, my Merit those
Shal perfet, and for these my Death shall pay.
Accept me, and in mee from these receave
The smell of peace toward Mankinde, let him live
Before thee reconcil'd, at least his days
Numberd, though sad, till Death, his doom (which I
To mitigate thus plead, not to reverse)
To better life shall yeeld him, where with mee
All my redeemd may dwell in joy and bliss,
Made one with me as I with thee am one.

                                        (ll. 1–44)

The story of Deucalion and the flood, told by Ovid in *Metamorphoses*
1.318 ff., parallels the story of Noah and the ark, except that Deucalion
and Pyrrha, as the only two survivors of the deluge, repopulate the earth
by throwing stones over their shoulders instead of resorting to the more
conventional method. What are they doing in a Christian epic? We know
that Milton read the Bible as history, but we can safely assume that he did
not read Ovid in the same way. It is at least possible, however, that he read
*Metamorphoses* in the way that the church fathers thought was safe, by

121

claiming, when classical texts spoke of virtues that accorded with Christian ones, that their authors were writing spiritual allegories without realizing it.

If this is how Milton read Ovid, then he saw Deucalion and Pyrrha as symbolizing the essentially good married couple. Roy Flannagan (659) points out that, like them,

> Adam and Eve also petition the deity (Themis, in the case of Decucalion and Pyrrha) for the benefit of future generations. It seems important that Ovid's pair are inherently good people (like their Old Testament analogues, Noah and his wife), wheras Adam and Eve are newly re-generate. Also, Pyrrha is described as "chaste," which suggests that Eve may have regained what Milton regarded as a kind of chastity or purity within the state of marriage, where the marriage bed is pronounced chaste.

If Milton did regard the regenerate Eve's condition as one of "a kind of chastity or purity" achieved through the act of repentance, he would again have been echoing the church fathers' view that God can allow the soul to move from a state of sin to a state of grace—that is, to become whole again—but cannot undo what has actually happened in the physical world: he cannot alter history. (This underlines the theological argument for confession, repentance, and atonement.)

Flannagan also notes Milton's representation of God and the Son as symbolic gardeners, "attentive to fertilizing the ground around their trees and attentive to the grafting process." But the Son is also an interpreter: "let mee / Interpret for him, mee his Advocate / And propitiation"—and this is especially interesting in the context of this study. We have seen that throughout medieval and Renaissance exegesis we are constantly reminded that God is beyond human comprehension: Christ speaks in parables to help us understand God's language; the Bible speaks in signs because we are "simple." Here, however, the process is, in a sense, reversed, and we understand that God, too, needs an interpreter in order to listen as well as to speak. For Adam, and presumably for God, this is a completely new situation, for before the Temptation and the Fall, they seem to have understood each other perfectly well without the need for any third party. It is only after the Fall that Adam's language is "mute" and that he is "Unskilful with what words to pray." In Milton's version of the story, banishment from the divine presence is therefore a punishment that entails not only physical and spiritual separations but also a linguistic one: the need for interpretation begins with the Fall. This fits very well with the idea of the poet as *vates,* as seer, and with the Renaissance fondness for pointing to the divine nature of poetry.

Certainly, the intermediaries between gods and humans have generally spoken in anything but the "real language of men": priests spoke in meter, then in Latin, oracles spoke in riddles, inspired humans spoke (and it seems still speak) "in tongues." We can now begin to understand the view of poetry, at least what the theorists we have seen called "good" poetry, as something akin to Scripture (and indeed the view of Scripture as a kind of poetry), an attempt, conscious or unconscious, to get back to God by translating him. We can talk of the physical world in terms comprehensible to everyone so long as we describe its contents as natural phenomena—a rose is a rose is a rose—but as soon as we decide to discuss it in terms of its divine origin, or to discuss God himself—as soon, that is, as we begin to talk in spiritual terms—ordinary language fails: we become "mute," like Adam, and have to describe attributes, to substitute characteristics for things. In other words, we have to use symbols and metaphors and allegories. I do not wish to claim that all allegories are spiritual allegories (it would need a very uneconomical reading indeed to back up such a claim). The point is that, if Milton thought of his poem as a kind of history—and he could legitimately think of it as a retelling of biblical history—he clearly thought of it as something else as well; and if it is something else as well, it is allegorical. After the evidence we have seen, it seems safe to claim that he saw it as conveying spiritual meaning. A worldly poem, even one dealing with a scriptural theme, is still secular; and if we think that a secular poem can have a spiritual sense we are still doing what Dante said we could do.

Finding spiritual meaning in nonreligious poetry will hardly seem revolutionary to a modern student, but for Milton, "spiritual" had a very specific reference whose sphere was limited by religious belief. The theology and rites of that belief were certainly not the same as for Dante's, but they do seem to have thought much the same thing about the *rules* for allegorical interpretation. Above all, they agree that poetry can ennoble humans and instill goodness, but they are both unable to discuss goodness in any other than a religious context. It is important to realize this, because it indicates that Dante, Milton, and all of the apologists for poetry are not saying, "Poetry as well as and as distinct from Scripture can lead to virtue," but, "Poetry can lead to virtue, and this makes it like Scripture." Reformation or no, interpretive theory at this point is still inseparable from religion.

Does this mean that *Paradise Lost* is a closed text? For it to be so it would have to be interpretable in one way only; or, as Augustine tells us, all roads of interpretation, however circuitous they might be, would have to lead to one meaning only. If we try to apply this to Milton's poem, we encounter serious difficulties, especially in the case of his representation of Satan, and a huge amount of learned ink has been used up in the debate over what Milton "meant" by him. William Blake, for example, held that Milton was unconsciously "of the Devil's party," and even that "Milton's Messiah is call'd Satan."

If more recent critics have been more temperate in their judgments, the suspicion that Milton's Satan is rather too likeable is one that has dogged the poem since its first appearance. The apparent ambiguity of his nature is very clearly seen in book 4, in which, as he flies to inspect the newly created Eden,

> horror and doubt distract
> His troubl'd thoughts, and from the bottom stirr
> The Hell within him, for within him Hell
> He brings, and round about him, nor from Hell
> One step no more then from himself can fly
> By change of place. Now conscience wakes despair
> That slumber'd, wakes the bitter memorie
> Of what he was, what is, and what must be
> Worse; of worse deeds worse suffering must ensue.
> Sometimes towards *Eden* which now in his view
> Lay pleasant, his grievd looks he fixes sad,
> Sometimes towards Heav'n and the full-blazing Sun,
> Which now sat high in his Meridian Towre:
> Then much revolving, thus in sighs began.
>   O thou that with surpassing Glory crownd,
> Lookst from thy sole Dominion like the God
> Of this new World; at whose sight all the Starrs
> Hide their diminisht heads; to thee I call,
> But with no friendly voice, and add thy name
> O sun, to tell thee how I hate thy beams

That bring to my remembrance from what state
I fell, how glorious once above thy Spheare;
Till Pride and worse Ambition threw me down
Warring in Heav'n against Heav'ns matchless King:
Ah wherefore! He deservd no such return
From me, whom he created what I was
In that bright eminence, and with his good
Upbraided none; nor was his service hard.
What could be less than to afford him praise,
The easiest recompense, and pay him thanks,
How due! Yet all his good proved ill in me,
And wrought but malice; lifted up so high
I sdeind subjection, and thought one step higher
Would set me highest, and in a moment quit
The debt immense of endless gratitude,
So burthensome still paying, still to ow;
Forgetful what from him I still receivd,
And understood not that a grateful mind
By owing owes not, but still pays, at once
Indebted and dischargd; what burden then?
(4. 18–57)

We are introduced here to a Satan distracted, even horrified, by doubt, one moreover who is racked by conscience. This leads to a theological irony because conscience, a good thing, in Satan's case leads to despair, and despair is a sin. In this way, what is positive in Adam and Eve, to whom conscience brings repentance, is turned to evil in Satan. He himself elaborates on this a few lines later, but before he does, the narrative voice of the poem explains the reason for his pang of conscience: it is not, as Satan implies, based wholly in the realization of his offence to God, who "deserved no such return," whom he acknowledges as his creator, and who "with his good / Upbraided none," but in the "remembrance from what state / [He] fell, how glorious once above [the sun's] Spheare / Till Pride and worse Ambition threw [him] down." It is only when this point has been made that he goes on to bemoan the fact that all God's good proved ill in him and turned to malice. He even manages to suggest that it was not really his fault: "lifted up so high," he seems to be saying, with the temptation of ultimate glory placed so close within his grasp, what could he have done but disdain the role of mere subject? It wasn't fair: God should not have tempted him. Satan's presentation of himself as the victim rather than the perpetrator of temptation is a way for him to identify with humans—he already plans to tempt Adam and Eve to sin—but also for us to see one aspect of ourselves reflected in him: he is in fact altogether too human for comfort.

It is absolutely essential for Satan to give the wrong reasons for his inconvenient attack of conscience, and absolutely essential that he should do so at this point in the poem, before his temptation of Eve, because if conscience were to lead to repentance rather than to despair, it would open up the possibility of forgiveness and redemption. This cannot be allowed, for without the temptation and the Fall in Paradise, there is no need for Christ to sacrifice himself: Satan and Christ justify each other's existence. I do not want here to confuse Milton's already heretical ideas.[3] Like all Christians, Milton believed that Christ Redeemer is there (or here) because humans continue to sin. Saying that Christ and Satan justify each other's existence does not mean that he believed humans continue to sin in order to keep Christ in a job.

But whom is Satan talking to? Nobody seems to be around, so presumably to himself. If this is so, he is either deceiving himself or he suspects that God is listening and is attempting to deceive him. In either case, his monologue can also be seen as a narrative device designed to involve the reader in the deception. We can either fall for it, and experience something like sympathy with his condition, or we can see his apparent wavering between continued sin and repentance as a plot to fool us; and even this makes him, I think, dangerously interesting, because the process of arriving at the point where we reject his words as a mere scheme has itself led us through the very process by which he attempts to deceive. If we see the trick, and reject Milton's Satan, we have effectively closed his text, or at least this part of it. We have made his Satan transparent and unambiguous—able to hold our attention so long as he is speaking, but, caught off guard, or alone as here, he turns out to be the same old tempter we always thought he was, and in this way he is very much like the witch Duessa in *The Faerie Queene,* who appears beautiful so long as we are blind, physically and spiritually, to see her as she really is. Moreover, in both cases, blindness is partly the result of a willingness not to see: the Redcrosse Knight sees in Duessa what his physical attraction for her wishes to see; and Eve, and later Adam, are both fascinated by the picture of themselves painted by Satan-as-Serpent. This, too, is important because it emphasizes the role of free will in the Temptation and Fall; that is, it emphasizes the presence of human as well as satanic culpability.

Can we decide to opt for the other, more interesting Satan? — can we, in other words, fall for the deception we have just attempted to expose? The question is a tricky one because answering yes would mean having to demonstrate that there really is another Satan to choose, rather than merely different aspects of the same one. But before we attempt an answer, it would be as well here to remind ourselves of what we are really trying to find out, which is whether Milton's Satan can — economically — be read as more than the "literal," "historical" one in the context of a spiritual sense to *Paradise Lost*. If he cannot, then the case, and the text, are closed, and we are left with the traditional figure, terrifying to the individual, over whose soul he may gain ascendancy, but ultimately powerless before God. If we say that he can, we must also say why.

I want to stress again the importance of economy in this question. We know that many critics of the sixteenth century referred to the "italianate Englishman" as "the devil incarnate," but I cannot, on this basis, economically claim that Milton thought Satan preferred to speak in Italian. Perhaps he did, but there is no evidence for this either in Milton's text or in Genesis, which does not even identify the serpent with Satan. A reading of *Paradise Lost* as political allegory would most likely wish to see Satan as a representation of Charles I, the Son as Cromwell, and so on; or more realistically still, would wish to see the struggle between good and evil as a representation of Protestant parliamentarianism, on the one hand, and an oppressive monarchy and corrupt church, on the other. Critical readings of the poem have gone through various phases of moving toward, then away from, political allegory: at present (2002) there is again a tendency to politicize.

The "historical," "literal" Satan is recognizable by attributes and actions: he is seductive, corrupt, perverted in a general rather than a narrowly sexual sense, proud and rebellious: he tempts, corrupts, perverts, leads humans into the sin of pride, which in turn leads them to rebel against the authority of God. When someone says the name "Satan," a reasonably educated hearer brought up in a Christian culture will most probably think of the attributes just mentioned — some or all of them, or closely related ones. In this way we can reasonably claim the name "Satan" to be a sign not only for a "literal" figure, but also for a group of attributes that, taken together, help to define the idea of "badness" or "evil." When someone says "So and so is a bad person" or "So and so is evil," however, our hearer is very likely to think of some or all of the same attributes. In this way we see that the qualities attributed to Satan are equally applicable to human beings (evil ones), and in this case it is possible to think of Satan as a literal figure who also parabolically stands for negative human capabilities. Satan thus represents not only the idea of evil but also its manifestation in those real human beings who are "in league with the devil"; and I do not mean so-called Satanists, but simply those people whom society and history has agreed to call "bad." On this basis I believe it is perfectly reasonable and very economical to read Milton's Satan as this parabolical representation of the human capacity for evil, as well as, if we wish, a literal figure of Christian belief.

### JOHN LOCKE: IDEAS, WORDS, AND ASSOCIATIONS

In book 2 of his *Essay Concerning Human Understanding* (1690), the philosopher John Locke analyzes the way in which the human mind associates one idea with another or others. The process of association is of course central to metaphor, symbol, and allegory, and therefore to poetry. Locke makes a distinction between "natural" associations (e.g., bee—honey; music—piano) and the association of ideas "not ally'd by Nature," and it is this second group that is the more important in the context of our study. The following passage, in which he discusses both groups, comes from chapter 33, *On the Association of Ideas:*

> Some of our *Ideas* have a natural Correspondence and Connexion one with another: It is the Office and Excellency of our Reason to trace these, and hold them together in that Union and Correspondence which is founded in their peculiar [i.e., particular] Beings. Besides this there is another Connexion of Ideas wholly owing to Chance or Custom; *Ideas* that in themselves are not at all of kin, come to be so united in some Men's Minds, that 'tis very hard to separate them, they always keep in company, and the one no sooner at any time comes into the Understanding but its Associate appears with it; and if they are more than two which are thus united, the whole gang always inseparable shew themselves together. (*Essay* 2.33.5)

The "Chance or Custom" that determine the association of ideas are the aleatory conditions we have discussed; but we must be careful here to remember that more than three hundred years have elapsed since Locke wrote his *Essay,* and that some things whose nature we today question were then considered natural as a matter of course. The association of Satan with certain characteristics and attributes that we made above, for example, is quite natural if Scripture is read as history and religious doctrine held to be truth: it is in the nature of Satan's being that he is corrupt, proud, rebellious and so on.

This is a very important point because what Locke says about chance and custom seems to indicate that interpretation depends upon the context of the interpreter, and this is absolutely central to the modern debate on "meaning" and reader response. Today, though I believe we would find it very difficult indeed to ignore the weight of two thousand years of Christian cultural history, we could choose to see Satan as harmless, or as the victim of a jealous and spiteful old man, or as a champion of initiative and originality against oppressive authority and vested interest. But for Locke, or for Milton, such associations would not be valid because the Christian tradition that holds Satan to be utterly evil was truth, and to think of him as anything other than evil would therefore have been contrary to the nature of his being and therefore not reasonable or logical. Therefore we would be wrong to say that Locke expresses a belief that *right* interpretation depends on the aleatory conditions of the interpreter. We can say only that he notes the way in which people make associations according to their own backgrounds. Our alternative readings of Satan would be quite illogical for Locke, whereas a modern critic might merely say they were not supported by the rest of Milton's text. As long as criticism insists on religion, the idea of truth remains ultimately stable and must lead back to a univocal world (though the path leading to it has by now become longer and more difficult), but we shall see that, for a modern critic, truth is highly problematic.

For the moment, here is Locke on "unnatural" associations:

> This strong combination of Ideas, not ally'd by Nature, the Mind makes in it self either voluntarily, or by chance, and hence it comes in different Men to be very different, according to their different Inclinations, Educations, Interests, etc. Custom settles habits of Thinking in the Understanding, as well of Determining in the Will, and of Motions in the Body; all which seems to be but trains of motion in the Animal Spirits, which once set a going continue on in the same steps as they have been

used to. . . . A Musician used to any Tune will find that let it but once begin in his head, the *Ideas* of the several Notes of it will follow one another orderly in his Understanding without any care or attention, as regularly as his Fingers move orderly over the Keys of the Organ to play out the Tune he has begun, though his unattentive Thoughts be elsewhere a wandering (*Essay* 2.33.6).

Custom, formed by personal taste, education, and other aleatory conditions that inform our responses to the physical world, "settles habits of thinking in the understanding." In other words, our understanding of the world, and the associations we make when we think about its contents, are informed by what we would today call our environment. This is important for poetry because it explains why A's poetry is different from B's, but also why C's interpretation of any given poem can be different from D's. Again, this seems to be moving close to what the critic Wolfgang Iser calls "Reception theory" and to the idea of reader-response theories generally, but there are still two crucial differences between Locke's ideas and those of modern criticism.

Firstly, Locke allows for different aesthetic responses on the basis of various conditioning factors that can be grouped together as "environment," but not as far as truth is concerned: truth is God. Secondly, Locke's purpose is definitely educational and instructional, which is made very clear in the following passage, where he explains the needs to prevent "wrong" associations from childhood:

This wrong Connexion in our Minds of Ideas in themselves, loose and independent one of another, has such an influence, and is of so great force to set us awry in our Actions, as well Moral as Natural, Passions, Reasonings, and Notions themselves, that, perhaps, there is not any one thing that deserves more to be looked after.

The *Ideas* of *Goblines* and *Sprights* have really no more to do with Darkness than Light; yet let but a foolish Maid inculcate these often on the Mind of a Child, and raise them there together, possibly he shall never be able to separate them again so long as he lives, but Darkness shall ever afterwards bring with it those frightful Ideas, and they shall be so joined that he no more can bear the one than the other. (*Essay* 2.33.9–10)

It is clear that for Locke these associations are a negative influence because they lead us away from the nature of things; the "intellectual defects" they cause are "contracted" like diseases, and can be prevented only by proper education (*Essay* 2.33.17).

This is bad news for poetry, which relies to a large extent on precisely such "unnatural" associations: there is nothing natural about the association of "rose" with "love": it merely seems natural because of "custom." The focus of Locke's attack shifts to "the Nature, Use, and Signification of Language" in his next chapter, but he ends the present one by turning his arguments against unnatural associations into an attack on the Roman Catholic Church: "Let the Idea of Infallibility be inseparably join'd to any Person, and these two constantly together possess the Mind, and then one Body in two Places at once, shall unexamined be swallowed for a certain Truth, by an implicit Faith, when ever that imagin'd infallible Person dictates and demands assent without enquiry" (*Essay* 2.33.17). It would be unfair to suggest that the substitution of "God" for "any Person" in this passage might have caused Locke a crisis of doubt comparable to that of Milton's Satan. God's existence is a matter of course for Locke, "evident and obvious to Reason"; for him, God seems to exist in space and time, for he "fills immensity as well as Eternity" and yet he is an immaterial, and "an Infinite Spirit"; he is of "infinite Duration," which is accompanied with "infinite Knowledge, and infinite Power, he sees all things past and to come." He sounds very much like the God described by Pseudo-Dionysius.

Further bad news for poetry is that Locke's view of it approximates Plato's:

Since Wit and Fancy finds easier entertainment in the World, than dry Truth and real Knowledge, *figurative Speeches,* and allusion in Language, will hardly be admitted, as an imperfection or *abuse* of it. I confess, in Discourses, where we seek rather Pleasure and Delight, than Information and Improvement, such Ornaments are borrowed from them, can scarce pass for Faults. But yet, if we would speak of Things as they are, we must allow, that all the Art of Rhetorick, besides Order and Clearness, all the artificial and figurative application of Words Eloquence hath invented, are for nothing else but to insinuate wrong *Ideas,* move the Passions, and thereby mislead the Judgement; and so indeed are perfect cheat: And therefore however laudable or allowable Oratory may render them in Harangues and popular Addresses, they are certainly, in all Discourses that pretend [i.e., claim] to inform or instruct, wholly to be avoided; and where Truth and Knowledge are concerned, cannot but be thought a great fault, either of the Language or Person that makes use of them. (*Essay* 3.10.34)

If interpretations of God, of the One, have not changed in the twelve hundred years since Pseudo-Dionysius, views on the use of language and on the value of poetry certainly have. For Locke, God is still recognizable by two basic characteristics: he is infinite and self-contradictory, and both of these characteristics render him finally unknowable: if he is infinite, and if as Locke says he knows all things past and to come, then clearly he is aware of things of which we are completely ignorant, and therefore contains aspects which we cannot possibly know; and we have already discussed how a self-contradictory God can never be perfectly defined: all we can do is describe attributes.

In the past, critics had accepted that one of the functions of poetry was to teach. Poetry could lead to virtue by describing the virtuous actions of historical or mythological figures, and the figurative language of certain passages of the Bible were understood as spiritual allegory. In this view, spiritual knowledge is knowledge that helps us to approach God and is therefore instructive in the best possible way, and if poetry can be interpreted as spiritual allegory there is no denying its educational value. It is this quality of poetry that Locke categorically denies: Wit and Fancy lead to "abuse" of language, and the ornaments they result in are useless except for causing delight, which Locke, unlike theorists of the preceding century, clearly divorces from any ability to teach. All figurative language does is "insinuate wrong *Ideas,* move the Passions, and thereby mislead the Judgement"; poetry employs the language of "Harangues and popular Addresses" and is no good "where Truth and Knowledge are concerned."

Locke was not a poet and was not interested in writing a *Defense of Poesy.* We can call him an idealist philosopher insofar as he sees philosophy as a practical way to improve society: he makes it clear in the passages we have seen that his aims are educational. In this sense he resembles the ancient philosophers, whose concern with abstract ideas—truth, morals, justice, and so on—was also a concern with the condition of the nation-state. He differs from the ancient philosophers in that the nature of philosophy itself has changed irrevocably since Plato and Aristotle. For them, it was natural to think of philosophy as including what we today distinguish as physics, chemistry, biology, mathematics, astronomy, and psychology, as well as subjects we can more easily accept as "philosophical," such as ethics. By the time Locke was writing, each of these subjects had already become far too specialized for anyone to think seriously of being expert in all of them.

We can think of what Locke says about language as Platonic in that he has no serious use for poetry in the context of his plans for social improvement. Unlike Plato, he would not go so far as to banish poets from the ideal state, but he certainly relegates their writings to the level of mere pleasure and entertainment, which, as we have seen, he distinguishes sharply from learning and knowledge. The history of poetry's reception still seems to be a continuous back-and-forth between Plato and Aristotle: poetry arouses the senses (Plato and Locke) and is therefore bad; poetry arouses the senses but can therefore be a good thing (Aristotle and the Renaissance apologists); poetry's use of figurative language only leads us away from the truth and creates pointless, even harmful associations of ideas (Plato and Locke); it is precisely through symbol and allegory that poetry leads us closer to God and therefore to the truth (Aristotle and the apologists). And so on. After Locke's sustained attack, we might now expect another apologist.

# 6

# TOWARD ROMANTICISM

## *HUMAN BEINGS AND THE NATURAL WORLD*

In 1700, the year of his death, John Dryden published *Fables Ancient and Modern,* a collection of verse translations from the works of Homer, Ovid, Boccaccio, and Chaucer, together with some of Dryden's own poems. If it were published today it would probably be called *Your Favorite Classics,* or *The Best of the Renaissance.* This is not to disparage *Fables:* it is precisely what the collection is—an anthology of tales by some of the authors most widely read during the two centuries leading up to its publication. Of course, all of the texts represented had been translated, and retranslated, before, but it is tempting to see the publication of *Fables* one year after the appearance of Locke's *Essay* as a kind of statement, a reaction against the growing rationalism of Hobbes and his successors that demoted poetry from its rank of divinely inspired philosophy in verse to a mere form of entertainment: civilized, perhaps, but ultimately unserious. It is at any rate interesting that Dryden chose at this point to publish a collection that, apart from his own original poems, consisted mostly of mythological and/ or allegorical works.

More than twenty years earlier, in his *Apology for Heroic Poetry and Poetic License* (1677), Dryden had reformulated the Renaissance claim for poetry (Kirsch 103) that one of its functions was to "delight a reasonable reader"— a *reasonable* reader, note—and that this delight is related to poetry's use of metaphor:

> Virgil and Horace, the severest writers of the severest age, have made frequent use of the hardest metaphors, and of the strongest hyperboles and in this case the best authority is the best argument. . . . Therefore catachreses [i.e., a misapplied word, as in Milton's *Lycidas*: "Blind

mouths!"] and hyperboles have found their place among [tropes and figures]; not that they were to be avoided, but to be used judiciously, and placed in poetry as heightenings and shadows are in painting, to make the figure bolder, and cause it to stand off to sight. . . . You are not obliged, as in history, to a literal belief of what the poet says; but you are pleased with the image, without being cozened by the fiction. . . . Imaging is, in itself, the very height and life of poetry. It is, as Longinus describes it,[1] a discourse, which by a kind of enthusiasm, or extraordinary emotion of the soul, makes it seem to us that we behold those things which the poet paints. (Kirsch 107)

To "make the figure bolder, and cause it to stand off to sight" sounds very much like the modern critical concept of defamiliarization, the surprised response elicited in a reader (and the technique that elicits it) when he or she encounters an unfamiliar association. The surprise is a lure that draws the reader further into the text. When we read, "My luve is like a red, red rose," we are so accustomed to the association rose/love that we find nothing remarkable in the line. Our response would not be the same, however, to "My love is like a green, green leek."

Secondly, if we can be "pleased with the image, without being cozened by the fiction," we have an answer, of sorts, to Locke's criticism of "unnatural" associations. Dryden's view, like Aristotle's, is that since human beings are always attracted to representation, poetry can be used, and has been used, to lead the reader toward virtue and knowledge—toward truth, in other words—because we will always follow what attracts us. The reader, at least the "reasonable" reader, will be able to differentiate between the fiction of the beloved being really "like a rose" and the idea of beauty that the idea "rose" conveys. Similarly, the reader will be able to distinguish between the fiction of, say, Midas dying of hunger because all the food he touched turned to gold and thus became inedible and the moral lesson conveyed by the story that greed for physical wealth leads to spiritual hunger and death.

But what is a "kind of enthusiasm, or extraordinary emotion of the soul"? Is it anything like "a state of vivid sensation"? And does it in that case have to do with "the manner in which we associate ideas in a state of excitement" (Wordsworth 1800)? A lot depends here on what Dryden means when he writes of the "passions": "It requires philosophy as well as poetry to sound the depth of the passions; what they are in themselves, and how they are to be provoked; and in this science the best poets have excelled" (Kirsch 107). In Locke's *Essay,* where he discusses how passions lead us into error, the idea is a complex one, but once we understand it we shall realize how central it is not only to Locke's rationalist view of poetry, but also to poetry itself in the course of the eighteenth century.

First of all, then, this is how Locke defines passion:

> *Power* being the Source from whence all Action proceeds, the Substances wherein these Powers are, when they exert this Power into Act, are called *Causes;* and the Substances which thereupon are produced, or the simple *Ideas* which are introduced into any subject by the exerting of that Power, are called *Effects.* The *efficacy* whereby the new Substance or *Idea* is produced, is called, in the subject exerting that Power, *Action;* but in the subject, wherein any simple *Idea* is changed or produced, it is called *Passion:* Which efficacy however various, and the effects almost infinite; yet we can, I think, conceive it, in intellectual Agents, to be nothing but Modes of Thinking, and Willing; in corporeal Agents, nothing else but Modifications of Motion. (*Essay* 2.22.11)

This becomes a lot easier to understand than it may seem if we first take a "corporeal agent" as an example. If I push with my hand against a tennis ball (which I discover conveniently on the table in front of me, waiting to be pushed in order to prove Locke's theory of cause and effect), the ball moves. How far it moves depends on various factors—how hard I push, the condition of the surface of the table, for example—but the essentials are clear: I push the ball, the ball moves. In this example I can think of myself as a cause; I can think of raising my hand and exerting pressure against the tennis ball as act; and I can call what happens to the ball, as a result of this act, effect. It seems odd to think of passion in a tennis ball, but if we now substitute *Romeo* for *tennis ball,* *Juliet* for *I, Juliet's beauty* for *Power,* and *distract* for *push,* we can easily guess that we shall soon have to substitute *falls in love* for *moves.* Now all we have to do is suppose *word* to stand for *cause, association* for *effect,* and remember that all words are signs that stand for ideas. Passion leads us into error, according to Locke, because it is a driving force: "Tell a Man, passionately in Love, that he is jilted; bring a score of Witnesses of the Falsehood of his Mistress, 'tis ten to one but three kind Words of Hers, shall invalidate all their Testimonies. *Quod volumus, facile credimus;* what suits our wishes, is forwardly [i.e., easily, soon] believed, is, I suppose, what every one hath more than once experimented [i.e., experienced]." In other words, once passion has empowered us (Shakespeare knew, in the case of Romeo and Juliet, that "passion lends them power"), reason, logic, probability, and plain common sense have little chance of resisting.

This is obviously important for poetry because the claim of both its detractors and its apologists is that it can arouse the passions, it causes in us "Modes of Thinking, and Willing" which Locke and Plato consider negative but of which Dryden and Aristotle write positively. This is indeed a crucial point, for if we agree with Locke it seems that we have now, with the publication of his *Essay,* reached the point at which the role of poetry as vehicle for the expression of the inexpressible can be abolished. There remains in this case only one truly obscure, truly open text, and that is the Bible; and that the Bible, or parts of it, should be obscure is only natural and proper since it is the inspired word of God. But what of all the other ancient texts whose meaning to this day proves very hard indeed to decipher? These, according to Locke, are best forgotten:

> But there being no Writings we have any great concernment to be very sollicitous about the meaning of, but those that contain either Truths we are required to believe, or Laws we are to obey, and draw inconveniences on us, when we mistake or transgress, we may be less anxious about the sense of other Authors; who writing but their own opinions, we are under no greater necessity to know them, than they to know ours. Our Good or Evil depending not on their Decrees, we may safely be ignorant of their Notions. (*Essay* 3.9.10)

This, we can assume with equal safety, is a reference to the commentaries of the church fathers, whose authority Locke rejects as a matter of course. But it is also a very clear statement of an attitude toward language that sees metaphor, except in one case, as a waste of time.

If, on the other hand, we think, with Dryden, that poetry can arouse the passions to good effect, we accept the need for metaphor, for Aristotle's "representation," for Augustine's "figurative language," in order to lead us toward truths our reason alone cannot find but that can be approached through "extraordinary emotion of the soul." The nature of this extraordinary emotion, and what it can bring about, will be the main focus of this chapter.

Like Milton, Dryden reworked existing texts (he had always been a prolific translator); like Dante, he claimed (in the preface) that the *Fables* could be read in a moral sense; and like earlier critics in general he insisted on poetry's dual function of teaching and delighting. If a poem about a fox and a rooster—one of the *Fables* is Dryden's reworking of Chaucer's "Nun's Priest's Tale"—can be read in a moral sense, it must be about something other than, or as well as, a fox and a rooster. The same holds for the lengthy passages he translates from Ovid's *Metamorphoses,* for the other extracts from *The Canterbury Tales,* and for the stories he takes from Boccaccio's *Decameron.* What makes it possible for all of these groups of texts to fulfil the same two functions of teaching and delighting? In order to answer this question I want now to take a rather technical approach, and I hope that readers will bear with me if the following begins to sound like Locke on cause and effect.

I am going to assume that, if a poem carries both a literal and a moral sense, each of these fulfils a different function or, rather, that each sense works on readers in different ways. Now I want to suggest that the initial "delight" a reader experiences from the poem is related to the literal sense: in the case of "The Nun's Priest's Tale," for example, the absurdity of the situation is (I think) likely to cause amusement. Readers will be able to accept the proposed connection between the moral sense and the idea of "teaching." However, I want to claim that the moral sense is also connected with a kind of "delight," and that this delight lies not in the moral sense itself but in the intellectual process of looking for it. Now, I realize that here I can be taken to have come perilously close to claiming that the purpose of reading a poem is to discover what it means. I cannot stress too much that this is not at all what I wish to say; and I should certainly be very disappointed if, after reading a poem several times over, I were forced to admit that all it had told me was *Thou shalt not kill* or *All parents should ensure their children eat lots of vegetables.* What I do wish to suggest is that part of the pleasure of reading a poem derives from precisely that process that so irritated Locke: from making, or recognizing, or believing we have recognized "unnatural" associations. In this sense, even lines that today seem clichés (because the associations they carry are too familiar) can be interesting. When I read "My luve is like a red, red rose," I can of course say "I know all about that," and toss the book aside in disgust, but I can also ask myself, again and again, *why* someone's love might be like a red, red rose. Whether, during this process of questioning, I happen to make the same associations as Robert Burns did when he thought of the line is of no consequence whatsoever, as well as being impossible to find out. It is the process itself that "delights." Finally, what enables us to perceive a moral sense (or a spiritual sense) through the literal one must be the association produced by "enthusiasm, or extraordinary emotion of the soul."

The approach just outlined differs from Dryden's in that it makes no claims for the meaning of a poem, which Dryden would have connected with the intention of the author. It agrees with Dryden's approach in that it sees "extraordinary emotion of the soul" as that which moves the mind to make associations. The problem with such a phrase is its vagueness. Locke expressed it in scientific terms as the "passion" that in intellectual agents (human beings) caused an effect (an idea). But he denied that the kind of idea we are discussing here was of any real value, which seems to indicate a belief that, except in the case of Scripture, which he makes a point of singling out ("Truths we are required to believe"), the literal sense of a text does not lead us to a spiritual one. This situation is interesting because it means we have now arrived back at precisely the same point where two earlier contemporaries, Aquinas and Dante, were putting forward precisely the same opposed views. The doctrinal differences between Locke's and Aquinas's respective religions are irrelevant here: both claim that only Scripture conveys anything important behind its mysteries.

The work of the Scottish poet James Thomson, born in the year Dryden published the *Fables,* restates the idea of poetry as teacher, as mediator between the physical and spiritual, with such force and such immediacy that it is difficult to read his poems in the context of what had been published by poets of the previous generation without seeing them as something completely new. The example I give here comes from *The Seasons* (1730):

> The western sun withdraws the shortened day;
> And humid evening, gliding o'er the sky,
> In her chill progress, to the ground condensed
> The vapors throws. Where creeping waters ooze,
> Where marshes stagnate, and where rivers wind,
> Cluster the rolling fogs, and swim along
> The dusky-mantled lawn. Meanwhile the moon,
> Full-orbed and breaking through the scattered clouds,
> Shows her broad visage in the crimsoned east.
> Turned to the sun direct, her spotted disk
> (Where mountains rise, umbrageous dales descend,

And caverns deep, as optic tube descries)
A smaller earth, gives all his blaze again,
Void of his flame, and sheds a softer day.
Now through the passing cloud she seems to stoop,
Now up the pure cerulean rides sublime.
Wide the pale deluge floats, and streaming mild,
O'er the skied mountain to the shadowy vale,
While rocks and floods reflect the quivering gleam,
The whole air whitens with a boundless tide
Of silver radiance trembling round the world.

("Autumn," lines 1082–102)

Perhaps we are today so used to seeing nature poetry that we have come to take it for granted. If this is so, we should think again about what it is we so calmly accept to be the job of poetry. Are we prepared, for example, to allow the western sun, as subject of a transitive verb, to "withdraw" the day? Are we really going to allow the evening to "throw" vapors? If we feel comfortable with this we shall have no problem with clustering fogs, trembling radiance, and quivering gleams; nor with "the pure cerulean" (the sky); nor with a floating "pale deluge" (moonlight); nor with a lawn being "dusky-mantled" (in shadow).

One response would be to point out that we can surely accept all this if we can accept talking roosters trained in the liberal arts; but there are crucial differences between Chaucer's (and Dryden's) fictions, and the day-withdrawing suns and vapor-throwing evenings of Thomson's poem. First of all, I am sure, beyond any doubt whatsoever, that not even the most overwhelmingly powerful enthusiasm or most wildly extraordinary "emotion of the soul" ever led Chaucer or Dryden to believe in the physical, literal existence of talking roosters. I do not feel so sure in the question of Thomson's perception of nature. Again, we are not obliged to believe the fiction; but a talking rooster is more obviously a fiction than the western sun withdrawing the shortened day. When I read Chaucer's or Dryden's version of "The Nun's Priest's Tale," I do not ask myself, "But how can a rooster talk?" and this is for the same reason that I do not ask myself how, in Ovid's story of Pygmalion and Galatea, a statue can suddenly come to life, or how Prospero can rule an island by magic in *The Tempest,* or how Puck can travel round the world in so short a time in *A Midsummer Night's Dream.* In the case of Thomson's poem, though I know perfectly well that the sun does not really "withdraw" anything and that fogs do not "cluster" of their own volition, I can easily see how an "unnatural" association might occur that connects the motion of the sun in the evening, or the way in which fog settles, with the actions *withdraw* and *cluster* as performed by human beings.

Thomson's personification of nature does not work in the same way as Chaucer's and Dryden's "humanization" of Chauntecleer/Chanticleer. We have, though, seen something similar to what Thomson does; for example:

> The air hung over all, which is as much heavier than fire as the weight of water is lighter than the weight of earth. There did the creator bid the mists and clouds to take their place, and thunder, that should shake the hearts of men, and winds which produce lightning and thunderbolts. To these also the world's creator did not allot the air that they might hold it everywhere. Even as it is, they can scarce be prevented, though they control their blasts, each in his separate tract, from tearing the world to pieces. So fiercely do these brothers strive together. But Eurus drew off to the land of the dawn and the realms of Araby, and where the Persian hills flush beneath the morning light. The western shores which glow with the setting sun are the place of Zephyrus: while bristling Boreas betook himself to Scythia and the farthest north. The land far opposite is wet with constant fog and rain, the home of Auster, the south-wind. Above all these he placed the liquid, weightless ether, which has naught of earthy dregs. (Ovid, *Metamorphoses* 1.52–68)

Both Thomson's text and Ovid's personify and gender nature: Ovid's winds are brothers, while in Thomson's poem the sun and moon retain their respective mythological sexes. But Ovid's text is also a religious one—like Milton, he takes the "official" version of the Creation and Fall and retells it in the form of an epic poem. Can we, though, merely on the basis of both Thomson and Ovid personifying nature, read *The Seasons* as a religious poem? For a text to be termed religious it must make denominational reference—it must talk about a *specific* religion. What name do we give to those texts that cannot be ordered into specific religious categories but that seem to speak about things normally discussed by them?

The following passage, again from "Autumn," is an example of the kind of text I mean:

Now black and deep the night begins to fall,
A shade immense! Sunk in the quenching gloom,
Magnificent and vast, are heaven and earth.
Order confounded lies, all beauty void,
Distinction lost, and gay variety
One universal blot—such the fair power
Of light to kindle and create the whole.
Drear is the state of the benighted wretch
Who then bewildered wanders through the dark
Full of pale fancies and chimeras huge;
Nor visited by one directive ray
From cottage streaming or from airy hall.
Perhaps, impatient as he stumbles on,
Struck from the root of slimy rushes, blue
The wildfire scatters round, or, gathered, trails
A length of flame deceitful o'er the moss;
Whither decoyed by the fantastic blaze,
Now lost and now renewed, he sinks absorbed,
Rider and horse, amid the miry gulf—
While still, from day to day, his pining wife
And plaintive children his return await,
In wild conjecture lost. At other times,
Sent by the better genius of the night,
Innoxious, gleaming on the horse's mane,
The meteor sits, and shows the narrow path
That winding leads through pits of death, or else
Instructs him how to take the dangerous ford.

("Autumn," lines 1138–71)

What is described in the first six lines above—the absence of order, the immensity of space, the synthesis, or confusion, of everything with everything—is both the state described at the beginning of the *Metamorphoses* and that at the beginning of Creation in Genesis. These are the opening lines from Ovid:

Before the sea was, and the lands, and the sky that hangs over all, the face of Nature showed alike in her whole round, which state men have called chaos: a rough, unordered mass of things, nothing at all save lifeless bulk and warring seeds of ill-matched elements heaped in one. No sun as yet shone forth upon the world, nor did the waxing moon renew her slender horns; nor yet did the earth hang poised by her own weight in the circumambient air, nor had the ocean stretched her arms along the far reaches of the lands. And, though there was both land and sea and air, no one could tread that land or swim that sea; and the air was dark. No form of things remained the same; all objects were at odds, for within one body cold things strove with hot, and moist with dry, soft things with hard, things having weight with weightless things. (*Metamorphoses* 1.1–20)

And the following are the first two verses from Genesis 1:

1. In the beginning God created the heaven and the earth
2. And the earth was without form, and void; and darkness was upon the face of the deep. And the Spirit of God moved upon the face of the waters.

A vast darkness and formlessness characterize the descriptions in all three texts, but Thomson's differs from Genesis and *Metamorphoses* in one crucial point: in these two, what is described is the state of primeval confusion *before* the order imposed by God had given earth its place in the universe and made it a viable habitat for humans and the other creatures. What Thomson describes takes us back to "one universal blot," the state of the universe immediately *after* Creation—or, if we prefer physics and evolution to Creation, to the first few fractions of a second after Big Bang (and in this case we can view Thomson and Ovid in the same way as the church fathers viewed classical authors, as telling the truth without realizing it).

The passage quoted from "Autumn" reminds us how close we are to that state and how powerful is the nature we like to think we have under control. It also reveals the unleashed power of God. Ironically, perhaps, we can now think of him, in Thomson's poem, in terms of the rationalist Locke's discussion of cause and effect: God is the power that acts to create the forces of nature, which in turn act upon the world we know with the effect of revealing him to us. All this means is that, in "Autumn," the power of nature can be read as a symbol for divine power. Divine power, and therefore God, is everywhere, containing, and contained in, everything in the natural world; and "everything" of course includes humans. This view of God takes us back to something else we have already seen. It has the effect of remystifying God and His creations, of making him more demonstrably and physically powerful; an Old Testament God, in fact, who is more interested in pyrotechnics and heavy symbolism than the more discreet, rather genteel God of the New Testament. We can read Thomson's nature, or Nature, as a reminder that in the civilized, orderly world of manners and human dealings, and with natural forces, as we like to believe, increasingly harnessed and tamed, the aspect of divine power that the processes of civilization have suppressed is still there, and that God is still as mysterious and unknowable as ever. Also, the stress on the infinite and on mystery in Thomson's text recalls the description of God's qualities in Pseudo-Dionysius.

So far, then, it certainly seems possible to read the passage from "Autumn" as allegory, with nature as it appears in this part of the poem symbolizing one aspect, at least, of divinity. But who is the "benighted wretch" whose wife and children are so concerned for his safety? Where is home? And where has he been? His journey is a difficult one, for we know that he "bewildered wanders through the dark." Guidance and security are associated with light, and being lost, with light's absence—there is no "directive ray / From cottage streaming or from airy hall"—except in the case of the "wildfire" or Will-o'-the-wisp, which leads travelers astray by its "deceitful" appearance until they are lost completely in a "miry gulf." Light is his one hope: the "meteor," which here refers to the "innoxious" glow produced by "St Elmo's Fire," or *ignus lambens,* during electrical storms, and which intermittently directs him through along the path that will ultimately lead him out of the "pits of death."

This very easily (very economically) supports an allegorical reading—the journey as allegorical motif representing the individual's physical and/or moral struggle against adverse forces has a long and venerable history. We know that the dark is traditionally associated with evil, the unknown, and is that state in which we cannot "see" because we are ignorant or because we lack faith; and in John 8:12, Christ says of himself, "I am the light of the world: he that followeth me shall not walk in darkness, but shall have the light of life." I do not believe that this by itself is enough to justify the reading light = Christ in Thomson's poem, but I do think that the text supports our association of physical darkness and light with spiritual ignorance and awareness, respectively. It is an allegory with a difference, however (or perhaps just an extremely old-fashioned allegory), in that God, in our allegorical reading of him, is represented by attributes

144

that stress the physical manifestations of his power—extremes of nature, flashes of light, the potential for chaos.

Thomson's treatment of nature is of interest to our study in the light of the work of the Scottish philosopher David Hume. His *Treatise of Human Nature* was published in 1735, and the *Enquiry concerning Human Understanding* appeared in 1748, and in both works, but especially in the *Enquiry,* he puts forward the view that humans, far from being chosen by God to govern the animal kingdom, are themselves part of it. They are, in other words, just as much a part of nature as other animals. This is not to say that he sees other animals as capable of the same advanced rational thought processes as humans: his claim is that many animals share with humans the ability to experience at least something similar to those emotions roused by the "passions"—love, hate, fear. In other words, humans' responses resemble those of other animals in extreme situations. It must be understood at this point that the word *animal* in this context is not used in a modern derogatory sense, as for example in the sentence: *He eats like an animal.* Hume uses the word to underline the view of humans as part of the natural world. He does not, though, seem to think of the existence of this natural world in terms of its reflecting the power of God. On those philosophers who claim that nothing exists except by his will, he says that

> they rob nature, and all created beings, of every power, in order to render their dependence on the Deity still more sensible and immediate. They consider not, that, by this theory, they diminish, instead of magnifying, the grandeur of those attributes, which they affect so much to celebrate. It argues surely more power in the Deity to delegate a certain degree of power to inferior creatures, than to produce every thing by his own immediate volition. It argues more wisdom to contrive at first the fabric of the world with such perfect foresight, that, of itself, and by its proper operation, it may serve all the purposes of providence. Than if the great Creator were obliged every moment to adjust its parts, and animate by his breath all the wheels of that stupendous machine. (*Enquiry* 7.1.22)

If we think of nature, the "fabric of the world," as contrived with "perfect foresight," we can imagine God, after the initial act of creation described by Ovid and in the first two verses of Genesis 1, folding his arms and saying, "Now get on with it." He does not now need to impose order on chaos since it will, because of the foresight with which it was originally planned, sort itself out without God. And indeed Ovid, though not Genesis, raises this possibility, for the separation of land from water and of sky from land, the imposition of order that in Genesis is carried out by God, is in *Metamorphoses* the work either of "God—or kindlier Nature" (*Metamorphoses* 1.21). In this way it becomes possible to think of nature as separate from God. Nature can still be read as a symbol for God because God can still be read as having given the initial spark to Creation, but at the same time nature is also becoming a power in its own right.

We can now at least question whether in any given case nature functions as a parabolic extension of God or independently of him. At this point, it is very difficult to continue to see the world as univocal, for if, as for example in Thomson's text, nature seems to be a symbol for something, but that something need not be God, then quite clearly it must be a symbol for something else. We shall see that this opening up of interpretive possibilities becomes increasingly important throughout the eighteenth century.

What Hume has to say on the association of ideas by the imagination is also very interesting indeed in the context of our study: "That we may understand the full extent of these relations [of cause and effect] we must consider, that two objects are connected together in the imagination, not only when the one is immediately resembling, contiguous to, or the cause of the other, but also when there is interposed betwixt them a third object, which bears to both of them any of these relations" (*Treatise* 1.4.4). We have already seen from Locke's discussion of cause and effect how two objects—we can call them A and B—can be related in the imagination by either "natural" or "unnatural" association. What is of particular interest in Hume's theory is the presence of a "third object," C, related to both A and B. Let us see what happens when we try to interpose a third object between two already related ones. In Oxford, there is a pub named "The Lamb and Flag." This pub name is so common in England, and therefore so familiar to me, that if someone, during a game of associations, were to say "lamb," I should almost certainly respond with "flag." But I also know that both the lamb and the flag are symbols for Saint John, and it is therefore also possible that either term might remind me of him. Once this association has been established, it is impossible that it should not work the other way: "lamb" will remind me of "flag," but "flag" will also remind me of "lamb"; "lamb" will remind me of "Saint John," but also the reverse is true; and so on—there will always be six possible associations. We could carry this to absurd extremes, and, from the example just given, create the association *whisky and soda: the Gospel according to Luke,* but this relation would make sense only to us. Absurd perhaps, but such relations happen in poetry (especially "difficult" poetry) because of the aleatory conditions that inform the associations made in the imagination of any given poet.

For the same reason, even the simple A:B relations often remain unfathomable in poetry, though we understand them, or at least accept them as normal, when, like *love: rose* they are familiar to our own, particular, culture. Hume regards this as a poetic mistake because it means that "the poet traces his events to too great a distance, and binds together actions, which, though not entirely disjoined, have not so strong a connexion as is requisite to forward the transition of the passions" (*Enquiry* 3.12). This implies that the job of poetry, or one of the jobs of poetry, is to excite the passions in order to "see" the connection; but Hume also knows that "all the colours of poetry, however splendid, can never paint natural objects in such a manner as to make the description be taken for a real landscape. The most lively thought is inferior to the dullest sensation" (*Enquiry* 2.1). "Inferior" probably means "less true" and "less intense." Nobody, I think, would seriously argue against the first proposed meaning, for the same reason that they would not argue that the word *ox* is also the physical object ox, rather than a sound intended to call an image of the physical object to mind. But we shall soon find people questioning "less intense."

This study began with the assertion that symbols and allegory were used in Scripture as a way of talking about something unknowable. They were needed because whatever is unknowable cannot be contained in language. We understand that even the word *ox* (or *cat,* or *tree,* or any word that stands for any physical object) *only* stands for an object—it does not really recreate that object in the physical world. But an ox is just that: a physical object (a very physical object, in fact) and we can see and touch an ox and satisfy ourselves of its existence. In the case of ideas like "beauty" or "ethics," we frequently need more words to explain them because beauty and ethics are not physical objects and are therefore more difficult to represent: we cannot see them or touch them, only discuss their characteristics or those attributes we consider necessary for their better definition—and even these characteristics and attributes are in a state of continuous flux. Sometimes, perhaps with the intention of saving time, but also, if we agree with Aristotle, because we take pleasure in representation, we use symbols: beauty becomes *rose,* for example.

At any rate, from what we have seen so far, the poetic use of symbols certainly does not always have the effect of saving time. In the case of the idea "God," things are even more difficult because God is not only the most complex idea we know (or don't know), he is *all* the ideas we know (as well as those we don't yet know and those we no longer know because we have forgotten them) since all ideas originate in him. This is why Augustine needed to see all words as symbols or signs. The world speaks of God, but God does not speak in words, he speaks in things: he opens his mouth and oxen, trees, cats, and so forth pop out. And even these things are themselves signs that stand for the ideas "ox," "tree," "cat" in God's mind. God speaks in what the Platonic tradition sees as symbols. In this way, the world can be thought of as a text. It is written in signs and can only ever be read, interpreted, and translated, never finally understood. This will hold as long as the poetic symbol is seen as standing for something unknowable to the intellect, to reason, and therefore unattainable—something that can be interpreted in a spiritual sense, something we feel rather than understand; and this will be the case as long as God and the mystery that always necessarily accompanies him are thought of as the "first causes" of symbols.

## *WILLIAM BLAKE*

Do we have to think of God in this way? Is God inseparably bound up with the idea of the poetic symbol? Or can we really "see," through poetry, more than our senses and our intellect allow? In the illuminated *There is No Natural Religion* (c. 1788), William Blake both asks these questions and provides an answer. The first part of the text consists of six claims derived from Locke's views on perception:

> The Argument: Man has no notion of moral fitness but from Education. Naturally he is only a natural organ subject to Sense.
> I. Man cannot naturally Percieve but through his natural or bodily organs.
> II. Man by his reasoning power can only compare & judge of what he has already perciev'd.
> III. From a perception of only 3 senses none could deduce a fourth or fifth.
> IV. None could have other than natural or organic thoughts if he had none but organic perceptions.

V. Mans desires are limited by his perceptions. None can desire what he has not perciev'd.

VI. The desires & perceptions of man untaught by any thing but organs of sense must be limited to objects of sense.

This is of interest to us not because of what it claims about our capacity for religion but because it clearly limits us to the world of reason. In particular, points I, V, and VI are relevant to poetry's use of symbol and deserve close attention.

Point I seems obvious enough: that we need our sense organs in order to sense—that is, to perceive—and are able to perceive *only* through them. This means that there is no such thing as "extra-sensory perception," and that what we feel but cannot perceive must therefore be illusory. If, then, we use a poetic symbol to stand for such a thing felt, that symbol must be a redundant one: there is nothing behind it. This view is supported by points V and VI, which propose that, if desires are those things we wish for in our imagination, they can be only those things we have experienced, since it is impossible to imagine something to which we have no relation or means of referring. It would be like trying to imagine a color we have never seen: it cannot be done. We can take this in two ways: when we feel what we think of as a spiritual yearning for "something more than this" we are (1) deluding ourselves or (2) in fact wishing for something tangible but that we have failed to recognize as such. The problem with this is that it leaves God out of the question altogether, and I am wrong to do this in the context of Locke's philosophy or Blake's use of it, because both Locke and Blake claimed to believe in God. I must, then, add the third possibility that (3) the "something more" is God and that all spiritual yearning is attributable to the soul's desire to return to him—which brings us directly back to Plato.

Now let us look at the second of Blake's texts:

I. Mans perceptions are not bounded by organs of perception. He percieves more than sense (tho' ever so acute) can discover.

II. Reason or the ratio of all we have already known is not the same that it shall be when we know more.

III. [text not extant]

IV. The bounded is loathed by its possessor. The same dull round even of a universe would soon become a mill with complicated wheels.

V. If the many become the same as the few, when possess'd, More!
More! is the cry of a mistaken soul, less than All cannot satisfy Man.

VI. If any could desire what he is incapable of possessing, despair must
be his eternal lot.

VII. The desire of Man being Infinite the possession is Infinite & himself Infinite.

Conclusion: If it were not for the Poetic or Prophetic character the
Philosophic & Experimental would soon be at the ratio of all things &
stand still, unable to do other than repeat the same dull round over
again.

Application: He who sees the Infinite in all things sees God. He who
sees the Ratio only sees himself only. Therefore God becomes as we are
that we may be as he is.

This complicated text becomes easier to understand if we begin with the
conclusion: it is the poetic or prophetic character that ensures that the limits of the world of reason are continually expanded. In this way, Blake
restates the idea of poet as *Vates,* or seer. We see God if we see "the Infinite
in all things" firstly because God is infinite and secondly, as Harold Bloom
points out in his commentary (Blake 894–95), because "to see the infinite
in all things is to see as God sees, which Blake believes is the only way to
see God." The logical next step, also taken by Bloom, is that in order to see
as God sees, to see the infinite, human beings must become as God—they
must themselves become infinite, and infinity is "a state to be attained only
by the individual utterly possessed by the Poetic Character" (Blake 895).
This explains why "More!" is the cry of a "mistaken soul": not because it
is wrong to cry for more, but because to be in the position to do so is,
according to Blake, to have limited ("bounded") the soul.

Seeing the infinite is one thing, but how to write about it? What kind
of language can we possibly use to define it? What words might be adequate? Surely, again, we can only describe infinity—perhaps, in fact, as "a
flashing darkness which is neither body nor figure nor shape, which has no
quantity, no quality, no weight, which is not in a place and does not see,
has no sensitivity, is neither soul nor mind, has no imagination or opinion, is neither number nor order nor greatness, is not a substance, not
eternity, not time"—that is, in precisely the same allegorical language used
by Pseudo-Dionysius in *On Mystical Theology* to describe God, the One.
Actually we would need to add the opposites of the qualities listed by
Dionysius in order to do slightly better justice to the idea of God's in-

finiteness—dark brightness, having body and figure and shape, both soul and mind, and so on—but I think the similarity between Dionysius and Blake will anyway be clear.

But if we want to describe Blake's approach as that of a mystic, we must be careful not to go too far. He is no mystic in the sense of the Renaissance hermetists, but only insofar as he believes that infinity—that is, God—can be found in everything is he conventionally and orthodoxically mystical. He does claim, though, that it is only through the unrestrained "Poetic Character" that infinity can be perceived. He makes this point again in another text in illuminated printing from the same period, *All Religions are One:*

> The Argument. As the true method of knowledge is experiment the true faculty of knowing must be the faculty which experiences.
> PRINCIPLE 1st. That the Poetic Genius is the true Man, and that the body or outward form of Man is derived from the Poetic Genius. Likewise that the forms of all things are derived from their Genius, which by the Ancients was call'd an Angel & Spirit & Demon.
> PRINCIPLE 2d. As all men are alike in outward form, so (and with the same infinite variety) all are alike in the Poetic Genius.
> PRINCIPLE 3d. No man can think write or speak from his heart, but he must intend truth. Thus all sects of Philosophy are from the Poetic Genius adapted to the weaknesses of every individual.
> PRINCIPLE 4. As none by traveling over known lands can find out the unknown, so from already acquired knowledge Man could not acquire more, therefore an universal Poetic Genius exists.
> PRINCIPLE 5. The Religions of all Nations are derived from each Nations different reception of the Poetic Genius which is every where call'd the Spirit of Prophecy.
> PRINCIPLE 6. The Jewish & Christian Testaments are An original derivation from the Poetic Genius; this is necessary from the confined nature of bodily sensation.
> PRINCIPLE 7th. As all men are alike (tho' infinitely various) so all Religions & as all similars have one source, the true Man is the source, he being the Poetic Genius.

This constitutes another restatement, this time of the idea popular with early Renaissance critics that poetry leads to an understanding of the "essence" or Platonic Idea of things, and thus reveals God and leads us to him: poetry is therefore divinely inspired.

But it also restates the idea that the world can be seen as a text. If all things contain "the Infinite," or God, then clearly all things can be understood as symbols for them, and if the world consists of symbols it consists of things we can interpret or "read"—it becomes an allegory, which tells, over and again, the story of God's work, and which is written in God's language, a language of signs. Northrop Frye puts it: "The material world provides a universal language of images and . . . each man's imagination speaks that language with his own accent. Religions are the grammars of this language" (Blake 894). Blake sees all religions as one because they all attempt to speak, though in different accents and using different grammars, about the same physical world. The medieval commentators understood this: it allowed Augustine, talking about possible interpretations of Paradise, to claim that we can interpret Scripture in any way we like. But the medieval commentators on Scripture also believed that everyone should speak in the same accent and use the same grammar, which is why Augustine needed to qualify his claim with the very clear condition: *provided that we also believe in the truth of the story as a faithful record of historical fact* (*City of God* 13.22).

What can Blake mean when he says that "the body or outward form of Man is derived from the Poetic Genius"? He seems to mean that the body is that manifestation of the soul that is perceivable by the senses. If this were so, it would fit very nicely with both the Christian notion of the body as temporary, worldly home for the soul, as well as with the Platonic view of physical bodies as mere representations of their essential Ideas. However, in another series of illuminated texts, *The Marriage of Heaven and Hell,* Blake constructs his argument in this way:

All Bibles or sacred codes have been the causes of he following Errors.
1. That Man has two real existing principles, Viz: a Body & a Soul.
2. That Energy, calld Evil, is alone from the Body, & that Reason, calld Good, is alone from the Soul.
3. That God will torment Man in Eternity for following his Energies.
But the following Contraries to these are True
1. Man has no Body distinct from his Soul for that calld Body is a portion of the Soul discernd by the five Senses, the chief inlets of Soul in this age.
2. Energy is the only life and is from the Body and Reason is the bound or outward circumference of Energy.
3. Energy is Eternal Delight.

We need to realize that Blake had a sense of humor and listed this collection of contradictions under the heading "The Voice of the Devil"—from the point of view of orthodox theology, Blake's refusal to distinguish between body and soul is indeed "diabolical"—but this does not mean we should not take his propositions seriously. If we read the second point of the Contraries above, that Reason is "the bound or outward circumference of Energy," in the light of the claims made in the second part of *There is No Natural Religion* and in *All Religions are One,* we can understand Blake's idea of Energy as the Poetic Character, the Infinite, whose "bound or outward circumference" is Reason, in much the same way as, in orthodox terms, the body houses the soul. This may sound rather far-fetched, but more simply it can be read as another way of expressing the claim made in the Application to *There is No Natural Religion:* "He who sees the Infinite in all things sees God. He who sees the Ratio only sees himself only." We can summarize Blake's view of the Poetic Character as follows:

All things contain the Infinite, or God;
the Infinite can be perceived by the Poetic Character; and
poetry can therefore reveal the Infinite in all things.

How does bearing these points in mind affect our reading of Blake's poetry? One of the things that happens is that we are able to see in "The Tyger" a good illustration of what Aquinas called the parabolical—a variant of the literal sense, rather than a separate sense altogether. Let us suppose that Blake, aided by the Poetic Character, perceived the infinite in his literal tiger and that his poem is an attempt to give expression to this quality. I am quite aware that I have no way of really proving what I suspect to be authorial intentions here, but I am prepared to take my chances on what seems a pretty safe bet in view of Blake's own comments on the nature of poetry. I will next assume that Blake published "The Tyger" when he felt satisfied that any further work on the poem would not be an improvement. This is important because it enables me to feel reasonably confident that, when I read Blake's descriptions of his *literal* tiger, I am seeing it more or less as he did. The problem with this is: where is the literal tiger? "Burning bright" hardly sounds like what real, physical tigers do (unless they are urgent cases for the inspectors from the humane society). And what are "forests of the night"? And who put the tiger's brain in a furnace, before subjecting it to surely horrific treatment on an anvil? Perhaps

I am being unfair in taking these obviously allegorical lines, dealing with obviously symbolic actions, out of context. Here is the complete poem:

> Tyger Tyger, burning bright,
> In the forests of the night;
> What immortal hand or eye,
> Could frame thy fearful symmetry?
>
> In what distant deeps or skies
> Burnt the fire of thine eyes?
> On what wings dare he aspire?
> What the hand, dare seize the fire?
>
> And what shoulder, & what art,
> Could twist the sinews of thy heart?
> And when thy heart began to beat,
> What dread hand? & what dread feet?
>
> What the hammer? what the chain,
> In what furnace was thy brain?
> What the anvil? what dread grasp,
> Dare its deadly terrors clasp!
>
> When the stars threw down their spears
> And water'd heaven with their tears:
> Did he smile his work to see?
> Did he who made the Lamb make thee?
>
> Tyger Tyger, burning bright,
> In the forests of the night:
> What immortal hand or eye
> Dare frame thy fearful symmetry?

The only word in the poem from which we can deduce a literal tiger is the name itself, "Tyger." All other ideas that might indicate a literal tiger—eyes, heart, brain—might also indicate the idea "human," "leopard," "hamster," or any other animal. The rest of the poem poses questions on the nature of an empirical maker who uses fire, anvils, and hammers to forge creations: God as blacksmith. Why does Blake not need to present us with a literal tiger? Because according to his own theory, the literal one is the same as the allegorical one. Or, rather: according to his own theory, he *has* presented us with a literal tiger, only a different aspect of one, the aspect that lies behind the physical, outward form "discernd by the five Senses" and that the "Poetic Character" can recognize—the "Infinite" in "tiger." The infinite is God, "he who made the lamb."

I know that I have not said enough about the symbol *tiger.* It is not enough to help myself to Blake's prose explications and discuss his poem in that context only (a miserly rather than an economical reading). It is not enough because it does not answer the question: If the Poetic Character can see the infinite in *all* things, why a tiger? Why not that leopard or hamster? And there is another point in the text of "The Tyger" that supports my dissatisfaction: If God is contained in and contains all things, the answer to the question "Did he who made the lamb make thee?" is so obviously "yes" that it does not need asking. There must be something about what "tiger" and "lamb" can symbolize that make the question—a surprised one, after all—a necessary one. But the poem does not say: *Here is a tiger, a fierce and bloodthirsty creature. Is it not surprising that such an animal should come from the same creator who gave us the gentle and timid lamb?* We ourselves are engaged to fill up the gaps from what we associate with literal tigers—the text need only mention the name "tyger" and we do the rest. The *literal* tiger is a pretty closed text: we do not think immediately of the meekness and self-sacrificing nature of tigers just as we do not normally think of the ferocity of lambs. And we remember this closed text of a tiger when we read the questions that the poem asks about it, especially the question associating it with the lamb. Locke, Hume, and perhaps Blake himself would say, "This is how symbols work—the associations we make depend on education and habit. We are simply used to thinking of tigers as fierce and untamable and of lambs as meek and gentle." Blake's use of symbol in "The Tyger" is different in that the poem blurs the usual distinction between symbol and symbolized, just as Blake blurs the distinction between body and soul in the prose texts we have seen. When Blake's writings are called condensed or obscure, it is perhaps because his work takes as given the necessity of symbolizing the inexpressible, and then hurries to get on with the business of discussing the infinite. In the case of this poem, once the name *tyger* has been mentioned, the poem immediately engages in this task.

When poems speak about the infinite, they very frequently do so by means of symbols that, in their literal senses, stand for physical power that clearly exceeds human capabilities. This seems a perfectly logical thing to do, but it also necessitates a certain kind of language and a very special scenario. In Thomson's poem, literal nature is overwhelming, frightening, threatening, uncontrollable (all adjectives that can apply to literal tigers, and all, arguably, applicable to the idea of infinity). But this is what the "Poetic Character" is able to perceive as positive also. It can do this because "the forms of all things are derived from their Genius," which seems to be the same thing as "the Infinite in all things," and we can therefore choose to accent either its "dark" or "bright" aspects.

## LYRICAL BALLADS

If Harold Bloom is right in his reading of Blake on "natural religion," we can perceive this infinite only if we are utterly possessed by the "Poetic Character." "Utterly possessed" sounds like madness—at the very least, it sounds like "a state of vivid sensation," the phrase used by William Wordsworth in his "Preface" to *Lyrical Ballads*. This collection was first published by Wordsworth and Coleridge in 1798, but without the preface, which was added in the second edition of 1800. Here is the first paragraph:

> The First Volume of these poems has already been submitted to general perusal. It was published, as an experiment which, I hoped, might be of some use to ascertain, how far, by fitting to metrical arrangement a selection of the real language of men in a state of vivid sensation, that sort of pleasure and that quantity of pleasure may be imparted, which a Poet may rationally endeavour to impart. (*Ballads* 241)

This raises all sorts of questions. How, for example, do we quantify pleasure? What kind of pleasure is it that a poet "may rationally endeavour to impart"? And is there such a thing as the "real language of men."

I shall take this last point first since the idea that there is indeed such a language is the basic assumption on which *Lyrical Ballads* is founded. Wordsworth begins by referring to the general debate on the association of ideas, but turns it into an attack on "poetic diction":

> It is supposed, that by the act of writing in verse an Author makes a formal engagement that he will gratify certain known habits of association, that he not only thus apprizes the Reader that certain classes of ideas and expressions will be found in his book, but that others will be

carefully excluded. The exponent or symbol held forth by metrical language in different areas of literature must have excited very different expectations: for example in the age of Catullus Terence and Lucretius, and that of Statius or Claudian, and in our own country, in the age of Shakespeare and Beaumont and Fletcher, and that of Donne and Cowley, or Dryden, or Pope. I will not take it upon me to determine the exact import of the promise which by the act of writing in verse and Author in the present day makes to his Reader; but I am certain it will appear to many persons that I have not fulfilled the terms of an engagement thus voluntarily contracted. (*Ballads* 225)

This is interesting first of all because of what it says about the relationship between author and reader, that the acts of writing *and* reading entail an agreement that certain things should be said in a certain way: that there are themes, for example, that are accepted as proper to poetry and that, it is also accepted, are to be expressed in a certain kind of language only. Closely related to this is the idea that metrical language "holds forth a symbol," so that it is the poem itself, the literary form, and not merely its intellectual content (what it says literally or allegorically), that is symbolic. If this is so, then different poetic forms should create different kinds of associations in readers' minds, and reading the first line of a sonnet that opens "My mistress' eyes are nothing like the sun" should lead us to expect a different development from that which we might expect from reading the first line of a limerick that opens "There was a young man from Japan." Also, beginning to read a text that we recognize as poetry should lead us to expect something different from what we would expect from a text that opens with, say, "milk one gallon, dozen eggs, two pounds bacon, tinfoil."

As this is very obviously the case, there seems to be something in Wordsworth's argument about metrical language and the implicit relationship it creates between author and reader. The nature of this relationship became one of the main focuses of critical debate in the twentieth century and remains so today. Wordsworth makes his own comment on it in the following, based on the brief "Advertisement" to the 1798 edition of *Ballads* but added to the 1802 "Preface": "They who have been accustomed to the gaudiness and inane phraseology of many modern writers, if they persist in reading this book to its conclusion, will, no doubt, frequently have to struggle with feelings of strangeness and aukwardness: they will look round for poetry, and will be induced to inquire by what species of courtesy these attempts can be permitted to assume that title" (*Ballads* 225).

Having thus generously refused to accept that gaudiness and inane phraseology might in fact be considered to constitute major elements of the real language of men, Wordsworth gives us a very concise, and very interesting, explanation of the purpose of *Lyrical Ballads*. Its aim is "to make the incidents of common life interesting by tracing in them, truly though not ostentatiously, the primary laws of our nature, chiefly as far as regards the manner in which we associate ideas in a state of excitement" (*Ballads* 244–45). This, too, raises a number of difficult questions. First of all, only someone who considers the incidents of common life uninteresting would think it necessary to make them interesting. Second, what is "common life" anyway? Third, "truly though not ostentatiously" seems to imply that expressions of truth usually demand or at least result in ostentation. Finally, how far can the language we adopt in a state of excitement be considered the real language of men?

In all of this we need to remember that Wordsworth's concern was with what he saw as the stilted, and therefore necessarily inexpressive, condition of contemporary poetry. With this in mind, we can understand his interest in states of excitement and what he calls "real" language. We can also take "ostentatiously" to refer to the undeniably turgid style of some of his contemporaries. We can think of the desire to reproduce a state of excitement as a desire to achieve natural language by surprising the speaker into forgetting his or her self-consciously rhetorical "poetic" style. For the same reason, Wordsworth decided to choose "low and rustic life" as the setting for many of the poems in *Lyrical Ballads*. Whatever our reactions today to an adjective like "low," we can follow, if not necessarily agree with, the reasoning that

> in that situation the essential passions of the heart find a better soil in which they can attain their maturity, are under less restraint, and speak a plainer and more emphatic language; because in that situation our elementary feelings exist in a state of greater simplicity and consequently may be more accurately contemplated and more forcibly communicated; because the manners of rural life germinate from those elementary feelings; and from the necessary character of rural occupations are more easily comprehended; and are more durable; and lastly, because in that situation the passions of men are incorporated with the beautiful and permanent forms of nature. (*Ballads* 226)

It would be mistaken to dismiss claims like "the manners of rural life germinate from those elementary feelings" as clichéd pastoral. If we do make this mistake it will be because we ourselves have unthinkingly accepted the associations that education and habit have taught us to make with "manners," "rural life," "elementary feelings," "rustic," and so on. If these ideas are now clichés, it is because we have helped to make them so. Wordsworth does not seek to romanticize, in the modern popular sense, the hardships of a life spent in agricultural labor, and his shepherds have better things to do than lounge about all day playing the flute. There is a world of difference between "The Passionate Shepherd to His Love" and holding that "the passions of men are incorporated with the beautiful and permanent forms of nature."

What kind of symbols can we expect from poetry that promises such plain speaking? After all, the 1802 "Preface" tells us that "the Reader will find that personifications of abstract ideas rarely occur in these volumes" (*Ballads* 231). The preface also speaks of the "rustic" language employed in the *Ballads* as "purified," and this will (I hope) remind readers of the other attempts at purification we have seen, also involving simplification and demystification, that collectively go under the heading Reformation. We must not be misled, however, into thinking of the publication of *Lyrical Ballads* as the beginning of an age of closed texts: there remain those "elementary feelings" and "permanent forms of nature," as well as those unpredictable states of "vivid sensation" and "excitement"; and I do not know of anyone who regards "The Rime of the Ancyent Marinere" as a closed text. In fact, we can see the attempt to simplify language in *Lyrical Ballads* as an opening up of texts, since what is being replaced is an elaborate but *known* poetic diction, while what replaces it is a "simple" but, in poetry, new language whose use must be reinterpreted.

The literary establishment reacted to this task with general disdain. The poet Robert Southey's response to *Lyrical Ballads* is a good example of an attitude toward poetry that makes a clear distinction between high and low culture and sees the everyday life of ordinary human beings as totally unfitting material for art:

> Of these experimental poems, the most important is the Idiot Boy. . . .
> Upon this subject the author has written nearly five hundred lines. . . .
> No tale less deserved the labor that appears to have been bestowed upon
> this. It resembles a Flemish picture in the worthlessness of its design and

the excellence of its execution. . . . The other ballads of this kind are as bald in story, and are not so highly embellished in narration. . . . In a very different style of poetry, is the Rime of the Ancyent Marinere, a ballad (says the advertisement) "professedly written in imitation of the *style,* as well as the spirit of the elder poets." We are tolerably conversant with the early English poets; and can discover no resemblance whatever, except in antiquated spelling and a few obsolete words. . . . We do not sufficiently understand the story to analyze it. It is a Dutch attempt at German sublimity. Genius has here been employed in producing a poem of little merit. (*Critical Review* 24 [1798]:197)

Southey was not so tolerably conversant with the early English poets as to recognize an allegory, even when it slapped him in the face, and his use of the word *genius* seems to be very different from Blake's. What he praises in "The Idiot Boy" is its "embellishment"—precisely the characteristic the "Preface" criticizes in poetic language; and his comments on Flemish painting, which in the sixteenth and seventeenth centuries produced a number of works celebrating the lower and middle classes whose language so interested Wordsworth, reveal an approach to art that has more to do with social prejudices than with critical acumen. (The French Académie was similarly dismissive of the impressionist painters, who reacted by establishing their own Salon des Refusés.) Southey in fact takes us back to the Renaissance ideal of noble art—not that it can spiritually ennoble human beings, but that it should take only noble deeds for its themes. For this reason, the theme of "The Idiot Boy" is "uninteresting," and for the same reason Wordsworth felt obliged to try to convince the readers of *Lyrical Ballads* that "incidents of common life" could be *made* interesting.

The following poem, however, "Lines left upon a Seat in a Yew-Tree," elicited a very different response from Southey:

> —Nay, Traveller! rest. This lonely yew-tree stands
> Far from all human dwelling: what if here
> No sparkling rivulet spread the verdant herb;
> What if these barren boughs the bee not loves;
> Yet if the wind breathe soft, the curling waves,
> That break against the shore, shall lull thy mind
> By one soft impulse saved from vacancy.
>   Who he was
> That piled these stones, and with the mossy sod

First covered o'er, and taught this aged tree,
Now wild, to bend its arms in circling shade,
I well remember.—He was one who own'd
No common soul. In youth, by genius nurs'd,
And big with lofty views, he to the world
Went forth, pure in his heart, against the taint
Of dissolute tongues, 'gainst jealousy, and hate,
And scorn, against all enemies prepared,
All but neglect: and so, his spirit damped
At once, with rash disdain he turned away,
And with the food of pride sustained his soul
In solitude.—Stranger! these gloomy boughs
Had charms for him; and here he loved to sit,
His only visitants a straggling sheep,
The stone-chat, or the glancing sand-piper;
And on these barren rocks, with juniper,
And heath, and thistle, thinly sprinkled o'er,
Fixing his downward eye, he many an hour
A morbid pleasure nourished, tracing here
An emblem of his own unfruitful life:
And lifting up his head, he then would gaze
On the more distant scene; how lovely 'tis
Thou seest, and he would gaze till it became
Far lovelier, and his heart could not sustain
The beauty still more beauteous. Nor, that time,
Would he forget those beings, to whose minds,
Warm from the labours of benevolence,
The world, and man himself, appeared a scene
Of kindred loveliness: then he would sigh
With mournful joy, to think that others felt
What he must never feel: and so, lost man!
On visionary views would fancy feed,
Till his eye streamed with tears. In this deep vale
He died, this seat his only monument.

If thou be one whose heart the holy forms
Of young imagination have kept pure,
Stranger! henceforth be warned; and know, that pride,
Howe'er disguised in its own majesty,
Is littleness; that he who feels contempt
For any living thing, hath faculties

161

Which he has never used; that thought with him
Is in its infancy. The man, whose eye
Is ever on himself, doth look on one,
The least of nature's works, one who might move
The wise man to that scorn which wisdom holds
Unlawful, ever. O, be wiser thou!
Instructed that true knowledge leads to love,
True dignity abides with him alone
Who, in the silent hour of inward thought,
Can still suspect, and still revere himself,
In lowliness of heart.

*Ballads* (1798)

Southey considered this poem "beautiful," and we can reasonably suppose he found its theme both a suitable one for poetry and sufficiently embellished. It is, after all, difficult to see how anyone could seriously claim the lines "what if here / No sparkling rivulet spread the verdant herb; / What if these barren boughs the bee not love" to exemplify "the real language of men," let alone describe them as "rustic." The lines are nonetheless important ones because they present a different picture of nature, not as pastoral idyll but as an emptiness (also a part of nature). From the seat beneath the yew, the "lost man" described in the poem was able to survey the landscape of the middle distance, and gaze upon it until "it became / Far lovelier, and his heart could not sustain/ The beauty still more beauteous." In other words, prolonged reflection on a particular object has the effect of (1) changing the appearance of the object in the imagination of the beholder, and (2) of revealing to the beholder a beauty in the object previously unrecognized.

I now want to suggest that what happens during the period of reflection is the attainment of the state of "vivid sensation," discussed at the beginning of the preface, that then affects "the manner in which we associate ideas"; further, that the revealed beauty that the heart "could not sustain" is that "elementary feeling" that leads to recognition of "permanent forms in nature"; and finally that these permanent forms are what Blake describes (though also not in "the real language of men") as "the Infinite in all things." Why, then, is the beholder in the poem, the builder of the seat beneath the yew, described as a lost man? Because "pride / Howe'er disguised in its own majesty / Is littleness," and because, in Blake's words,

"If any could desire what he is incapable of possessing, despair must be his eternal lot." If I am right in my reading of these lines from the yew-tree poem, we can say that the recognition of permanent forms, or the infinite, has failed insofar as the beholder of the scene of natural beauty remains spiritually alone. He has not allowed his vision of permanent forms to include himself as part of nature; or, in Blake's terms, he has not relinquished the Ratio in favor of the Infinite. If this seems too vague, we can try thinking of this failure to connect with nature as intellectual pride: a tutored, analytical approach to nature may well lead to a theoretical acceptance of the unity of all things, but not necessarily to the "lowliness of heart" that according to the preface is requisite for its practical application. This places the beholder, the lost man of the yew-tree poem, in a position similar to that of Milton's Satan who, when he considers the beauty of the newly created Eden—a beauty whose essence he very well comprehends—experiences a sense of loss and isolation that, for a time at least, overcomes even his own pride and disdain; for both of these characters it is a beauty that can be perceived by the intellect, but not wholly shared in.

Why did Southey think the yew-tree poem beautiful? Modern criticism is impatient of such statements ("I like this poem because I find it beautiful") because it holds the perception of beauty to an extremely personal reaction, too dependent on aleatory conditions and therefore insufficient in itself as a basis upon which to build a serious analysis. Of course, this does not mean that we are no longer allowed to find things beautiful or to like them because we think they are. But if we are to use beauty as a criterion, we must have some idea of what it is we mean, and what it is we mean must be applicable to more than the poem we happen to be discussing. A good theory is one that has been tested with consistent results on as many subjects as possible. Southey's poetic taste was clearly different from Wordsworth's; but Southey was no fool, and he understood that there is indeed a pleasure that the poet can "rationally endeavour to impart." Since he used the adjective *beautiful,* which we can safely associate with the idea of pleasure, to describe two other poems in *Lyrical Ballads,* Coleridge's "The Dungeon" and the "Lines Written Above Tintern Abbey," it will be a good idea to look at these poems also and try to find what they have in common with the lines on the yew tree. I am also going to discount the possibility that the pleasure we are discussing involves recognizing a simple confirmation of one's own personal opinions. This is certainly crucial, for if we cannot do this, the criteria of pleasure and beauty become purely subjective reactions and thus useless for the kind of reading that the *Ballads* preface demands of us.

Like the yew-tree poem, "Lines Written a few miles above Tintern Abbey" describes the contemplation of a landscape, and again the beholder is alone, physically distanced from the scene of human activity before him. Solitude is an important element in both poems because it means that there is nothing to distract the beholder's attention from the object of contemplation—there are no extraneous conditions that might affect the chain of associations created in the beholder's imagination. The objects noted—farms, orchards, hedgerows, wreaths of smoke—are all "forms of beauty" (l. 24) that the speaker of the poem has carried with him, in memory, "in lonely rooms, and mid the din / Of towns and cities" (lines 26–27). The poem then makes the suggestion that the mere memory of these forms of beauty can move humans to virtue: the feelings aroused by the memory are ones

> Of unremembered pleasure; such, perhaps,
> As may have had no trivial influence
> On that best portion of a good man's life;
> His little, nameless, unremembered acts
> Of kindness and of love.
>
> (lines 32–36)

Moreover, the poem connects these acts of kindness and love to a "more sublime" human faculty in which we cannot fail to recognize what Blake called the Poetic Character:

> that blessed mood,
> In which the burthen of the mystery,
> In which the heavy and the weary weight
> Of all this unintelligible world
> Is lighten'd:—that serene and blessed mood,
> In which the affections gently lead us on,
> Until, the breath of this corporeal frame,
> And even the motion of our human blood
> Almost suspended, we are laid asleep
> In body, and become a living soul:
> While with an eye made quiet by the power

> Of harmony, and the deep power of joy,
> We see into the life of things.
>
> (lines 38–49)

I think that what we have read of the preface, together with the two poems we have seen so far from *Lyrical Ballads,* justifies a reading of "the life of things" as equivalent to both "the beautiful and permanent forms of nature" and "the Infinite in all things." Also, it is not stretching the imagination too far to assume that this is what Southey recognized as beautiful in "Tintern Abbey" and "Lines left upon a Seat in a Yew-Tree." We now need to find out whether a reading of Coleridge's poem "The Dungeon" will produce similar results.

The poem is in fact taken from Coleridge's tragedy *Osorio* and is a soliloquy spoken by the imprisoned hero Albert, a victim of the Inquisition. The first nineteen lines discuss the injustice of an authority that is sustained by the poverty and ignorance in which it keeps those under its rule, and the useless cruelty of physical punishment for the crimes that are the inevitable result of those states. The way in which poverty and ignorance lead to corruption is described, to horrifying effect, in terms of psychological and physiological processes:

> Is this the only cure? Merciful God?          5
> Each pore and natural outlet shrivell'd up
> By ignorance and parching poverty,
> His energies roll back upon his heart,
> And stagnate and corrupt; till changed to poison,
> They break out on him, like a loathsome plague-spot;          10
> Then we call in our pamper'd mountebanks[2]—
> And this is their best cure! . . .
> . . . . . . . . . . . . . . . . .
>                    So he lies          16
> Circled with evil, till his very soul
> Unmoulds its essence, hopelessly deformed
> By sights of ever more deformity!

Evil breeds evil, and fire does not purify the soul—it merely burns, and the pain it causes brings human beings into such proximity with the indignity of their sufferings that healing becomes an impossibility. Lines 20 to 30 offer an alternative. Nature is presented as redeemer, and succeeds in this role where violence and punishment fail because of its irresistible power for good:

> With other ministrations thou, O nature!
> Healest thy wandering and distempered child:
> Thou pourest on him thy soft influences,
> Thy sunny hues, fair forms, and breathing sweets,
> Thy melodies of woods, and winds, and waters,
> Till he relent, and can no more endure
> To be a jarring and a dissonant thing,
> Amid this general dance and minstrelsy;
> But, bursting into tears, wins back his way,
> His angry spirit healed and harmonized
> By the benignant touch of love and beauty.

The lost soul is separated from nature and is therefore in a state of disbalance: "wandering and distempered," a "jarring and a dissonant thing," an "angry spirit." Nature counters this discord with its own harmony, which is manifested both physically in "fair forms," in "melodies of woods, and winds, and waters," and spiritually in "the benignant touch of love and beauty." Nature is thus perfect, being spiritually and physically good. The speaker here, and the character described in the yew-tree poem, are both moved to tears, a sense of rebelonging, and in the yew-tree poem because of his inability to make the leap of faith (and act of humility) necessary to allow his readmittance into society.

It is easy to see a religious significance to nature in both of these poems, especially in "The Dungeon." In each, nature can be seen as holding out the possibility of redemption; in each nature teaches by example, rather than by the threat of punishment (so that free will is also a factor in the redemptive process); and in each it is the physical, outward form of nature that leads to an understanding of spiritual content, the "permanent forms" or "Infinite in all things" in the same way as the physical Christ, Word made flesh, leads to God, who is also the infinite in all things. Though the "fair forms" of nature work in different ways in each text—through direct observation in the yew-tree poem, through memory in "Tintern Abbey," and as a proposition in "The Dungeon"—it is always the idea of an infinite, unifying spirit that lies behind them.

As with Blake, nature is more than nature: it is a language of symbols speaking of the infinite in each object that the senses perceive. In this sense, the natural world is still very much like the one so painstakingly codified and categorized in medieval encyclopedias and bestiaries. Unlike Blake, however, Wordsworth describes in some detail the process by which the symbol leads to the symbolized. We can partially explain it by using the yew-tree poem as an example: the beholder reflects on an object, here a landscape, in a particular state of mind that the *Ballads* preface calls one of "vivid sensation." In the beholder's imagination, the object, the landscape, takes on characteristics other than those that were immediately apparent in it (in the case of the yew-tree poem, this means that the intrinsic beauty of the scene is revealed to the beholder). In effect, the landscape becomes another one place—one where various associations are created. In other words, we can say that the beholder turns the original, literal landscape into a symbolic one, which he then interprets in an allegorical sense (in this case a spiritual one). Of course, the original landscape remains a literal one, but we can clearly read it as symbolic also because we know from the text that it has conveyed a spiritual message to the beholder.

This sounds like the understanding of symbols as explained by the early commentators on Scripture and later applied to secular literature by Dante. But, yet again, there is a difference in that an extra step has been added to the process of interpretation. For Augustine and Aquinas, certain scriptural texts were, at the same time, both historical narrative and allegory. In the yew-tree poem, however, symbols seem to work in two distinct ways. In lines 25–29 we read:

> And on these barren rocks, with juniper
> And heath, and thistle, thinly sprinkled o'er,
> Fixing his downward eye, he many an hour
> A morbid pleasure nourished, tracing here
> An emblem of his own unfruitful life.

Here there is no intermediate stage between symbol and symbolized: the literal landscape itself is interpreted as a reflection of the beholder's "unfruitful life." This is the way allegory works for the church fathers (except, of course, for the fact that we are here discussing secular poetry). However, in the lines immediately following, something happens to the literal landscape before it begins to function as a symbol:

And lifting up his head, he then would gaze        30
On the more distant scene; how lovely 'tis
Thou seest, and he would gaze till it became
Far lovelier, and his heart could not sustain
The beauty still more beauteous . . .
. . . . . . . . . . . . . . . . . . . .
On visionary views would fancy feed        41
Till his eye streamed with tears.

The landscape becomes "still more beauteous." This seems to be a necessary development before "visionary views" can present themselves to the imagination and we are able to perceive the "permanent forms" of nature that in turn lead to a real understanding of "kindred loveliness" (l.38).

How does this transformation occur? According to the preface, it seems to happen during the actual process of writing poetry:

> I have said that Poetry is the spontaneous overflow of powerful feelings: it takes its origin from emotion recollected in tranquillity: the emotion is contemplated till by a species of reaction the tranquillity gradually disappears, and an emotion, similar to that which was before the subject of contemplation, is gradually produced, and does itself actually exist in the mind. In this mood, successful composition generally begins, and in a mood similar to this it is carried on (*Ballads* 246).

Finally, all of this happens to the poet in particular because he (no mention yet of poet as woman) is

> endued with more lively sensibility, more enthusiasm and tenderness, who has a greater knowledge of human nature, and a more comprehensive soul, than are supposed to be common among mankind; a man pleased with his own passions and volitions, and who rejoices more than other men in the spirit of life that is in him; delighting to contemplate similar volitions and passions as manifested in the goings-on of the Universe, and habitually impelled to create them where he does not find them (*Ballads* 237).

How are we to read this? A man of more than average soul, sensibility, and tenderness sounds like an aspiring saint, while a man "pleased with his own passions and volitions," on the other hand, sounds like an egotistical monster. The really interesting claim is that the poet habitually creates "volitions and passions" where he does not find them occurring naturally. In other words, the poet *creates* what Locke called unnatural associations, sees connections where there are in fact none, and creates something out of nothing. It turns out that the medieval commentators were right and anything at all can be a symbol. What they most definitely did *not* mean by this was that symbolic representation depended on the volitions of the poet. For them, the universe spoke always of God and therefore everything in it was a potential symbol for him—it depended on how Scripture used the object in question. When Blake talks of the infinite in all things, which is God, the difference between his approach and theirs is that he allows secular texts to work in the same way as Scripture. What they have in common is that the symbolized remains ultimately unknowable.

The approach to symbolic representation put forward in the preface to *Lyrical Ballads* and in the poems themselves is different in several ways. First, according to the preface, the language of poetic representation need not be mysterious or mystical: it can be—indeed, it should be—the "real language of men." Second, though what is finally revealed as the symbolized is "kindred loveliness," the preface stresses the personal nature of both relationships involved—that between what we have called the beholder and the symbol and that between the beholder and his or her interpretation of it. One possibility opened up by this personal relationship is demonstrated in the yew-tree poem, where the beholder perceives "kindred loveliness," but rejects or cannot share in it. Another characteristic of this relationship is the emphasis it places on the poet's own role in creating the symbol; and where the medieval allegorists (and Blake) could help themselves to a ready-made universe of symbols, we now have to create our own by first attaining a state of "vivid sensation" and "excitement." This cannot be the same thing as divine inspiration, because if it were we could treat secular texts in the same way as Augustine treated the Old Testament. All the same, "kindred loveliness" and "permanent forms" remain ideas, and rather vague ideas at that. This vagueness could easily be resolved if we were to substitute "God" for "the Infinite" and "permanent forms" and, in the Christian tradition, "Holy Spirit" for "kindred loveliness." But the *Ballads* preface does not do this; and Blake's visionary Christian poetry was the exception, rather than the rule. If "permanent form" and "God" are not always the same thing, then God is no longer always the ultimate symbolized, the medieval equation of symbol with allegory can no longer function, and the univocal world has finally collapsed.

# SYMBOL AND ALLEGORY

## IDEAL WORLDS AND REAL WORLDS

"Symbolism," wrote the German poet Johann Wolfgang von Goethe (1749–1832), "transforms the experience into an idea and an idea into an image, so that the idea expressed through the image remains always active and unattainable and, even though expressed in all languages, remains inexpressible." Here Goethe recognizes the central paradox of much poetry. Logically, we must reject the notion that something inexpressible can be expressed even in one, let alone in all languages. Yet a poem is a text. It uses words that readers attempt to interpret. Until quite recently, interpreting a text was generally taken to mean discovering its meaning, and in the same tradition that meaning was taken to refer to the "message" the author of the poem intended to send. However, modern criticism now appreciates the impossibility of knowing precisely what an author's intention was. For one thing, most of the authors read by students of literature are likely to be dead authors, and communication beyond the grave is not accepted as an academic method. But even if a living author were to say: "This poem of mine means such-and-such, and this symbol I use stands for so-and-so," we recognize the right of every reader to add: "But I, because of my own personal experience and because of the aleatory conditions affecting my own life, always and automatically associate the same symbol with something different."

Goethe's definition of symbolism, and the hypothetical reader's response I have just given, are both possible only in a system of interpretation that allows for personal symbols. This is because, in a world where all symbols are seen as having the same ultimate source, they must also be seen as standing ultimately for the same thing. In the case of the medieval tradition of interpretation, the source was God. Goethe's definition retains a similarity with the medieval one insofar as there is still an "inexpressible," but what it "expresses" is no longer automatically attributable to a divinity. A modern reader will recognize this "inexpressible" in the sudden feeling caused by, say, gazing at the ocean, or the stars—most people, I think, will be able to confirm such an experience. The same people, in my experience, cannot put this feeling into words in such as way as to really define it or to offer a logical explanation of it (they tend to use words associated with the ideas of vastness, eternity, infinity, oneness, and so on). It seems not to matter whether we are talking about stars or oceans, whales or dolphins, music or poetry, or mountains or fishing—the feeling seems to be very similar in all cases.

There are problems specific to the world of personal symbols and personal responses—the problem of "meaning"—and these will form the subject of this final chapter. For the time being, here is Goethe's definition of allegory: "Allegory transforms experience into a concept and a concept into an image, but so that the concept remains always defined and expressible by the image." The difference between this and symbolism is obvious: it lies in the fact that what is expressed by the image in allegory is not a nebulous idea or feeling, but something "defined and expressible." This makes symbolic texts far more open than allegorical ones, and, perhaps for this reason, by the end of Goethe's century the critical emphasis was definitely upon symbolism, in France especially, with Baudelaire (1821–67) restating that the Platonic world of ideal forms was attainable though poetry; with Verlaine's claim, in his poem "Art Poétique" (1874), that it is above all the musicality of "pure" poetry that can lead to this ideal world through suggestion; with the article in *Le Figaro* by Jean Moréas (1886) claiming that Romanticism was dead; and with Stéphane Mallarmé (1842–98), who claimed that symbolism involved gradually evoking an object "so as to reveal a mood" through "a series of decipherings" (Mallarmé 1891).

In England, the period between Goethe and the French symbolists is that of the later Romantics and the Victorians, and one in which the personalization of symbols becomes more and more apparent; but it seems to be the personalization of reactions to symbols that now poses the problem for students. We can still read Wordsworth's "Steamboats, Viaducts, and Railways" (1835) as an expression of the "permanent forms" of nature even if the objects symbolizing those forms have changed so radically since the publication of the *Lyrical Ballads* "Preface" that to a modern reader they may well seem anomalous:

> Motions and Means, on land and sea at war
> With old poetic feeling, not for this,
> Shall ye, by Poets even, be judged amiss!
> Nor shall your presence, howsoe'er it mar
> The loveliness of Nature, prove a bar
> To the mind's gaining that prophetic sense
> Of future change, that point of vision, whence
> May be discovered what in soul ye are.
> In spite of all that beauty may disown
> In your harsh features, Nature doth embrace
> Her lawful offspring in Man's art; and Time,
> Pleased with your triumphs o'er his brother Space,
> Accepts from your bold hands the proffered crown
> Of hope, and smiles on you with cheer sublime.

Even Tennyson's poem "The Kraken" (1830) manages, by the use of a single phrase from the Book of Revelation ("the latter fire") to use a new understanding of science—in particular of geological time—to make mythological creatures refer back to an essentially Christian view of the unity of all things in nature:

> Below the thunders of the upper deep,
> Far, far beneath in the abysmal sea,
> His ancient, dreamless, uninvaded sleep
> The Kraken sleepeth: faintest sunlights flee
> About his shadowy sides; above him swell
> Huge sponges of millennial growth and height;
> And far away into the sickly light,
> From many a wonderous grot and secret cell
> Unnumbered and enormous polypi
> Winnow with giant arms the slumbering green.
> There hath he lain for ages, and will lie
> Battening upon huge sea worms in his sleep,
> Until the latter fire shall heat the deep;
> Then once by man and angels to be seen,
> In roaring he shall rise and on the surface die.

But a later poem by Tennyson, the short "Flower in the Crannied Wall" (1869), presents a very different approach. Where earlier poems used nature to symbolize ultimate unity in God, this one seems to accept this as a possibility but at the same time to admit that this acceptance brings us no nearer an understanding of what that unity means:

> Flower in the crannied wall,
> I pluck you out of the crannies,
> I hold you here, root and all, in my hand,
> Little flower—but if I could understand
> What you are, root and all, and all in all,
> I should know what God and man is.

The poem also introduces the possibility of chance into our conception of the universe: how did the flower get into the crannied wall in the first place? If it were planted by human hand, we would have a nice analogy to God's creation. But what if it is there merely because a seed was carried there by the wind? Did God want the wind to drop the seed in precisely that spot? There is always the answer "God works in mysterious ways," but in this poem it is self-evidently not a satisfactory one. The flower certainly symbolizes *something,* and can indeed be read as standing for that "Infinite" and those "permanent forms" we have already discussed; but the poem is not content simply to have made the point—it wants to understand it in a way that involves more than just recognition.

If the nature of poetic symbols was being reassessed, a contemporary of Tennyson's was producing remarkable allegorical poems—dramatic monologues that reworked, or reevaluated, Renaissance themes as Renaissance poets had reworked medieval ones. The poems of Robert Browning (1812–89), especially the dramatic monologues, are, stylistically at least, so different from the work of his contemporaries that at first reading they seem not to belong to the same period at all. But Browning and Tennyson both give expression to some of the major intellectual and spiritual concerns of their time—religious doubt, the role of the artist, the problem of good and evil. Browning's case is interesting because many of his poems are truly allegorical, and the allegorical mode is now usually associated with the Middle Ages. By "truly allegorical" I mean allegorical in the senses we have discussed in earlier chapters: the medieval and Dantesque senses. What makes Browning's allegories different is that they also manage to

173

include the "defined and expressible" of Goethe's definition. This depends on an understanding both of Browning's own religious faith and of his own understanding of himself as poet. I admit that these two conditions, particularly the second one, are very vague indeed and seem about to lead us astray along a devious path toward the author and away from the text. All the same, Browning did have religious faith, and he was concerned with the role of the artist in society.

We can redirect our attention toward the text, and keep our nebulous conditions in mind at the same time, by looking at the poem "Fra Lippo Lippi"—a dramatic monologue given to the painter and friar Filippo Lippi, also a profligate, and periodic consumer of copious quantities of wine, general scapegrace, and protegé of Cosimo de' Medici, the Florentine ruler who recognized Filippo's enormous abilities. In other words, the poem is about a man of religious faith (in spite of certain forgivable weaknesses) with an interest in the role of the artist in society. It is allegorical because there is a "literal" Filippo, based, however loosely, on the historical one, who narrates, talks to himself, and responds to unspoken (i.e., unwritten) questions by officers of the night watch who have stopped him on his way home to the Medici residence: the poem makes sense as narrative, as a dramatization, as an entertaining historical reconstruction; but the words of this literal character constitute, among other things, a discourse on the possibility of interpreting art in a spiritual sense, or the possibility of art representing the spiritual world. In the following lines, the Filippo of the poem "quotes" the words of a prior who objects to the painter's too realistic representation:

> "How? what's here?
> Quite from the mark of painting, bless us all!
> Faces, arms, legs and bodies like the true
> As much as pea and pea! it's devil's game!
> Your business is not to catch men with show,
> With homage to the perishable clay,
> But lift them over it, ignore them all,
> Make them forget there's such a thing as flesh.
> Your business is to paint the souls of men—
> Man's soul—and it's a fire, smoke . . . no, it's not . . .
> It's vapor done up like a newborn babe—
> (In that shape when you die it leaves your mouth)
> It's . . . well, what matters talking, it's the soul!

Give us no more of body than shows soul!
Here's Giotto, with his Saint a-praising God,
That sets us praising—why not stop with him?
Why put all thought of praise out of our head
With wonder at lines, colors, and what not?
Paint the soul, never mind the legs and arms!
Rub all out, try at it a second time.
Oh, that white smallish female with the breasts?
She's just my niece . . . Herodias, I would say—
Who went and danced and got men's heads cut off!
Have it all out!"

("Fra Lippo Lippi" lines 175–98)

The prior's criticism of what he is observing is a compendium of medieval opinion in the Aristotelian tradition expressed by a rather unimaginative representative of church authority: the idea that art can lead to spiritual awareness becomes in the prior an exhortation to paint "no more of the body than shows soul."

Our prior is no Neoplatonist, for he does not see beauty in the human body—at least, he does not see that kind of beauty that is the outward manifestation of "the Infinite in all things," though he does seem to develop a more finely tuned aesthetic sense when it comes to his young niece's breasts. But he does not, or cannot, see the human form as beautiful in itself, as part of creation. We know that we are meant to find his instructions to "paint the soul" ludicrous, not only because he might just as well have said "Go and fetch the Moon" but also because of his own spectacular failure to represent the soul with language. His words seem a mockery of Pseudo-Dionysius's description of the all-encompassing and self-contradictory One, and his "what matters talking!" is absurd because it undermines his own authority, which depends very much on preaching, expounding Scripture, the words of the Mass and of absolution: "talking" matters a great deal. If he does not think of words as signs, the importance of other kinds of signification does not, however, escape his comprehension. One example he gives of the "right" kind of sign is the painting by Giotto he mentions, "with his Saint a-praising God / That set us praising," and his suggestion that we—Filippo, art, philosophy, the world and its history—should "stop with him" sounds rather like the suggestion a dinosaur might make to the effect that it really would be better for everyone if that ice age didn't come any nearer.

In a sense, the prior is right, if only he knew it. What he is witnessing (at least in my interpretation of Browning's Filippo's prior's reported commentary) is the end of the approach to interpretation of the age he symbolizes. His formulation of that approach is not a very good one, but Browning's Filippo cannot allow it to be a good one since this would obviously weaken his own argument. The lines immediately following the prior's are given to Filippo, and he uses them to tell us what is wrong with the old interpretive theory:

> Now, is this sense, I ask?
> A fine way to paint soul, by painting body
> So ill, the eye can't stop there, must go further
> And can't fare worse! Thus, yellow does for white
> When what you put for yellow's simply black,
> And any sort of meaning looks intense
> When all beside itself means and looks naught.
> Why can't a painter lift each foot in turn,
> Left foot and right foot, go a double step,
> Make his flesh liker and his soul more like,
> Both in their order? Take the prettiest face,
> The Prior's niece . . . patron-saint—is it so pretty
> You can't discover if it means hope, fear,
> Sorrow or joy? won't beauty go with these?
> Suppose I've made her eyes all right and blue,
> Can't I take breath and try to add life's flash,
> And then add soul and heighten them threefold?
> Or say there's beauty with no soul at all—
> (I never saw it—put the case the same—)
> If you get simple beauty and naught else,
> You get about the best thing God invents:
> That's somewhat: and you'll find the soul you have missed,
> Within yourself, when you return him thanks.
> "Rub all out!" Well, well, there's my life in short,
> And so the thing has gone on ever since.
>                                    (lines 198–222)

The point being made in the first seven lines of this extract is that an imperfectly executed representation of the body is unlikely to lead to a clear perception of the soul. A beautiful body, even one "with no soul," is, according to Browning's Filippo, "about the best thing God invents," and the understanding of the body as God's work leads to the discovery of one's own soul. This is a rather problematic theory because it excludes those bodies not thought beautiful. Perhaps our painter has had a few drinks too many this evening, or perhaps he assumes we take as a given that the appreciation of purely physical beauty is a subjective reaction anyway. At any rate, the concern he expresses is with progress, and this clearly allegorical passage works by having him stopped by the representatives of civil authority in his progress back to the Medici residence—the place where he is allowed to paint as he wishes—just as his artistic progress was halted by a representative of church authority.

This Filippo, though, seems to think that progress is not a rejection of the church itself but a desire to extend interpretive possibilities. He sees that the physical is a part of creation, but more than a world of symbols that all stand for God; nor is it necessarily a stumbling block placed by God in the way of the soul. (In this way, Blake could celebrate his tiger for its perfection of *physical* form, just as much as he could celebrate his lamb as symbol for Christ.) This Lippi understands that "The world and life's too big to pass for a dream" (l. 231); and even while he creates his unauthorized works, he is constantly aware of "the garden and God there / A-making man's wife: and, [his] lesson learned, / The value and significance of flesh." This constitutes an interpretation of the nature of humans as more than mere clay, more than a perishable casing for an eternal spirit that longs to return to its creator. Despising the flesh and the senses (aesthetic response is response of the senses) is therefore the same thing as despising a part of God's work of creation. This can also, however, be read as a reflection of the Victorian idea that God's intention was to create an imperfect world as a kind of experiment—a testing ground for humans. It follows from this notion, at least in Browning's use of it, that perfection is represented by heaven and that the human soul must be immortal in order to attain that state. If God wanted an imperfect world, the imperfect humans who inhabit it are nonetheless created according to God's will, and their form, including its physical aspect, is therefore something that demonstrates God's work and can be celebrated as such.

Those forms that do not accord with traditional ideas of beauty and perfection find a champion in poet and Jesuit priest Gerard Manley Hopkins (1844–89). His poem "Pied Beauty" (1877) is essentially a celebration of the variety of physical forms, but these forms are clearly related to the all-inclusive nature of God, and we can here allow ourselves to be

177

reminded, not only by the idea of variety but also by the unusual use of language used in the poem, of the self-contradictory (because all-inclusive and all-creating) One as described by Pseudo-Dionysius:

> Glory be to God for dappled things —
>    For skies of couple-colour as a brindled cow;
>        For rose-moles all in stipple upon trout that swim;
> Fresh-firecoal chestnut-falls, finches wings;
>    Landscape plotted and pieced — fold, fallow, and plough;
>        And all trades, their gear and tackle and trim.
>
> All things counter, original, spare, strange;
>    Whatever is fickle, freckled (who knows how?)
>        With swift, slow; sweet, sour; adazzle, dim;
> He fathers-forth whose beauty is past change:
>        Praise him.

Especially the contrasts made between "swift, slow; sweet, sour; adazzle, dim" recall Dionysius's "flashing darkness." But though this poem uses words in an exciting and unusual way, it does not represent a new approach to poetic symbolism: every object named in this text, and every quality the text endows it with, is, of necessity, part of the old univocal world in which all phenomena are signs that speak of God and thus lead us to him. In this way, "Pied Beauty" is an allegorical poem in the sense Augustine would have acknowledged, a retelling of the story of Creation.

Hopkins did not particularly like Browning's work. Occasional comments he made imply that he thought it vulgar (in the modern sense; i.e., crude). I have claimed here that "Fra Lippo Lippi" is essentially an allegorical poem, while the example I have taken from Hopkins's work, "Pied Beauty," can be read in the old allegorical senses as laid down in the tradition of Augustine and Aquinas. Given Hopkins's religious background, this is not necessarily surprising, but there is another way of thinking about the differences between their respective approaches to poetry, and it is closely connected with Goethe's definitions of symbolism and allegory. Goethe thought that in symbolism the idea expressed by the image remained undefined and unattainable (God, for example), while an allegory, he says, tells us about a concept that, though also presented through an image, can be defined. Perhaps his distinction between idea and concept is a useful one to retain here, and in what follows I shall therefore use *idea* to mean the undefined and *concept* to mean the defined.

But before we use Goethe's theory to look at the two poems we have just seen, I want to bring in another witness, and a rather unlikely one, too. The Utilitarian philosopher John Stuart Mill (1806–73) turned to poetry, he tells us in his autobiography, during a period of depression, and he published a number of essays on the subject. I shall quote a passage from his essay *The Two Kinds of Poetry,* in which he discusses association, poetic representation, and the relationship between poem and its subject matter in a way that helps to formulate a working distinction between symbol and allegory and at the same time to clarify Goethe's comments:

> Whom, then, shall we call poets? Those who are so constituted, that emotions are the links of association by which their ideas, both sensuous [i.e., related to the senses] and spiritual, are connected together. This constitution belongs (within certain limits) to all in whom poetry is a pervading principle. In all others, poetry is something extraneous and superinduced: something out of themselves, foreign to the habitual course of their every-day lives and characters; a quite other world, to which they make occasional visits, but where they are sojourners, not dwellers, and which, when out of it, or even when in it, they think of, peradventure, but as a phantom-world, a place of *ignes fatui* and spectral illusions. Those only who have the peculiarity of association we have mentioned, and which is one of the natural consequences of intense sensibility, instead of seeming not themselves when they are uttering poetry, scarcely seem themselves when they are uttering anything to which poetry is foreign. Whatever be the thing which they are contemplating, the aspect under which it first and most naturally paints itself to them, is its poetic aspect. The poet of culture sees his object in prose, and describes it in poetry; the poet of nature [i.e., *by* nature; the "born" poet] actually sees it in poetry. (*Essays* 31–32)

Mill's description of the person who "sojourns" rather than "dwells" in the realm of poetry might well be a reference to himself—he would certainly have agreed. In fact, he made the distinction between the "poet of culture" and the "poet of nature" in order to refer to Wordsworth and Shelley, respectively, both of whom, by the way, he considered great poets who produced "true and enduring poetry" (*Essays* 34), so that "poet of culture" is not to be understood as a derogatory term.

Mill paraphrases, from the point of view of a philosopher interested in association, Wordsworth's own description of the creative process by beginning with the idea that, in Wordsworth, "the poetry is almost always the mere setting of a thought." The word *setting* has both musical and theatrical associations—a text may be set to music or a mise-en-scène—and this certainly recalls what Wordsworth has to say about ideas being set in metrical language. Mill admits that "the thought may be more valuable than the setting"—that is, that we can clearly see that the poem's intellectual content is what is valuable in it—but adds that "there can be no question as to which was first in his mind: what he is impressed with, and what he is anxious to impress, is some proposition . . . some truth, or something which he deems such." Mill then echoes Wordsworth's description of the writing process when he claims that "he lets the thought dwell in his mind, till it excites, as is the nature of thought, other thoughts, and also such feelings as the measure of his sensibility is adequate to supply."

Shelley, for Mill, is "the very reverse of all this":

Where Wordsworth is strong, he is weak; where Wordsworth is weak, he is strong. Culture, that culture by which Wordsworth has reared from his own inward nature the richest harvest ever brought forth by a soil of so little depth, is precisely what was wanting to Shelley: or let us rather say, he had not, at the period of his deplorably early death, reached sufficiently far in that intellectual progression of which he was capable. . . . For him, intentional mental discipline had done [i.e., would have done] little; the vividness of his emotions had done all. He seldom follows up an idea; it starts into life, summons from the fairy-land of his inexhaustible fancy some three of four bold images, then vanishes, and straight he is off on the wings of some casual association into quite another sphere. . . . The thoughts and images are suggested by the feeling, and are such as it finds unsought. (*Essays* 36–37)

It seems we can read Mill's terms "thought" and "feeling" as roughly synonymous with Goethe's "concept" and "idea." This becomes a more concrete proposition when we read the following paragraph from the same essay:

The difference, then, between the poetry of a poet, and the poetry of a cultivated but not poetical mind is that in the latter, with however bright a halo of feeling the thought be surrounded and glorified, the thought itself is still the conspicuous object; while the poetry of a poet is Feeling itself, employing thought only as the medium of its utterance. In the one feeling waits upon the thought; in the other, thought upon feeling. The one writer has a distinct aim, common to him with any other didactic author; he desires to convey the thought, and he conveys it clothed in the feelings which it excites in himself, or which he deems most appropriate to it. The other merely pours forth the overflowing of his feelings; and all the thoughts which those feelings suggest are floated promiscuously [i.e., indiscriminately, confusedly] along the stream. (*Essays* 33–34)

If we accept Mill's critical approach (many of his contemporaries did not) and consider it in the light of Goethe's distinction between symbol and allegory, we need to reassess our view of Wordsworth's "Yew-Tree" and "Tintern Abbey" as expressions of "permanent forms" that cannot be defined. This becomes necessary because, though on the one hand they seem to employ symbols (nature) in Goethe's sense to express an inexpressible universal, on the other hand they are also, according to Mill, the product of a process that begins with a thought (i.e., a concept), which then produces an image, and these two approaches to interpretation are apparently incompatible. We can see that Goethe's distinction has in some ways made things easier, but that it has also brought with it problems of its own, especially in cases such as those we are discussing in which two very reasonable-sounding theories overlap. (The same, of course, could be said of Mill's theory).

In fact, this is not such a problem after all. No one is obliged to choose one theory over another. In practical terms, say that a student is given the task of writing an essay on "Tintern Abbey" taking into account contemporary, or more or less contemporary, interpretive theories—he or she is presented not with a choice between a "right" and a "wrong" approach, but with the opportunity to make use of both (or of as many as happen to be available), exploring the interpretive possibilities that each has to offer. In the present example, this means that our student can reasonably discuss "Tintern Abbey" in terms of what Wordsworth wrote in the preface about "permanent forms" and think of nature as a symbol that leads us to them. Also, especially if we feel that a relation between "permanent forms" and "undefined" can be sustained, it is useful and productive to read the poem according to Goethe's definition of symbolism. On the other hand, if we

181

are prepared to think of "permanent forms" as a concept that can be satisfactorily expressed, we can justify thinking of "Tintern Abbey" as an allegorical poem and then see what happens when we compare it with other allegorical poems. If we agree with Mill in seeing the poem first and foremost as a text constructed around a "thought," a "proposition" to be communicated and understood, we have made a connection between Mill's "thought" and Goethe's "concept." And if we feel that we can economically develop this connection, we end up with a series of relations that looks something like: *idea—feeling; concept—thought;* and then, *idea—feeling—symbol; concept—thought—allegory.* Perhaps this seems rather technical, but it is only a reduction into more manageable terms of some of the things Goethe and Mill wrote about poetry using more words than can be easily remembered.

We should remember that these approaches to "Tintern Abbey" (and that all approaches to all poems) exist *at the same time.* Whether we happen to agree with one approach and not with another is of only secondary importance: the interest lies in trying them all out and seeing what happens when we do. I now want to try out another approach and see if turning an idea or a concept into an image is anything like "evoking" an object little by little so as to "reveal" a mood through which, or in which, an ideal world can be attained. But we first need to know what an ideal world is.

## SYMBOL AND IMAGE: T. E. HULME, EZRA POUND, T. S. ELIOT

An ideal world might be the kind of place Plato was talking about—a world of ideas or forms that we experience at second hand through the objects representing them physically. Some ideas, however—erotic love, for example—do not have physical representations in the same way that a physical table represents the idea of a table. In order to replace this missing physical form, we invent symbols or endow known physical objects with symbolic values. So, in the case of erotic love, we can refer to mythological characters like Eros, Aphrodite, or Cupid, or to a natural symbol like the rose. We can then write allegorical poems about roses budding and opening, roses in full bloom, roses fading, the short life of the bloom, and so on; and about the tricks played on humans by gods and demigods with a mean sense of humor. Plato was less philosophically interested in this kind of love than in the heavenly variety, the love of God that fills the human soul with constant yearning to return to its creator, and he told the allegorical story of how the soul sprouts wings in its endeavor to do so, carrying us higher and higher up a spiritual ladder toward God as we leave the worldly and the physical further and further behind. We know that Plato's argument against art was that it makes this upward progress impossible because it takes us away from God's ideas, rather than closer to them. (There is, of course, a nice irony in the fact that he used a powerful poetic device in order to illustrate his understanding of the soul's relationship with God.) We also know that thinking of everything as God's idea provides an ultimate unifying element that, if we want to call ourselves Neoplatonic mystics or hermetists, we can then use to connect everything with everything else. Even if we prefer other labels, we can still, as we have seen, talk about the "Infinite in all things" and about "permanent forms" in nature, but in order to do this we have to side with Aristotle, rather than with Plato: God (presumably) wants virtuous human beings; virtue involves (among other things) recognizing God; art can lead to virtue by representing it. We also know that we can equate "permanent forms" and the "Infinite in all things" with God, and that we can see art as revealing both.

An ideal world needs an idealistic philosophy to sustain it, and histories of philosophy traditionally distinguish between objective and subjective idealism: Plato's theory of Forms, according to which visible nature is the physical manifestation of essential ideas that can nonetheless be directly recognized by human beings, is an example of objective idealism. According to subjective idealism, on the other hand, it is human reason and understanding upon which reality depends for its existence: the world that may or may not exist outside a relationship with an observer is of no interest except as a possibility that exists only because that observer can imagine such a world and thus establish a relationship with it. The difference here between recognizing and imagining lies in the emphasis placed by subjective realism on the role of the observer (i.e., the subject of the transitive verb *to observe*): the imagined world is the result of the observer's own activity and not a thing-in-itself existing independently of human experience.

If, as the French symbolist poets claimed, there is an ideal world to which poetry can lead us by evoking an object little by little in order, "by a series of decipherings," to "reveal a mood," our perception or understanding of it must be dependent on attaining this mood, since the symbolists made it the final rung in their own Heavenly Ladder. The problem

183

is that "mood" is a subjective reaction dependent on association—not all readers will make the same ones because the same object will evoke different reactions in different people. The same goes for "a series of decipherings"—these, too, must depend on association, again dependent on the reader's own history and environment. Even if the symbolists meant the mood of the author, and thought it to be the job of the reader to decipher it, the same conditions apply. In this way, their claims for poetry have a lot to do with subjective idealism.

In English poetry and poetics, the symbolists' ideas began to be combined with that expressed in the preface to *Lyrical Ballads*—that poetry should be written in the "real language of men." According to this approach, by using "ordinary" language to create vivid images, art can beautify the ordinary. The philosopher and poet T. E. Hulme (1883–1917) gives a good example of how this works in his *Notes on Language and Style* (c. 1907), ideas he jotted down for future use in extended essays. About half of these ideas were published, still in note form, in T. S. Eliot's journal *Criterion* (1925). I will cite an example: "The beauty of London only seen in detached and careful moments, never continuously, always a conscious effort. On top of a bus, or the sweep of the avenue in Hyde Park. But to appreciate this must be in some manner detached" (Hulme 27).

And it is not only the detachment of the observer that evokes a perception of beauty but the suddenness of the apparition: a "light-haired woman with upturned face in Regent Street," for example. Literature is "a method of sudden arrangement of commonplaces. The *suddenness* makes us forget the commonplace." Or again: "Literature, like memory, selects only the vivid patches of life. The art of abstraction. If literature (realistic) did really resemble life, it would be interminable, dreary, commonplace, eating and dressing, buttoning, with here and there a patch of vividness" (Hulme 27). Or, to put it yet another way: "Life composed of exquisite moments and the rest shadows of them" (Hulme 27). It is difficult to see how there can be a universal vivid or "exquisite" moment unless it is the same thing as a perception of the "Infinite" or of the "permanent forms" discussed by Blake and Wordsworth; or unless it is a perception of God in all things as discussed by medieval and Renaissance exegetes, poets, and theorists.

Why should poetry be interested in making a sudden arrangement of commonplaces? Because poetry is for the entertainment of "bankers and other sedentary armchair people in after-dinner moods," "for use of clerks in love to send to sweethearts," and to evoke "temporary moods (in the-atres) of cultivated artificial people." This view of poetry leads Hulme to discuss the relation between author and reader:

> Just as Aristotle asserts that Matter the unlimited contains Forms em-bedded in it, and that they are not thrust upon it from some ideal world, so all the effects that can be produced by the literary man (here assum-ing his apprenticeship and marshalling of isolated moments to produce a mystic separation, aided by old metaphors), are to be found dormant, unused in the reader, and are thus awakened. (Hulme 20)
> The new art of the Reader. (i) The relation between banker and poetry (ii) Sympathy with reader as brother, as *unexpressed* author. (Hulme 14)

The idea of the reader as "unexpressed author" must not be confused with the view held by some modern critical theories that it is the reader who creates the text through the act of reading. This view denies to texts the possibility of ultimate, fixed meaning because we can read only in the con-text of our own history, and the associations we make will therefore be different from those made by other readers with different histories. Ac-cording to Hulme, however, to see the reader as the "unexpressed author" is to see the reader as a potential sharer in the *same* emotion as that expe-rienced by the author:

> The effort of the literary man to find subtle analogies for the ordinary street feelings he experiences, leads to the differentiation and importance of those feelings. What would be unnoticed by others, and is nothing when not labelled becomes an important emotion. A transitory artificial impression is deliberately cultivated into an emotion and written about. Reason here creates and modifies an emotion, e.g. standing at street cor-ners. Hence the sudden joy these produce in the reader when he remem-bers a half-forgotten impression. "How true!" (Hulme 23)

In fact, what Hulme describes here is the process of writing, and only the final sentence refers directly to the reader, but it is clear from this that Hulme is writing about something he believes is transferable from author to reader through the medium of the text. The first reader of any text, however, is its author, and the "sudden joy" of recognition might just as easily be one felt by the poet during composition as by the reader.

The most extensive of Hulme's notes on poetry is the following, in

185

which he discusses his change of opinion on the process leading to the creation of a poem:

It was formerly my idea that a poem was made somewhat as follows. The poet, in common with many other people, occasionally experienced emotions which strangely moved him. In the case of the greengrocer this was satisfied by reading Tennyson and sending the lines to his beloved. The poet on the contrary tried to find new images to express what he felt. These lines and vague collections of words he gradually built up into poems. But this I now see to be wrong; the very act of trying to find a form to fit the separate phrases into, itself leads to the creation of new images hitherto not felt by the poet. In a sense the poetry writes itself. This creation by happy chance is analogous to the accidental stroke of the brush which creates a new beauty not previously consciously thought of by the artist.

The form of a poem is shaped by the intention, vague phrases containing ideas which at past moments have strongly moved us. As [i.e., depending on whether] the purpose of the poem is narrative or emotional the phrases become altered. The choice of a form is as important as the individual pieces and scraps of emotion of which the poem is made up. In the actual making accidental phrases are hit upon. Just as musician in striking notes on piano comes across what he wants, the painter on the canvas, so the poet not only gets the phrases he wants, but even from the words get a *new* image.

*Creative* effort means *new* images.

The accidental discovery of effect, not conscious intellectual endeavour for it.

The theory that puts all phrases in a box and years later starts to arrange *all wrong*.

Start creating *at once,* and in this very process new ideas spring up, accidentally.

So *condemn* card system, red tape leads to nothing.

The living method of arranging at once in contemporary notebooks. (Hulme 25–26)

This amounts to a clear rejection of the Romantic theory that poetry is made by recollecting states of vivid emotion in later moments of tranquility. For Hulme the image must be captured immediately, not only in order to retain its power but because the process of its formulation leads the poet to unexpected associations (Hulme mentions "Lobster and me," as an example), and it is these that constitute the "new" of art. What is formulated is still an emotion experienced in the past, but the association with a particular object or situation is immediate and accidental, rather than the result of contemplation or effort. Therefore, when Hulme talks of the relation between form and intention, it becomes clear that he sees the search for poetic form not as a rigid metrical or lexical process, nor even as a wholly conscious intellectual exercise, but rather as a series of more or less free associations (more or less free because some associations may have been rejected by the poet during the writing process) based on a wholly personal set of aleatory conditions.

What kind of poetry will this produce? Presumably a body of work consisting of vivid images that seem to recall *something* to the reader, but that, without a system like the medieval one to classify the physical universe, must always refer to something that defies ultimate meaning. This sounds like Goethe's definition of symbolism, except for Hulme's insistence on the accidental discovery of effect, where Goethe presents what seems to be a more methodical and controlled progress from experience to idea to image. Let us now take an example from Hulme's own poetry, the two rhyming couplets of "Above the Dock" (published 1912):

> Above the quiet dock in mid night,
> Tangled in the tall mast's corded height,
> Hangs the moon. What seemed so far away
> Is but a child's balloon, forgotten after play.

We can understand, or "see," the literal situation easily enough. The moon is seen through the spaces between the cords attached to a ship's mast: that is all.

But something is being symbolized here—we know this because the poem itself tells us so. We know that the moon is not really "tangled" or hanging in the ship's ropes, but it takes only a minimal effort of even the dullest imagination to see how it appears as though it were, and from this point the same imagination could probably make the association with a balloon. But the further association, the development of this image of the moon, comes in the final one-and-a-half lines: there is a difference between just any old balloon and a child's balloon forgotten after play. In the sense we are discussing, this is the point at which interpretation begins, and it will depend on the associations made by the reader with the ideas *far, child, forgotten,* and *play;* or, better, *after play.* We are presented with a single, very clear image and left to make something of it. The poem is a good illustration of Hulme's ideas on commonplaces—doubly so, in fact, since I understand not only that the moon is a (poetic) commonplace that we tend to forget about unless something happens to remind us that it is still there, but also that children tend to drop their toys when they grow bored with them. Humans have been making associations with the moon since the beginning of written history, and presumably before it, and the chances of hitting upon precisely the same one that occurred to Hulme are practically zero. This is irrelevant; and I suspect that, though the image itself is a very clear one, Hulme had no very clearly *defined* idea as to what it symbolized to him. All I can do is allow the image to create associations in my own mind and see what happens. A child's balloon forgotten after play is something discarded as irrelevant and no longer interesting—a forlorn, rather sad object. Of course, balloons cannot really be sad, but this kind of "unnatural" association works in precisely this way, by attributing human characteristics to inanimate objects. If we follow this idea through, we could see the balloon/moon as, for example, a person with whom we used to be, but are no longer, in love; or we could reverse the roles and see ourselves as the rejected ones. It is much more interesting though, in my opinion, to be less specific, and to see our lost love as a symbol for all lost loves; or better still, having arrived at the idea of loss, to read the balloon/moon as a symbol for all human loss: I agree with Aristotle in finding the universal more fun than the particular.

Am I justified in my depressing reading of these lines? I think so, because of "What seemed so far away" and because of "but" in the last line. Something that seems far away seems unattainable, and when we think of things as unattainable it is usually because we think it would be pleasant to attain them. Our sense of loss is thus accompanied by one of disillusion when we discover that, after all, what we desired is "but" a child's balloon; nor is the association we have just made between "child" and ourselves likely to be a comfortable one. Hulme thinks that disillusion is necessary to both poet and reader—"literary man" must always be first disillusioned, then consciously creative of illusion.

It is important to understand that by "illusion" in this last sentence, Hulme is talking about the fact that we are prepared to accept for a moment that the moon is, or at least is like, a child's balloon caught in ship's rigging: this is the illusion that the poet deliberately creates. The mood or feeling created by this illusion, however, is by no means illusory, though it may have as many different aspects as the poem has readers. Another poem that lends itself very well to this kind of reading is the two-liner by Ezra Pound entitled "In a Station of the Metro":

> The apparition of these faces in the crowd:
> Petals on a wet, black bough.

There is so much that could be said about this poem that it is impossible here to offer a reading that would do it anything like justice, but we can at least make a start that will demonstrate how beautifully it is constructed.

My first response is to ask why the faces are an apparition. An apparition is either something that suddenly appears as if from nowhere; or it is a ghost. I can easily imagine literal petals on a literal wet, black bough, and equally easily associate them with human faces against a dark background. This is enough for me to paint a first picture. I know more or less where we are—the poem's title tells me—but in my reading the faces belong to bodies emerging into the rain from a station of the Paris subway (I have a particular station in mind, but it is irrelevant) because I need a wet, black background against which to place them, and I have decided that the stairwell leading up from the platforms will do very well. "These" singles out a number of faces that catch the attention—Hulme gave a similar example when he wrote of the faces of people at a Baptist meeting, seen through a window by a chance observer passing along the street. The second line, in my reading, contrasts life with death. If there are petals, it is spring, which brings new life to the natural world, but these petals lie upon a wet, black bough, as though the tree that brought them forth were itself dead and rotted through. The faces are an apparition—they either appear suddenly and unexpectedly—and life from a dead tree is certainly unexpected—or they are ghosts, reminders of what spring looked like when the tree was alive.

But I can interpret this tree imagery as a kind of spiritual allegory. I know that the poem was written during a time of terrible social and political upheaval in early-twentieth-century Europe. I also know that Pound became extremely right-wing politically and supported Mussolini's Blackshirts in Italy, and that his belief in *fascisti* politics entailed a further belief in neoclassical (or pseudoclassical) ideals of order and discipline that were supposed to inform everything from education to architecture and art.

Why is all of this relevant? Because of the meter of the poem. The first line is hexametric, and the hexameter is the line of classical Latin poetry. In contrast to this, the second line begins with a trochee rather than an iamb, which causes an uneasy transition from one stressed syllable, the last of the first line, to another, the first of the second line. The trochee is followed by a pyrrhic, which is in turn followed by three single, more or less stressed syllables that slow the line down until it finally ceases with an exhalation on "bough." In comparison with the smooth elegance of the first line, this is complete chaos, and it is very tempting (for me) to read the poem's physical structure, its transition from order to disorder, as symbolic of Pound's belief that Europe was going down the drain because it had abandoned its classical—or, more precisely, Renaissance—ideals, with Europe a dead branch from which springs only an apparition, a ghost of life. There are other readings: we can see the faces as a hopeful sign, for instance, a symbol of life returning; or the poem might simply be saying "I saw some beautiful faces today"; but I think the one I have just put together reasonable, economic, and supported by the text. Nobody is obliged to agree—just to come up with an equally or more reasonable and economic one.

Both of these poems share the suddenness that Hulme held was a necessary quality of an image (in Pound's poem, it is underlined by "apparition") and the elevation, or at least the singling out, of the commonplace: people in a subway station, the moon over the dock. Also, the association made in each—moon/child's balloon; faces/petals—is understandable even in a literal sense so long as we understand the implied "like" in each: the moon is *like* a child's balloon; the faces are *like* petals on a wet, black bough. But what are we to do with lines such as the following from T. S. Eliot's "The Love Song of J. Alfred Prufrock"?

> I should have been a pair of ragged claws
> Scuttling across the floors of silent seas.

"Scuttling" and "claws" are easy to identify with crustacea (and indeed with Hulme's "lobster"—"The lobster and me"—from the notes published by Eliot), but why this "I" should have been a crab or a lobster takes a little more time to work out. Most critics agree that the image suggests age: the stiff movement of crabs (and perhaps also the fact that they move sideways, rather than forwards, and thus at least seem not to make any progress) can be readily associated with the infirmities of age, while "crabbed" and "crabby" suggest a capricious and irritable old man. Further, the couplet occurs at a point in the poem where growing old is actually the issue. In my reading, "should have been" is used in the way that someone who is fond of impersonating others "should have been" an actor, and thus we have something like an ironic aside, a comment uttered by a man regretful of lost opportunity and youth. We do not need to know what those opportunities were—rather, each reader knows what they were: this is a gap we can fill in ourselves. At any rate, it should be clear that we need to see our crab as a symbolic one, otherwise we should be left with a man who seems to think he would be better suited to life as a literal crustacean. In fact, we find ourselves yet again in a situation similar to that faced by those medieval commentators on Scripture when they realized that their book of books, the Truth, the Bible, sometimes very obviously said more than one thing at the same time. The difference between modern critics and them is that modern critics do not wish to limit interpretation as rigidly as their medieval counterparts.

Now, the reading above of the couplet from "Prufrock" is by no means sufficient. For one thing, the lines need to be read in the context of the complete poem. But even as they stand, I know very well that they say more than "I grow old." More precisely, "I grow old" is more than a statement concerning chronology. I feel justified in this claim because of what Aristotle said about particulars and universals, and because of what Augustine and Dante said about allegory. If, as Aristotle suggests, it is the job of poetry to speak of universals rather than particulars, I have a right to expect it to do so. And if Augustine is right in finding allegory where the literal sense seems to make no sense at all, then the couplet from Prufrock is certainly allegorical. For Augustine, making no sense meant contradicting the laws of Scripture, while for us today it means, rather, contradicting the laws of nature, logic, or language. (Augustine would say that if something contradicts the laws of nature, logic, and language, then it also necessarily contradicts the law of Scripture. For him, everything in Scripture must be logical and must be in accordance with the laws of nature.) But when we read poetry, we still automatically apply the same basic formula and suspect that, if something seems to make no literal sense, it must stand for something else. Something is wrong with a pair of claws scuttling across the seabed. My mind does not like the idea of claws without a body, so it supplies one, and in this context, the floors of silent seas, the body it supplies belongs to a crab or a lobster because it finds these the most obvious possibilities. With the same justification, other minds have supplied the idea *apple* where the Bible says simply "fruit." However, my mind is prepared to accept bodiless claws so long as they occur in poetry because it is used to the idea that poetry involves "unnatural" associations.

How does this couplet work? First of all it uses the common symbolistic device of taking a part to represent the whole—claws, or ragged claws, for crab. It then uses similarity of characteristic and effect to represent the concept—stiff, slow movement for old age. But it then uses the concept *age* itself to represent a wider understanding of it than the literal concept *grow old*. To age is, among other things, to approach death, and death, as we have seen, has been the subject of poetry in more than one sense. There is a spiritual death as well as a physical one, and to become aware of spiritual death is to reflect on life—a sudden, awful awareness that the life in question has been empty of spiritual content, focused on the gratification of physical desires and the fulfillment of physical functions, for example. If we apply this idea to the couplet from "Prufrock," it gives us another way of looking at those claws. Their function in the real world is to attack, defend, and feed—all related to the gratification of desires and the fulfillment of physical functions, and they are all that is left, in this image, of our potential crab. In other words, they can be seen as symbolizing the kind of life we have just described. I do not expect crabs to be tortured by metaphysical angst (though I may be doing their intelligence and sensibility an injustice), but a man who suggests, however ironically, that his life can be summed up by the image of their feeding apparatus is certainly aware of what that missing body represents.

This is very oblique, personalized, "intellectual," and "difficult," and much of Eliot's poetry uses this kind of indirect symbol. A single image is presented to the reader, who must then respond to it. Whether this response is the result of a conscious effort, to produce a "series of decipherings," or or that of an unconscious chain of "unnatural associations" depends wholly on the reader, who may of course accept or reject as many possible readings as he or she wishes.

### THE CASE OF ROBERT GRAVES

Not everyone was happy with this new kind of symbolism: it seemed to be exclusive of too many readers, too "elitist," and it is true that the most famous product of this genre, "The Waste Land," is not an easy poem to

192

read. (It is also true that Eliot's tongue-in-cheek explanatory notes to the poem do not make things any easier.) One of the loudest voices raised in protest was that of the English poet Robert Graves. His criticism is not always very rational: it is frequently self-contradictory and too obviously based in social and even racial prejudices, thinly disguised as a plea for a supposed cultural integrity. All the same, there is no doubt that Graves was a gifted poet, and some of the points he raises in criticism of "intellectual" poetry were taken up and developed by some English poets of the next generation who formed the loosely connected group that became known as "the Movement."

Graves's argument against what he perceived as the overintellectualization of poetry is founded on a complex and very personal interpretation of classical myth and a particular understanding of the origin and function of poetry, but he distinguishes between two basic kinds: "true" poetry and "Apollonian." "True" poetry is composed "at the back of the mind" and is "an unaccountable product of a trance in which the emotions of love, fear, anger or grief are profoundly engaged, though at the same time power-fully disciplined; in which intuitive thought reigns supralogically, and personal rhythm subdues meter to its purposes." Poetry written under the guidance of Apollo, rather than through inspiration by a personal muse, is composed "in the forepart of the mind"—

> wittily, should the occasion serve, always reasonably, always on a pre-conceived plan, and derived from a close knowledge of rhetoric. Pros-ody, Classical example, and contemporary fashion. It may, of course, disguise simple statement in masquerade dress, but if so, observes all masquerade conventions; whether the dress chosen be medieval dou-blet, pastoral smock, Roman toga or pseudo-Homeric armour. The pleasure [it] offers is consciously aesthetic. (*On Poetry* 286–87)

Whatever we think of the division of the brain into a "forepart" and a "back," the distinction Graves makes between two kinds of poetry is a use-ful one. Most important for our study is the description of the creative process for "true" poetry, the "unaccountable product of a trance." We would expect the kind of image produced in such a state to seem uncal-culated and natural (though not in Locke's sense), where the "Apollonian" poet would produce a clever but obviously contrived, "intellectual" imagery. Here Graves is clearly thinking of Pound and Eliot (though in other essays he makes similar comments on the work of modern poetry in general), whose enthusiasm for French symbolist and surrealist poetics he found particularly distasteful because, in his view, they were too cerebral and pseudohistorical, and for this reason antiinspirational.

In fact, the difficulty of *not* writing the kind of poetry he criticizes is a recurring theme in Graves's own poetry, and despite the sometimes eccentric, neomystical views he expresses in his critical writings, the poems themselves often demonstrate an acute awareness of what has become a central point of modern critical theory. A paradox of poetry is that its concern is still with truth, which sounds as though it ought to be a point at which we can ultimately arrive, but that words, as signs, stand always for ideas that can be more nearly defined only by other words—and so on. His poem "The Cool Web" takes this paradox for its theme:

> Children are dumb to say how hot the day is,
> How hot the scent is of the summer rose,
> How dreadful the black wastes of evening sky,
> How dreadful the tall soldiers drumming by.
>
> But we have speech, to chill the angry day,
> And speech to dull the rose's cruel scent,
> We spell away the overhanging night,
> We spell away the soldiers and the fright.
>
> There's a cool web of language winds us in,
> Retreat from too much joy or too much fear:
> We grow sea-green at last and coldly die
> In brininess and volubility.
>
> But if we let our tongues lose self-possession,
> Throwing off language and its watery clasp
> Before our death, instead of when death comes,
> Facing the wide glare of the children's day,
> Facing the rose, the dark sky and the drums,
> We shall go mad no doubt and die that way.

Children are "dumb"—mute, without the language to order and categorize experience, which remains inexplicable and therefore disturbing.

But the poem implies that when we "spell away" the child's unseen, or unformulated, terrors of the "overhanging night," we are not only employing language literally in order to rationalize fear, but also invoking a demon of logic, a "Black Goddess"[1] who, while bestowing the gift of eloquence, removes us immeasurably from the truth the poet had hoped to use that eloquence to represent. Language—eloquence, rhetoric, poetic devices—here constitutes the "retreat" from human experiences that without its rationalizing effect would be horrifying and unmanageable. But to retreat is to capitulate in the face of an overwhelming power. Once we decide, as inevitably we must, to ally ourselves with language, we become irrevocably enmeshed in its "web" of half-truth and paraphrase that seeks perpetually to recreate and define but may only ever describe. Language relentlessly "winds us in" toward itself and toward death. But what kind of death is it that language brings? Certainly an ironic one, for we die "coldly," at furthest remove from the heat of the day and of the scent of the summer rose we had sought to escape, so that "too much joy" and "too much fear" become equivalents to "too much life." The implication is that "real" life is characterized by extremes that human nature dictates we should flee in an act of psychological self-preservation, but that the poet, rejecting the security of mere "volubility," attempts to re-live. The irony is that the only material at the poet's disposal from which to reconstruct these extremes is language. If we do reject it, however, if we do "let our tongues lose self-possession," we must again experience the full intensity of too much joy or fear unfiltered by words, and this, the poem tells us, will lead to madness caused by our inability to perfectly quantify and express them.

But what if there were a perfect language, somehow capable of distancing us from "too much" human experience yet simultaneously reproducing it? What would such a language look like? One of its characteristics would certainly have to be an ability to unify the intellectual and spiritual comprehensions of ideas, for without this ability it would either convey purely worldly interpretations or very likely be so utterly spiritual as to be unintelligible. Our perfect language must be able to convey *everything*, but in such a way that the human mind can comprehend it. It would be something like God's language, for only that can express unspeakable mysteries. But we know that God's language—dictated by him to his faithful secretaries on earth to produce what Blake called the Great Code of Art—though it necessarily expresses everything, had to be translated in order to be understood, and we know that for the medieval commentators this meant attributing theologically acceptable (and, in their view, there-fore logical) symbolic meanings to difficult (i.e., open) passages of Scrip-ture as well as to the natural world.

But we know also that some commentators had been quite happy to think of Scripture as a pretty open text—Origen, for example; and we have seen that Pseudo-Dionysius tried another way of getting around the prob-lem of expressing the inexpressible: he used oxymoron ("flashing dark-ness," etc.) to create an image, behind which lay an idea—God—that every-one could name but no one could define. Now, when Graves talks about the rose's "cruel scent," he is in one important sense doing the same thing as Pseudo-Dionysius. He does not use oxymoron, and he would certainly not have agreed that he was talking about a Christian God, but he does offer a response to the question, How can we express the inexpressible? Indeed, he offers the only response, because the only way to talk about such ideas that lie beyond rational knowledge is to use a language whose signs can have no logical literal meaning and are therefore open to inter-pretation. So what is our response to the rose's cruel scent? Bear with me if my own attempt to deal with this question seems long-winded. (Even criticism can only describe but not define.)

It cannot be denied that the poet is the poem's first reader. At the very latest, Graves read each word of each of his poems simultaneously with the act of writing the words on paper, though of course we can safely as-sume that he had already "read" each word before the physical act of writ-ing began, unless we believe that in all his writing he was merely a vehicle for the inspired utterances of the White Goddess. Like any other poet, Graves made conscious choices (as well, almost certainly, as unconscious ones) of particular words or phrases over others, decided on and ex-panded particular metaphors, preferred this or that simile to such-and-such, and so on. In other words, the first literary critic to occupy himself with the collected poems of Robert Graves was Robert Graves.

It is useful to remember this because it enables us to ask what kind of literary critic he was: how far did his adherence to a particular "school" of critical thought affect his choice of poetic language? This is not to suggest that Graves went about the business of writing poetry by saying, for exam-ple: "I am a vehement opponent of modernism and therefore I shall con-sciously write in the most unmodernist way I can conceive." Nevertheless, when Graves put down the steel-nibbed pen he continued to use through-out his career and claimed, "This poem is finished" (or, perhaps, with

Valéry, "This poem is abandoned," which is more or less the same thing), he was also saying, "For the moment and to the best of my ability I have fulfilled the criteria of good poetry as I understand them" ("for the moment" because Graves was an assiduous reviser of his own work). One of those criteria concerns what Graves called "goodness." Quinn (96) quotes a remarkable passage from the essay "Politics and Poetry," which Graves co-wrote with Laura Riding for *Epilogue 3* (Graves, *Common Asphodel* 283–84) and that contains a description of this quality:

> The goodness of poets and poetry is unquestionable, but it is not a goodness to be piously exemplified in a partisanship of humanitarian causes. . . . Let it be declared as clearly as possible that the goodness of poetry is not moral goodness, the goodness of temporal action, but the goodness of thought, the loving exercise of the will in the pursuit of truth. . . . The poet is concerned with truth which is not a historical product but which is always there of itself because it *is* reality: he is concerned with final truth only.

According to what Graves says here, "goodness" may be worldly and "temporal," in which case it is manifested in "humanitarian causes"—in good deeds; or it may be outside, beyond time—in this sense we can say it is "metatemporal." This metatemporal goodness is also "goodness of thought." Thought, or at least good thought, is therefore also metatemporal: it exists outside and independently of time and is not subject to its constraints. Human beings, however, are not so lucky (not even poets), and the thoughts that human minds generate—their responses to objects and ideas—are sadly temporal: they can at best be what Graves calls "moral."

If this is true, it is difficult to see how we can have any "good" thoughts at all unless they come from somewhere other than our minds. Such thoughts must exist somewhere in metatime, where presumably they have always existed, and we would have to receive them rather than generate them ourselves (ignoring for now the question of from whom or from where). But what is "the loving exercise of the will"? In the passage quoted above, Graves tells us it is the same thing as "goodness of thought" if it is something we undertake "in the pursuit of truth." (There may be other kinds of loving exercise of the will, and there must be exercises of the will other than loving ones, but Graves doesn't mention them.) Both *exercise* and *will* are highly problematic terms because of the strong temporal associations of what they are usually taken to signify in the combination Graves employs—an exercise of the will is, after all, a very worldly and human affair. But, for the "good" poet, it must be possible to exercise the will in such a way as to at least attempt to transcend the temporal, since his concern is with "final truth," which is itself metatemporal and "not a historical product." Alternatively it is this kind of loving exercise of the will that constitutes the "goodness" that in turn qualifies our poet as a good one, and this seems to be the implication of the passage quoted by Quinn: we should have to ask Graves, who unfortunately now exists only in metatime, unable to make further obscure pronouncements on poetry.

But we can certainly say that his concern to place poetry and what it speaks of beyond the historical seems similar to Aristotle's ideas in the *Poetics* on universals and particulars. The comparison is slightly misleading because Aristotle's universals equate roughly to "possibilities" rather than to "final truth," the concept set up by Graves in opposition to "the historical product." They agree, though, in subordinating history to poetry, and they agree that it is something in its language other than certain rhetorical devices that differentiates poetry from other forms of writing. Aristotle thinks that Herodotus would still be history even if it were written in verse, and Graves sees the politically engaged poem as polemic, rather than an expression of final truth, however competent its author's use of poetic forms.

What kind of truth is it that is "always there of itself because it *is* a reality"? And what kind of language could possibly be used to express it? The poet whose "goodness" is "unquestionable" surely makes it his business to find answers to these questions. In fact he must make it his business to ask them in the first place. He must maintain that there is indeed such a truth and such a possible language since without these his goodness would either not exist at all or it would turn out to be the ordinary, far less interesting moral kind.

We know from "The Cool Web" some of the characteristics this language must *not* have. It must not become, nor lead us into, mere volubility, which means that we must not become *too* fluent; that is, glib. An older meaning of *voluble* is "rotating," and if we take this into account we learn that our language must also be one that does not lead us round in circles. This sounds very reasonable (and wholly unremarkable), as though the demand were for a language just precise and concise and logical enough for safe everyday use. And according to Graves's poem, this is exactly what happens: we use language to explain our emotions to ourselves and in this way render them harmless. Indeed, without such a language, everyday life would be impossible because we should all be immobilized by constant terror or joy. Graves mentions volubility in a negative sense: "We grow sea-green at last and coldly die / In brininess and volubility," and in the context of the rest of the poem we can take this to indicate that, while he accepts the necessity of a language that allows us to go about our daily business in relative peace, he regrets at the same time the ultimate cost of its acquisition—the relinquishing of the very experience we have invented words to escape. A language capable not only of adequately describing but of truly recreating the experience of the "overhanging night" or the rose's "cruel scent" would be intolerable and we could not bear to use it.

But poetry is not our daily business: it is, Graves tells us, "the loving exercise of the will in the pursuit of (final) truth," and he seems to be imply-ing that this truth is somehow represented by the cruel scent of the rose and by the overhanging night. We know that the night is not really sus-pended above our heads, and we can reasonably discount any exercise of free will on the part of the rose's scent that might make it decide to act cru-elly toward us. But as soon as we concentrate on "rose" and "night" rather than on the attributes Graves decides to give them, we recognize their sym-bolic values. For a long time in poetry, they have been used to signify ideas other than literal roses and nights. ("I am the rose of Shar'on, and the lily of the valleys," declaims the ecstatic singer in the Song of Solomon; "I call to remembrance my song in the night," says Psalm 77; or perhaps Psalm 91 is more to the point: "Thou shalt not be afraid for the terror by night.") The terror of the night and the beauty of the rose (or rather, what Graves thought they signified) are clearly so all-inclusive and all-consuming that they cannot be named. We must approach them obliquely through a Per-seus's shield of language: we see them reflected, but we do not see *them*. If poets really were gods instead of people who have license to play at being them, language would certainly be very different. We have seen what would happen: we should create real oxen each time we said "ox." I do not think that Graves believed "ox" to signify "final truth," but he does equate "rose" and "night" with extremes of emotional experience, and these in turn he associates with an underlying human condition.

We know that the signs *rose* and *night* sometimes refer to, respectively, a family of flowers and (loosely) the period between sunset and sunrise, but it is equally obvious that in "The Cool Web" Graves intends something different, just as Blake, when he says "O rose, thou art sick," can be safely assumed not to be referring to diseases of plants. Both Graves and Blake, and every other poet who has ever used the sign *rose* as a symbol for something other than a particular kind of flower, use it as a sign with "no literal or univocal meaning." It seems then that our perfect language must be capable not only of saying everything, but of saying, in effect, and at the same time, nothing at all.

This raises the question of whether Graves (in our example) intended *rose* to signify something specific. Was he trying to express a particular or only a vague idea; something clearly defined, or something intuitively "understood"? It would be easy to say that Graves was talking about something spiritual: Graves himself may well have done so. But what does that mean? Saying this would merely replace one problem with another. Unless Graves intended his poem as a highly complex practical joke, he was consciously using *rose* as a symbol for something, or a group of somethings, that everyday, nonpoetic linguistic usage cannot adequately describe. In order to allow his readers to infer that *rose* signifies something other than (or something in addition to) a kind of flower, Graves needed to use a code, and it had to be a code that readers would immediately recognize as such, even if they were unable to agree on how to decode it.

He writes about this something, this "final truth," in so magisterial a way that it sounds wholly knowable, but we must admit it is equally likely that he adopted this tone merely to make his *Epilogue* essay rhetorically effective—that he was employing a trick of dialectics in order to win an argument. This is important because what Graves thought about the nature of final truth must affect his understanding, and therefore his choice, of the symbols he used to represent it. If he perceived final truth only vaguely, by an intuitive recognition that elicited powerful emotional responses but whose object remained opaque and intangible, then his use of *rose* to convey it corresponds to the definition of symbolism proposed by Goethe.

This must not be taken to imply that Graves's *rose* is completely open to limitless interpretation. I defy anyone to seriously claim that *rose* means "raspberry jelly" (or even "God the Father, God the Son, and God the Holy Spirit"). Graves was writing in the same tradition, that of Blake's Great Code of Art, that allows "I am the Rose of Shar'on," "O rose, thou art sick," Othello's "When I have pluck'd thy rose, / I cannot give it vital growth again," together with all the other instances in poetry of *rose* used as a sign to convey an impression of great beauty, usually a beauty so great that it transcends the purely physical. There are other codes—there may even be one in which *rose* signifies "raspberry jelly"—but Graves chose this particular one because he rightly believed that his readers would recognize it as one proper to poetry.

## MEANING AND INTERPRETATION

I have discussed Graves's poem at some length because it takes us straight to the heart of the current academic debate on meaning and interpretation. "Poems must always be read in their historical context," wrote Graves in his essay "Pulling a Poem Apart" (*On Poetry* 272). He also held, with Ben Jonson, that only poets have the right to judge poetry. Let us judge Graves in his own historical context. He studied English literature at Oxford just after World War I, before we began "to swim in the foul tidal basin of modernism" and when all that was required of undergraduate students was "a close attention to the primitive roots of our language and the long history of our literature" (*On Poetry* 279). The problem with a historical context is that we never know how historical it is. We learn about history from reading texts. Texts are composed of words, and, as we know, words are signs that stand for ideas; and throughout this book we have seen (I hope) just how problematic interpreting those signs has proved to be.

Since the mid-twentieth century, academic criticism has focused more and more on the reader as central to the idea of textual meaning, in particular those critical approaches that come under the general heading of reader-response theories. Again, this must not be taken to mean that interpretation has become (or should become) a kind of free-for-all. On the contrary, for Eco,

> the notion of unlimited semiosis does not lead to the conclusion that interpretation has no criteria. To say that interpretation . . . is potentially unlimited does not mean that interpretation has no object and that it "riverruns" for the mere sake of itself. . . .
>
> . . . Even the most radical deconstructionists accept the idea that there are interpretations which are blatantly unacceptable. This means that the interpreted text imposes some constraints upon its interpreters.

The limits of interpretation coincide with the rights of the text (which does not mean with the rights of its author). . . . Let us be realistic: there is nothing more meaningful than a text which asserts that there is no meaning. If there is something to be interpreted, the interpretation must speak of something which must be found somewhere, and in some way respected. (*Limits* 6–7)

For Eco, "economy," in the sense used throughout this book, is the criterion of a useful reading of literary texts: it tells us how far, or in which direction, we can allow our associations to go without them becoming absurd.

Other critics have adopted a more radical approach. Susan Sontag, for example, discussing the "old" and "new" methods of criticism, found that

the old style of interpretation was insistent, but respectful; it erected another meaning on top of the literal one. The modern style of inter- pretation excavates, destroys; it digs "behind" the text, to find a subtext which is the true one. . . . To understand *is* to interpret. And to interpret is to restate the phenomenon, in effect to find an equivalent for it. Thus, interpretation is not (as most people assume) an absolute value, a ges- ture of mind situated in some timeless realm of capabilities. Interpreta- tion must itself be evaluated, within a historical view of human con- sciousness. (Quoted in Iser, *Act of Reading* 10–11)

There is a contradiction here in that, if, as seems very reasonable, inter- pretation must itself be subject to constant evaluation and reevaluation, and if, as seems equally reasonable, interpretation is not an "absolute value," then there cannot be a "true" subtext behind the primary one since whatever subtext is discovered is necessarily in a state of flux, nonabsolute and dependent on the evaluation of the interpretive act.

Erecting a new meaning "on top of the literal one" is a good descrip- tion of the allegorical methods we have discussed, but we have seen also how the world to which poetic language refers can no longer be automat- ically understood as univocal, so that the new meaning is not an ultimate and indisputable truth in the Augustinian-Thomist sense, but rather, where an allegorical sense can be assumed because the literal one seems illogical or absurd, an inexpressible and unattainable idea in Goethe's sense.

There are social and political implications in what Sontag says about the "respectful" attitude of older criticism. She was talking not about the rights of the text that Eco suggests should be respected, but about the idea of canonicity, of a body of "great" texts generally accepted as representing the highest literary achievements of a particular culture or linguistic group. The idea of a canon has come under heavy attack during the past few decades because it was perceived as too exclusive—of women writers, for example, or of the work of Asian, Caribbean, and African authors writing in English. For our study, the idea of a literary canon is interesting because the criteria for admission into it have traditionally been connected with the fundamental idea of literature as representation in the sense proposed by Aristotle. Students will understand, therefore, that even if the rejection of an established canon can be traced to political and sociological ideals expressed in a distaste for the idea of a kind of literary Country Club whose membership consists solely of dead white males, its effects are—or, perhaps, will become more generally recognized as—immeasurably more far-reaching and demand what amounts to a complete reevaluation of the function of literature.

From Aristotle to Augustine to Aquinas to Dante to the English apologists of the sixteenth century, right through to Blake and well into the twentieth century, the interpretation of poetry depended on two crucial assumptions. First, it was taken for granted that the text carried a deducible meaning—that intended by its author—that it was the duty of the reader to discover. Second, for the poem to qualify as good, this meaning had to be clearly connected to at least one of the four allegorical senses proposed by the medieval commentators. These four senses were in turn related ultimately, but through the Christian tradition, to Aristotle's claim that good poetry was interpretable in a moral sense and had therefore a didactic, educational function: good poetry taught virtue by representation, and by encouraging the reader to seek for "final truth," "permanent forms," and "the Infinite in all things." The rejection of the idea of a literary canon necessarily entails the rejection of the criteria it imposes on texts. But if those criteria have indeed been rejected, have they been replaced by others, or do we now expect something completely different from poetry? What, in other words, is now the meaning of "aesthetic response"? One contemporary critic who addresses this question is Wolfgang Iser, and I now want to discuss some of the ideas he formulates in *The Act of Reading,* which first appeared in 1976; and in the more recent *Prospecting: From Reader Response to Literary Anthropology* (1989). Iser's work has generally been better received in Europe than in the United States, where *The Act of Reading* was severely criticized by the more radical (or more extreme) Stanley Fish. The debate resulting from their respective positions is highly relevant to our study since it focuses on the nature of perception and, therefore, of interpretation.

The basic premise of *The Act of Reading* is a very logical and straightforward one—that a text can only then produce a response when someone reads it. Whatever happens when someone does read it, however, is obviously something that depends on both reader and text. The effects a text has on us, and our responses to it (i.e., to those effects), are therefore "neither [solely] of the text nor [solely] of the reader; the [unread] text represents a potential effect that is realized in the reading process." In other words, interpretation—the reading process—can be said to involve an *interaction* between text and reader, a relationship in which each has effects on the other. The text affects the reader by eliciting responses; the reader affects the text by "creating" it—by interpreting it and thus endowing it with a meaning he or she finds acceptable. It would in fact be more precise to say that the text represents an indefinite number of potential effects, since a text has an indefinite number of potential readers, each of whom carries along a different set of aleatory conditions that will influence reading. Iser (*Act of Reading* ix) therefore thinks that a theory of aesthetic response must be based on "the poles of text and reader, together with the interaction that occurs between them."

Iser (*Act of Reading* 18) offers another very logical justification for his approach to interpretation and, at the same time, sums up the rationale of reader-response theories generally when he points out that if interpretation's concern is to convey meaning, the text itself can hardly have done so already:

> How can the meaning possibly be experienced if—as is always assumed by the classical norm of interpretation—it is already there, merely waiting for a referential exposition? As meaning arises out of the process of actualization, the interpreter should perhaps pay more attention to the process than to the product. His object should therefore be, not to explain a work, but to reveal the conditions that bring about its various possible effects. If he clarifies the *potential* of a text, he will no longer fall into the fatal trap of trying to impose one meaning on his reader as if that were the right, or at least the best, interpretation.

In *Prospecting,* Iser sees literary texts as containing "gaps" that the reader sets out to fill by interpretation. In so doing, the reader is fulfilling a desire for textual (or logical) "consistency" or harmony. But the consistency that any reader believes to have discovered must be bound up with "subjective factors and, above all, the habitual orientations of the reader." It is for this reason, Iser claims, that modern literary works contain so many apparent inconsistencies: "not because they are badly constructed, but because such breaks act as hindrances to comprehension, and so force us to reject our habitual orientations as inadequate. If one tries to ignore such breaks, or to condemn them as faults in accordance with classical norms, one is in fact attempting to rob them of their function."

It must be pointed out that talking about texts as being well or badly constructed, and as having a particular function, comes very close indeed to talking about the intentions of the author, and this is precisely what reader-based theories seek to avoid. When he comes to discuss what he calls the "repertoire" of the literary text, it is easy to see why his insistence on a historical understanding of the way the text functions, though it may sound very reasonable to many readers, is too "classical" for those modern critics who in their turn insist that the reader, and therefore the text (since it is the reader who creates the text through the act of reading), are in fact autonomous of historical context:

> The repertoire of a literary text does not consist solely of social and cultural norms; it also incorporates elements and, indeed, whole traditions of past literature that are mixed together with these norms. It may even be said that the proportions of the mixture form the basis of the differences between literary genres. . . . There are [texts] in which the repertoire is dominated by elements from earlier literature—lyric poetry being the prime example. Striking effects can and have been gained by reversing these proportions, as has happened in the twentieth century, for instance, in the novels of James Joyce, with their countless literary allusions, and in the lyrics of the Beat Generation, who incorporated into their verse a wide range of social and cultural norms drawn from our modern industrial society. (Iser, *Act of Reading* 79)

For some modern critics, the problem with "whole traditions of past literature" and poetry "in which the repertoire is dominated by elements from earlier literature" is the implication that an adequate interpretation can be carried only if the reader has sufficient literary-historical knowledge to recognize the elements and traditions to which the new text refers. This would undermine the importance of the role played by the reader in the interpretation, which of course is not what reader-response theorists want to hear.

The same modern critics might also feel justified in inferring a too conservative view of the importance of history in Iser's text. In the view of the more radical forms of reader-response, the interpretation of a reader who lacks historical knowledge must be just as valid as an interpretation by a reader who possesses it. This, too, is something that Iser's comments can be read as denying. For this reason, perhaps, the American critic Fish thought Iser's approach, or parts of it, at least, "hopelessly conservative" and "reactionary" (Iser, *Prospecting* 67). Students will realize how relevant all this is to our theme—what caused the disagreement between two critics is the subject of this book: how do we interpret? More precisely, how do we interpret those parts of a literary text that demand interpretation because they are obscure, because they seem illogical, because they must refer to something other than or as well as what they seem to be saying they refer to—in other words, because they employ metaphor, symbol, allegory?

One point raised by Fish is of particular interest to us here. It concerns the idea of the world as text and recalls our discussion of the medieval exegetes. I shall again quote from Iser's *Prospecting,* from a passage in which Iser discusses objections to his approach formulated by Fish and in which Iser claims that the world as text is not a valid metaphor:

> One should not confuse reality with interpretation of reality. My interpretation of the world may well be as much a product of linguistic acts as my interpretation of a literary text, but I maintain that there are substantial differences between the things being interpreted.[2] First, the real world is perceivable through the senses, whereas the literary text is only perceivable through the imagination—unless one believes that reading the words sunset, music, silk, wine, and scent is the same as seeing, hearing, touching, tasting and smelling the real things. Second, all known experience suggests that the real world (uninterpreted) lives and functions independently of the individual observer, whereas the literary text does not. Third, our contact with the real world has immediate physical or social consequences, whereas our contact with the literary text need not, and indeed rarely does have any such consequences. It is precisely these restrictions of the literary text that make it an unsuitable metaphor for reality. (Iser, *Prospecting* 66)

This seems to contradict the passage above in which Iser stresses the way in which the literary text "incorporates elements, and, indeed, whole traditions of past literature": thinking of the world as text is itself just such a tradition. When I read the word *sunset,* I do not for a moment believe I am seeing a real sunset, but I do see a pretty accurate picture of one in my mind. The real world is also perceivable through the imagination, and the imagination is in this case prompted by a sign, the word *sunset,* which stands for the real thing, a real sunset. It is doubtful how far this mental picture of an imagined sunset, based on my experience of real sunsets seen in the real world, can accurately be described as "interpretation" of reality; but it is quite certain that neither I nor anyone else in his right mind *confuse* it with reality. There are substantial differences between humans and lions, but nobody will take issue with the description of Achilles as a lion because there are also recognizable similarities—Achilles is ferocious, predatory, physically strong, and inspires fear in his enemies. If I say "Achilles is a lion," I am not implying that Achilles has a tail, and nobody, moreover, thinks that is what I am doing. Of course, Iser's second and third points in the passage above—that the text (at least, the interpreted text) does not exist without human intervention, and that there are not necessarily any physical or social consequences resulting from our contact with the text—are both reasonable. All the same, we can still justify a view of the world as text on the basis of certain similarities between the two ideas, most importantly the similarity that we are obliged to interpret each of them if we wish to find its "meaning," however subjective that meaning might be.

Fish and Iser differ on the idea that a text contains "gaps," which, according to Iser, exist independently of the reader. For Fish, as for Locke, perception cannot be "innocent of assumptions" (Holub 26), and therefore any such gaps cannot exist before an act of interpretation has taken place. Ironically, the medievals thought the same thing. The difference between them and Fish is that there was only one possible context governing the assumptions of which our perception is not innocent. Fish agrees with them in seeing human perception—and therefore human responses—as dependent on a code or convention (Holub 26). He disagrees with them in his rejection of an ultimate, universal code determining the responses of every individual within a particular cultural group.

The debate on perception is philosophical rather than literary-critical in origin, but in the Western tradition philosophical concerns have been related to poetry at least since Plato banned poets from his ideal republic. A debate on the nature of perception is of obvious importance to what we think about interpreting literary texts (or interpreting anything at all) since what we see as a matter for interpretation necessarily depends on our perception of things. Unfortunately, once we accept this as a general rule, we must also accept that it applies to our theoretical approaches, and, understandably perhaps, most modern critics do not seem particularly pleased to do so. At any rate, in the absence of the Grand Unified Theory provided by a worldview based on Creation and God's unalterable law, and until physics does indeed come up with a grand unified theory of everything, we are left with the problem of perception and interpretation. It is only a problem, however, as long as we insist on seeing the job of literary criticism as discovering a text's meaning—a single and irrefutable interpretation based on the intention of the author—and modern critics (even Iser and Fish) agree that this cannot be done.

What are we to do? If we reject a reading of literary texts based on authorial intentions, or on ultimate truth, Blake's "Infinite in all things," Wordsworth's "permanent forms," or on a world of signs speaking of God and Creation, the idea of searching for "final truth" in a text becomes absurd. Perhaps for this reason, much modern criticism has become *metacritical*—that is, its focus is on the criticism of critical methods, and this has meant a definite move toward philosophical questions. These, in turn, are closely related to problems of linguistics and semiotics. But it is often difficult for the undergraduate student, faced with ragged claws scuttling across the floors of silent seas, to see how metacritical debate is of practical relevance to the assignment due in three days' time. There is nothing to stop us reading any poem in the context of Augustine's, or Aquinas's, or Dante's four interpretive senses. Devout Christians are likely to see this approach as relevant indeed. But even a devout Christian (or believer of any faith at all) should not deny that there are today other very widely accepted theories of reading and that in an academic environment these cannot be simply ignored.

I believe that students could do a lot worse than to bear in mind Eco's criterion of economy. If Locke and Fish are right, what is economical will depend in part on the personal beliefs and experience of the reader and in part on the text itself. The reader's experience determines the reader's perception, and the text as a whole affects the likelihood of a reading of a part of it being useful. A sophomore student of mine once announced that a poem he had been given to read was about abortion. This reading was not impossible in that I was unable to really prove its impossibility, but it was very unlikely. The poem was by John Donne, and we simply know that when Donne was alive, as far as poetic themes were concerned, abortion was about as important an issue as space travel. Certainly, there were words in the poem that could very easily be interpreted by a modern reader in such a way as to relate them to the issue of abortion, but if I am allowed to do this, I must also be allowed to relate the telephone directory to the idea of racial segregation or the production of Scotch whisky because it contains the names Black and White. My student made the mistake of asking what the poem meant and trying to find this out as though he were solving a mathematical problem.

There is a difference, though, between economy and parsimony. I shall use the first four stanzas of W. H. Auden's poem "A Summer Night" to explain what I mean:

Out on the lawn I lie in bed,
Vega conspicuous overhead
    In the windless nights of June,
As congregated leaves complete
Their day's activity; my feet
    Point to the rising moon.

Lucky, this point in time and space
Is chosen as my working place,
    Where the sexy airs of summer,
The bathing hours and the bare arms,
The leisured drives through a land of farms
    Are good to a newcomer.

Equal with colleagues in a ring
I sit on each calm evening
    Enchanted as the flowers
The opening light draws out of hiding
With all its gradual dove-like pleading,
    Its logic and its powers:

That later we, though parted then,
May still recall these evenings when
    Fear gave his watch no look;

> The lion griefs loped from the shade
> And our knees their muzzles laid,
> And Death put down his book.

Let us respond to the stanzas by testing some of the approaches we have seen. If we agree with Plato and see poetry as morally corrupting, then we can forget about interpretation altogether, and I do not recommend his approach to students given a reading assignment. Aristotle is more promising, but to really agree with him we need to think of poetry as having a moral function, and this is in itself problematic because of Aristotle's association of "moral" with "educational." We may or may not think of poetry in this way, but I suspect the number of people who have been moved to virtue by reading a poem is in fact rather small. Besides, we would be severely limiting our interpretive possibilities if we were to read poetry *only* with the aim of being instructed. This does not mean that we have to reject entirely Aristotle's idea that actions and ideas represented in poetry can move us to, or at least make us aware of, moral virtues. To illustrate this point, I am now going to cheat and discuss what Auden himself had to say about his poem. He says that, one summer evening in June 1933, he was sitting in a garden with three colleagues when he suddenly felt himself "invaded by a power" that led him to feel that for the first time in his life "[he] knew exactly what it means to love one's neighbor as oneself." He felt certain, too, that his colleagues were experiencing the same feeling, and he was, so he tells us, later able to confirm this in one case. The existence of these colleagues suddenly seemed "of infinite value," and he "knew" that as long as this feeling lasted it would be impossible for him deliberately to injure another human being. He admits that the memory of this experience has not prevented him from making use of others, but that it has made it much more difficult for him to deceive himself about doing so.

I admit, immediately, that this is extremely weak evidence. Auden wrote this passage almost thirty years after the event; he was influenced by his socialist beliefs; he was writing in the context of "the various factors that brought me back to the Christian faith in which I had been brought up" and was therefore manipulating the past to provide himself with a good piece of religious propaganda—these are all valid responses to the passage quoted here. But the point is that the stanzas can very easily be interpreted in an Aristotelian sense: as a description of the experience of one individual that leads to that individual's awareness of a human virtue, Christian or otherwise, expressed as "loving one's neighbor as oneself," and at this point we can say that the poem may well inspire others to the same awareness.

However, if we read the lines only in Aristotle's sense, we soon reach a dead end: what are we to do with a poem once we have decided that it is morally improving and thus fulfils its function? Let us see if we can do better with Augustine's four senses. The problem here, though, is ultimately the same as with Aristotle: we know we are supposed to think of these four senses in a particular context, and this will necessarily influence our perception of the ideas we think the lines convey and thus impose an external limit on our interpretation. The problem is based in the notion that poetry has a function that has to do either with the intention of the author to communicate something to the reader or with an unwritten law stating that poetry is to do certain things and not others. What happens if we rid ourselves of this notion? One very useful result is that we are allowed to reinterpret the senses proposed by the medievals. We can, for example, interpret moral and mystical in contexts other than strictly religious. We are by no means obliged to do this, but again, since (at the time of writing) we are no longer in danger of being burned at the stake for attempting it, it is certainly worthwhile to make use of the interpretive freedoms we feel we now have.

Can we reinterpret the literal sense? The answer to this is that modern linguistics and epistemology does precisely that. In the absence of any final truth—God, for example, or, on a rather different level, authorial intentions—the idea of being is connected with the idea of perception: there are no "givens" we can rely on, and we should in fact allow for every possible interpretation in every possible context. Even so, it might easily be argued that what is possible is also dependent on perception. But if, as seems to be the case, we have no way of being sure about authorial intentions, we can limit our possible readings and contexts to the most likely, or least unlikely, as we found it sensible to do in the case of the student's reading of the poem by Donne. We can then begin with the most frequent dictionary definitions of words and see where they lead us. In this way, the first two lines of the poem by Auden, "Out on the lawn I lie in bed, / Vega conspicuous overhead," can be understood literally to mean that the speaker in the poem was, on a certain evening, lying outside on the grass while either the star Vega or the stars of the constellation Vega/Lyra were shining brightly. Of course, we could leave it at that and move on to the next line, but I am not happy with what I have: I want the two lines I have just read to tell me more than that such-and-such a person was lying on the grass on a starry night. This may be unreasonable of me, but I think I am justified, and for two reasons. First, I suffer from the prejudice that encourages me to expect more than a literal-informative message from poems, and if I read one that seems to say no more than "I am happy" or "I am in love," or even "The Spectral Type A0Va Vega is the fifth brightest star," my immediate response is to ask "Who cares?" The ideas these statements convey are not unimportant in themselves, but, in the case of the first two at least, have been heard and read so often that their interest as statements of fact is small. I would be more interested if the same things were said in a novel, unusual way or were set in an unexpected context. In other words, I make the demand of poetry that it offer me more than bald fact.

Second, I know that I am reading a poem, and I also know that, in poetry, stars are frequently mentioned in a particular mood, or seem to evoke a particular mood: I am, or allow myself to become, a model reader, and accept the rules of a kind of game that is played between text and interpreter and in which the text drops certain hints to let the interpreter know what is going on. We do not have to accept these rules, but if we do, we acknowledge a poetic code according to which stars are very often associated with the kind of emotion, that sense of an indefinable infinite that we discussed at the beginning of this chapter. Each reader will have personal variations on this state of mind, but only up to a point and only within a general context: I do not believe an astronomer would take the poem to be a discourse on astronomy. If he did, he would be making the same error of judgment as the student who claimed Donne's poem to be about abortion, by interpreting *only* in the context of his own personal experience. Our experience will always influence our interpretations, but the claim that we must, inescapably, interpret only in the context of that experience is untrue. I, for example, have never fought in hand-to-hand to combat with a Greek hero (or with anyone else), but I can read the *Iliad* and understand how Hector felt at the prospect of fighting Achilles because I know what anger is and what fear is and how it sometimes comes into conflict with a sense of duty. Poetry, Aristotle tells us, is not about particulars. Here the particulars are who fought whom, and how, and who died. The "universals" are the fear and the anger and the conflict, and these are part of the basic human condition experienced by everyone.

Augustine and Aquinas made a clear distinction between the moral and the mystical senses, but Dante, Aquinas's contemporary, already suggests that all senses other than the literal can be grouped together under the heading "allegorical." One aspect of our interpretive freedom today is manifested in our ability to think of the ideas "moral" and "mystical" as nonreligious. We should remind ourselves that, as far as philosophical discourse is concerned, "morals" is the same thing as "ethics," even though in common usage the two concepts often seem to be thought of as different ones: nobody talks about "business morals," for example, while sexual license is generally termed immoral rather than unethical. (In fact, even histories of philosophy refer to the study of ethics in the same breath as they refer to "moral philosophers.") The moral sense of these stanzas, whether we think in terms of religion or not, can be seen in the awareness that the *agape,* or brotherly love, described is a good thing: it is promoted as an *ethos,* a way of life that would, if it were possible to achieve, improve the human condition generally. The experience itself can be thought of as mystical in the way that Blake's perception of the "Infinite" is mystical: a sudden and inexplicable sense of "oneness"—or, to use Goethe's definition yet again, a sense of something that, "even though expressed in all languages, remains inexpressible."

Poetry has changed since Goethe, since Auden, and certainly since the medieval exegetes wrote about allegorical interpretation; but it has not changed so profoundly as we might think. Art no longer represents life but performs it, Iser claims in *Prospecting.* Yet a performance is a representation, and Aristotle, from whom the Western tradition inherited the view of art as representation, was speaking of the theater. Poetry still uses what Augustine called "figurative language"—it does not, in Auden's words, "call a spade a spade"—and since figurative language depends on perception and association, the reader still has to interpret. It remains useful for us to think of the world as text because everything in it is potentially a poetic theme and, in this sense, a potential allegory. Since the aim of interpretation, the result we are supposed to arrive at, is no longer proscribed, it seems most sensible, and most productive, to use the freedom we have to explore as many interpretive avenues as possible whenever we approach a poem. I believe that we should always bear in mind the criterion of economy, but perhaps this, too, is, after all, a matter of perception. Even if we know that a rose is a rose is a rose is a rose, we can still ask: Yes, but what *is* a rose?

# NOTES

## 1. THE WESTERN TRADITION

1. For a fuller discussion of the ideas on Augustine, Aquinas, and Dante in this overview, see Eco's *The Limits of Interpretation* (1994 edition), especially the first chapter. I am greatly indebted to this work and to Eco's *Interpretation and Overinterpretation* for many of the ideas discussed throughout this book.

2. Reading and listening to poetry played a much more important role than it does today in education and society—even a central role—so that we should not be surprised at the notion of soldiers being influenced by it.

3. *dithyramb:* a Greek hymn performed by a chorus using a mime to describe the adventures of the mythological Dionysus. Dryden uses dithyrambic verse in "Alexander's Feast."

4. Dante later echoes this idea in the *Convivio* (see my chapter 3).

## 2. RELIGION, PHILOSOPHY, AND INTERPRETATION IN THE MIDDLE AGES

1. *Aleatory* means "depending on chance"—literally "on the throw of a die," from Latin *aleator,* a dice player.

2. *Hermetic drift* is the term used by Eco in *Limits* to indicate a chain of association unlimited by any logical context. The example given by Eco (27) to show various kinds of association is the following: Peg—pig—bristle—brush—Mannerism—Idea—Plato. Renaissance hermetism is discussed in my chapter 3.

3. To interpret a word syntagmatically means to read it in its context; that is, in the context of the words preceding and following it. If, walking in a garden and pointing to a bush, I say, "That is a rose," my hearer will most likely understand from *rose* that I am referring to a particular kind of flower. Paradigmatically, without the interpretive constraints created by the word *that,* in

215

this situation—the garden, my pointing out the bush—*rose* might be taken to stand for "Blood of Christ," "love," a reference to the famous stripper Gypsy Rose Lee, and so on.

4. A *closed* text is one that denies free interpretation; an *open* text invites it. The terms are from Eco's *The Open Work* (1989). The idea of open texts is essential to modern interpretive theories such as reader response."

## 3. DANTE, HERMETISM, AND RENAISSANCE ITALY

1. See Aristotle, on representation, in chapter 1 for a similar view of the ways in which texts can be read.

2. The pre-Copernican universe was geocentric: after Earth at the center, there followed the spheres of the Moon, Mercury, Venus, the Sun, Mars, Jupiter, Saturn; then the sphere of the "fixed" stars, the "crystalline sphere"; the *primum mobile,* or "First Moveable," whose motion was thought to have caused that of all the others; and finally the Empyrean Heaven, or High Heaven, which was the "habitation of the blessed."

3. In classical and Renaissance models of education, the *trivium* and *quadrivium* were the divisions into three and four subjects, respectively, of the material to be studied.

4. The philosopher Marcus Tullius Cicero, 106–43 B.C.E.

5. The fictive sense *is* the literal sense.

## 4. ENGLAND IN THE LATE MIDDLE AGES AND THE RENAISSANCE

1. Harrington is quoting from the *Georgics,* 1. 184ff. The following is the Loeb (1999 ed.) translation: "Often, too, it has been useful to fire barren fields, and burn the light stubble in crackling flames; whether it be that the earth derives thence hidden strength and rich nutriment, or that in the flame every taint is baked out and the useless moisture sweats from it. . . . Much service does he do the land, who with the mattock breaks up the sluggish clods, and drags over it hurdles of osier."

2. A reference to Robert Greene (1558–92), one of the so-called "University wits" and known for his dissipated lifestyle as well as for his literary portraits of the London underworld, which include *The Defense of Cony-Catching* (1592) and *Friar Bacon and Friar Bungay* (1589).

3. "Who taught the parrot to say his 'hello'?"

4. See Nathaniel Owen Wallace, "The Responsibilities of Madness: John Skelton, 'Speke Parrot'; and Homeopathic Satire," in *Studies in Philology* 82 (1985). I disagree with Wallace's reading of Parrot as "mad." For a fuller dis-

cussion, see Brittan, "Skelton's 'Speke Parott': Language, Madness, and the Role of the Court Poet," in *Renaissance Forum* 4, no. 1 (1999).

5. This stanza refers specifically to the widely detested Cardinal Wolsey (1475–1530). Wolsey, the son of a butcher, gained enormous power under Henry VIII and attempted, unsuccessfully, to secure his own election to the papacy.

6. Another example of a poem that rejects traditional notions of courtly beauty (and gender roles) is the anonymous "The Nutbrown Maid" (pub. 1503), in which the eponymous heroine is held up to men as a moral example. I cite only the final stanza of thirty:

> Here may ye see that women be
> In love, meek, kind, and stable.
> Let never man reprove them than
> Or call them variable;
> But rather pray God that we may
> To them be comfortable.
> God sometime proveth such as he loveth,
> If they be charitable.
> For sith that men would that women
> Be meek to them each one,
> Much more ought they to God obey
> And serve but him alone.

## 5. PHILOSOPHY AND REPRESENTATION IN THE SEVENTEENTH CENTURY

1. The "Seven Wise Men of Greece," whose number included the "first" philosopher, Thales, and who are recorded as the authors of concise ("gnomic") formulas (e.g., "Know thyself").

2. The Muses were the daughters of Mnemosyne and Zeus or, in another tradition, of Uranus and Ge (i.e., of Heaven and Earth). They were divine singers, but also presided over all forms of thought: eloquence and persuasion, history, mathematics, and astronomy. Their names and respective areas of influence are: Calliope (epic poetry), Clio (history), Polyhymnia (mime), Euterpe (flute playing), Terpsichore (light verse and dance), Erato (lyric choral poetry), Melpomene (tragedy), Thalia (comedy), and Urania (astronomy).

3. Especially in the treatise entitled *On Christian Doctrine*, Milton expresses theological views that have been considered heretical by the Anglican Church, notably his unorthodox views on polygamy and his subordination of the Son to God the Father, where tradition sees the Trinity as three coequal entities.

## 6. TOWARD ROMANTICISM

1. The Greek rhetorician and Neoplatonic philosopher known by his Latin name Cassius Longinus (c. 213–73 C.E.) After teaching at Alexandria and Athens, Longinus became adviser to Zenobia, queen of Palmira, whom he incited to resist Roman authority. Both he and Zenobia were executed on the order of Emperor Marcus Aurelius.

2. Swindlers, but here a reference to priests.

## 7. SYMBOL AND ALLEGORY

1. The White Goddess is Graves's idea of the personal muse. Writing under her influence ensures that the resulting poem is a "true" one—that is, it is not influenced by political or social agendas, literary fashions, or other extraneous considerations. The Black Goddess is her opposite, under whose influence poetry loses integrity (as does the poet) and becomes "Apollonian." "Apollonian" poetry, named after the son of Zeus and Leto, among whose various roles was that of god of music, was for Graves the polished, "intellectualized" poetry of Virgil, whose work he held in contempt. For the same reasons, according to Graves, modernist poetry is Apollonian, in particular the work of Eliot and Pound. Graves's book on poetic myth, also called *The White Goddess,* appeared in 1948.

2. Iser's mention of his interpretation of the world as the possible product of "linguistic acts" is a reference to (1) the idea that the world can be seen as text because it consists of signs which must be interpreted—a notion Iser disagrees with; and (2) the idea that interpretation is necessarily logocentric (word-based) because any attempt to interpret must use words, which, because they are themselves signs, always require further interpretation.

# WORKS CITED

Aquinas. *Summa Theologiae.* Trans. Fathers of the English Dominican Province. c. 1948. Westminster, Md.: Christian Classics, 1981.

Aristotle. *Poetics.* Trans. and ed. Richard Janko. Indianapolis: Hacket, 1987.

———. *Politics and Poetics.* New York: Heritage, 1964.

Auden, W. H. *Collected Shorter Poems, 1927–1957.* London: Faber & Faber, 1966.

Augustine. *De doctrina christiana.* In *Works,* ed. Marcus Dods. Vol. 1. Edinburgh: T. and T. Clark, 1872a-78.

———. *Confessions.* Harmondsworth: Penguin, 1986.

———. *City of God.* Harmondsworth: Penguin, 1986.

Blake, William. *Poetry & Prose.* Ed. Geoffrey Keynes. London: Nonesuch Press, 1927.

Browning, Robert. *Complete Works.* Ed. Charlotte Parker and H. E. Clarke. New York: T. Y. Corwell, c. 1898.

Burrow, J. A. *Ricardian Poetry.* London: Routledge & Kegan Paul, 1971.

Chaucer, Geoffrey. *The Canterbury Tales.* Ed. A. C. Cawley. London: Dent, 1958.

Cowper, William, and Thomson, James. *The Works of Cowper and Thomson.* Philadelphia: J. Grigg, 1832.

Dante Alighieri. *Divina Commedia.* A cura di Tommaso di Salvo. Bologna: Zanichelli, 1989.

———. *Opere Minori,* Firenze: A. Salani, 1938.

Di Cesare, Mario A. *George Herbert and the Seventeenth-century Religious Poets.* New York: Norton, 1978.

Dryden, John. *Poems.* Ed. James Kinsley. 4 vols. Oxford: Oxford Univ. Press, 1958.

Eco, Umberto. *The Limits of Interpretation,* Bloomington: Indiana Univ. Press, 1994.

——. *The Role of the Reader.* Advances in Semiotics Series. Bloomington: Indiana Univ. Press, 1984.

——. *The Open Work.* Cambridge: Harvard Univ. Press, 1989.

Eco, Umberto, with Richard Rorty, Jonathan Culler, and Christine Brooke-Rose. *Interpretation and Overinterpretation.* Cambridge: Cambridge Univ. Press, 1992.

Ficino, Marsilio. *Sopra lo amore: Ovvero, Convito di Platone.* Lanciano: Carabba, 1934.

——. *Opera omnia.* Torino: Bottega d'erasmo, 1959.

Flannagan, Roy, ed. *The Riverside Milton.* Boston: Houghton Mifflin, 1998.

Goethe. *Werke.* Leipzig: Bibliographisches Institut, 1926.

Graves, Robert. "The Dedicated Poet." In *On Poetry: Collected Talks and Essays.* New York: Doubleday, 1959.

——. *New Collected Poems.* Garden City, N.Y.: Doubleday, 1977.

——. *The Common Asphodel: Collected Essays on Poetry, 1922–1949.* London: Hamish Hamilton, 1949.

Gregory Smith, G. *Elizabethan Critical Essays.* 2 vols. Oxford: Oxford Univ. Press, 1959.

Holub, Robert C. *Crossing Borders: Reception Theory, Poststructuralism, Deconstruction.* Madison: Univ. of Wisconsin Press, 1992.

Hopkins, Gerard Manley. *Poems of Gerard Manley Hopkins.* 2nd ed. Ed. Robert Bridges. London: Oxford University Press, 1930.

Hulme, T. E. *Notes on Language and Style.* Ed. Herbert Read. Seattle: Univ. of Washington Chapbooks, no. 25, 1929.

Hume, David. *A Treatise of Human Nature.* 1739; reprint, Oxford: Clarendon, 1964.

——. *An Enquiry concerning Human Understanding.* Ed. Tom Beauchamp. Oxford: Oxford Univ. Press, 1999.

Iser, Wolfgang. *The Act of Reading: A Theory of Aesthetic Response.* Baltimore, Md.: Johns Hopkins Univ. Press, 1978.

——. *Prospecting: From Reader Response to Literary Anthropology.* Baltimore, Md.: Johns Hopkins Univ. Press, 1989.

Kirsch, Arthur C., ed. *Literary Criticism of John Dryden.* Lincoln: Univ. Nebraska Press, 1966.

Langland, William. *Piers Plowman* (C-text). Ed. Derek Pearsall. Exeter: Univ. Exeter Press, 1994.

Lawton, David. *Faith, Text, and History.* Charlottesville: Univ. Press of Virginia, 1990.

Locke, John. *An Essay on Human Understanding.* Ed. P. H. Nidditch. Oxford: Clarendon, 1975.

Mead, G. R. S. *Thrice-greatest Hermes: Studies in Hellenistic Theosophy and Gnosis*. London: Theosophical Publishing Society, 1906.

Mill, John Stuart. *Essays on Poetry*. Ed. F. Parvin Sharpless. Columbia: Univ. of South Carolina Press, 1976.

Origen. *De principiis*. Ed. Alexander Roberts and James Donaldson. Edinburgh: T. and T. Clark, 1885.

——. *Origen*. Trans. Walter Mitchell. New York: Sheed & Ward, 1955.

Osborne, Charles, *W. H. Auden: The Life of a Poet*, London: Eyre Methuen, 1979.

Ovid, *Metamorphoses*. Trans. Frank Justus Miller. 2 vols. Cambridge: Harvard Univ. Press, 1994.

Pico della Mirandola. *De hominis dignitate*. Firenze: Valecchi, 1942.

Plato. *Republic*. New York: Collier & Son, 1901.

——. *The Apology*. In *The Trial and Death of Socrates*, ed. and trans., B. Jowett. New York: Heritage, 1963.

Pound, Ezra. *Selected Poems*. Ed. T. S. Eliot. London: Faber & Faber, 1934.

Skelton, John. "Certayne bokes, co[m]pyled by mayster Skelton, Poet Laureat. . . . " [1545]. Early English Books, 1475–1640. Ann Arbor: Univ. Microfilms International, 1938.

Southey, Robert. *Critical Review*, 2nd ser., 24 (October 1798):187–204.

Spenser, Edmund.s *Complete Poetical Works*. Ed. Robert E. N. Dodge. Boston: Houghton Mifflin & Co., 1908.

Spingarn, J. E., ed. *Critical Essays of the Seventeenth Century*. 2 vols. Oxford: Oxford Univ. Press, 1957.

Tennyson, Alfred. *Poetical Works*. London: Macmillan, 1911.

Virgil. *Eclogues, Georgics, Aeneid 1–6*. Trans. H. Rushton Fairclough. Cambridge: Harvard Univ. Press, 1999.

Wordsworth, William, and S. T. Coleridge. *Lyrical Ballads*. 1798; with prefaces of 1800 and 1802. Ed. H. Littledale. Oxford Univ. Press, 1930.

# INDEX

allegory: *allegoria in factis,* 21, 40, 42, 61, 63; *allegoria in verbis,* 21, 40, 61, 63; Aquinas on, 30–35; and association, 128–33; Augustine on, 20–29; in the *Canterbury Tales,* 64–66; Dante on, 40–48; and Elizabethan criticism, 78–89; Goethe on, 171; in *Lyrical Ballads,* 160–69; in *Paradise Lost,* 117, 120–28; in *Piers Plowman,* 57–63, 66; in Pound's poetry, 189; and Puritanism, 116–28; in the *Republic,* 8; sexual, 94–95; in Spenser's poetry, 86–89; and symbol, 30; in Thomson's "Autumn," 139–45

Aquinas, 2–3, 23, 30–35, 38, 40, 42, 48, 50, 53, 56, 58, 60–62, 67–68, 106, 139, 152, 167, 202–3, 208, 213

Aristotle, 13–29, 41, 66, 77–78, 80, 88, 92, 133, 137, 147, 183, 191, 203, 212–13

art (in general), 1, 11, 74–75, 78, 93, 97–98, 103, 105

Ascham, Roger, 78

association, 25–28, 35, 82, 99; and aleatory conditions, 129–30; in David Hume, 196; and imagination, 100–102; in J. S. Mill, 179–82; and *Lyrical Ballads,* 156–69; and memory, 99–101; and "mood," 184; "natural," 128, 146; and perception, 213; and reason, 100–102; in T. E. Hulme, 183–89; unfamiliar, 135; "unlawful" (or "unnatural"),

100–104, 106, 129–33, 135, 138, 141, 188, 192

Auden, W. H., 209–13

Augustine, 1–4, 12, 20–29, 47–50, 53, 56, 58, 61, 63, 67–68, 73–74, 106–7, 113, 114, 116, 118, 124, 137, 148, 152, 167, 169, 178, 191, 202–3, 208, 211, 213

Bacon, Francis, 99, 103–5

Baudelaire, Charles, 171

Bewe, 95

Bible: allegorical sense of, 2–3, 21–23, 27–28, 32–33, 48, 104, 117–18, 191–92; anagogical (mystical) sense of, 2, 27, 32, 38; as fable, 36–37; as God's work, 2–3, 32; literal sense of, 1, 2, 21–23, 26, 28, 32–33, 42, 117, 129; Locke on, 137, 139; moral sense of, 2, 32, 33; Neoplatonic interpretation of, 50; parabolic sense of, 34, 37, 117; Song of Solomon, 76–77; spiritual sense of, 2, 32–33; as symbolic, 1, 21, 27; translations of, 69–73, 120

Blake, William, 1, 148–56, 162, 166, 169, 184, 195, 203, 208, 213; on the Bible, 151–52; and God, 149–56; on perception, 148; and Plato, 149; on the "poetic character," 150–51; and reason, 148; "The Tyger," 153–56

Boccaccio, Giovanni, 56, 138

Browne, Sir Thomas, 3

223